THE STALLED REVOLUTION

Is equality for women an impossible dream?

By

Eva Tutchell
John Edmonds

United Kingdom – North America – Japan
India – Malaysia – China

Emerald Publishing Limited
Howard House, Wagon Lane, Bingley BD16 1WA, UK

First edition 2018

Reprints and permissions service
Contact: permissions@emeraldinsight.com

British Library Cataloguing in Publication Data
A catalogue record for this book is available from the British Library

ISBN: 978-1-78714-602-0 (Print)
ISBN: 978-1-78714-601-3 (Online)
ISBN: 978-1-78714-990-8 (Epub)

ISOQAR certified
Management System,
awarded to Emerald
for adherence to
Environmental
standard
ISO 14001:2004.

ISOQAR
REGISTERED
Certificate Number 1985
ISO 14001

INVESTOR IN PEOPLE

CONTENTS ²⁹³.

ACKNOWLEDGEMENTS

When Sheila Rowbotham first decided that there should be a women's liberation conference in 1970, her intention was 'to put women back into history'.

At this time of anniversaries, *The Stalled Revolution* is a tribute to the women who made Britain a better place. We record their struggles and we celebrate their victories.

In the course of writing our book, we interviewed many people and talked informally with several others. All were helpful, informative and encouraging. We are extremely grateful for their support.

In particular we wish to thank:

Marie Bailey, Pauline Barrie, Kim Beat, Karen Butler, Bea Campbell, David Charles, Miriam David, Jo Delaney, Carole Easton, Richard Ennals, Jane Everton, Heather Fallows, Christopher Forster, Sophie Gilpin, Philip Hedley, Jack Hodgkinson, Ashleigh James, Annabel Jones, Susanna Jones, Glenys Kinnock, Katie Learmonth, Deborah Mattinson, Paul Miller, Charlotte Proudman Ricky Romain, Elizabeth Roberts, Sheila Rowbotham, Lynne Segal, Sam Smethers, Hazel Taylor, Ann Traynor, Suzy Tutchell, Sarah Veale, and David and Jane Whitworth.

Colleagues and friends also kindly read and commented on sections of the book and we thank them for giving their time so willingly: Marianne Coleman, Jayne Grant, Beatriz Lees, Margaret Littlewood, Jane Miller and Liz Nichols.

In the following pages we record many extraordinary women. We dedicate our book to them and to the thousands more whose names may be forgotten by history but whose achievements illuminate our lives.

1

The Two Great Anniversaries

In the spring of 2017, the government agreed to erect a statue of Millicent Fawcett in Parliament Square.

The decision was well reported but many newspapers evidently did not expect their readers to know much about Millicent Fawcett. One newspaper ran the headline:

> 'Who was Millicent Fawcett, the woman behind
> Parliament Square's first female statue?'[1]

The statue has considerable symbolic significance. It marks the hundredth anniversary of one of the most important events of the twentieth century. On 6 February 1918, the Royal Assent was granted to the Act that allowed women to vote in parliamentary elections. Later in that year over 8 million women voted for the first time in a General Election.

Millicent Fawcett led the Votes for Women campaign for nearly 30 years. In 1918 she and her allies won a glorious victory and, at the time, she was one of the most famous women in Britain.

But her fame has not lasted.

Emmeline Pankhurst, the other great leader of the campaign to secure votes for women, is rather better known.[2] Most people have heard of the suffragettes, whom she led, but they know very little about the nature of their struggle. When the film, *Suffragette*, was shown in 2015, the prejudice shown by the British establishment and the hardship suffered by the campaigners caused gasps in many cinemas.

This lack of knowledge is extraordinary. The campaign by women to secure the right to vote in parliamentary elections is one of the most momentous and inspiring stories of the last two hundred years. It changed the status of women in Britain and has a profound effect on the way we live today. Yet most people know less about the Votes for Women campaign than the marriages of Henry VIII.

The Second Anniversary

The year 2018 should also be commemorated for a second anniversary. It marks fifty years since the beginning of the great upsurge of feminist feeling that came to be known as the Women's Liberation Movement.

The pioneers of the Women's Liberation Movement have no statues to record their achievements and, although many of these pioneering women are still alive, they are even less well known than Millicent Fawcett and Emmeline Pankhurst. This is partly the result of modesty. The Women's Liberation Movement was self-consciously egalitarian. It elected no leaders and rejected the cult of personality. But its achievements are all around us.

The Women's Liberation Movement inspired the two great Acts of Parliament that were passed in the 1970s: the Equal Pay Act and the Sex Discrimination Act. Britain is far from being an equal society but many of the opportunities enjoyed by twenty-first century women can be traced back to the efforts of the Women's Liberation Movement.

The movement aimed to transform the way women were regarded and treated. Changes in popular culture illustrate the extent of the Movement's influence Pictures of nude women were taken down from workplace walls, the so-called Beauty Contests lost their popularity and eventually even the Benny Hill Show, with its cohort of young women squealing as most of their clothes were 'accidentally' removed, eventually disappeared from our television screens.

Surprisingly, the work of the Women's Liberation Movement has fallen out of the popular consciousness. There appears to be an assumption that these changes in the role and status of women just arrived automatically as a matter of course. This is a dangerous piece of mythology. If we do not recognise the significance of the campaigns that won these important victories, we may delude ourselves into thinking that further improvements will come without effort.

There is also the need to establish a proper balance to the recollection of British history. It was said by a writer[3] in *The New Yorker*, and repeated many times since, that the women's movement was the most successful revolution of the twentieth century. Yet it is scarcely celebrated in this country. Indeed, unless they happen to sit on the throne, the achievements of women scarcely feature in popular accounts of our history. The coincidence of the two great anniversaries gives us an opportunity to restore these great victories, and the women who won them, to their proper place in the collective memory of Britain.

Extraordinary Women

We were able to interview many of the most committed members of the Women's Liberation Movement. They all offered advice and encouragement to women campaigners.

> Sheila Rowbotham told us that, 'it is no longer enough to point out what we don't like. We have to work out what sort of society we do want'.

> Lynne Segal looked ahead: 'We do not simply want equality with men; we want to change the value system… We have visions of a better life'.

> Bea Campbell says we must persuade people to be open to change: They should "be prepared to be enlightened, enraged, amused and above all provoked'.[4]

> Miriam David insisted that, 'it is time for another women's movement.… It seems to me that feminism is everywhere and yet nowhere (is it) influential or powerful'.[5]

For the suffrage campaigns we have relied on the autobiographies of the two leaders and the writing of their many supporters. Millicent Fawcett was an elegant and intelligent member of the British political class, demure when she wanted to be but with a turn of phrase that could skin an opponent. She was generous and often funded parts of the campaign with her own money. Everyone speaks of her warmth and humanity which inspired wonderful admiration and loyalty in her supporters. On her death one supporter wrote,

> 'We were unspeakably proud of her.'[6]

Emmeline Pankhurst was a very different character, single-minded to an extraordinary degree, feared by the government and demanding unquestioning obedience from her followers. Slim and beautiful, Rebecca West called her, 'a reed of steel'.[7]

She was an extraordinary public speaker although Ethel Smyth, Emmeline's close friend, tells us that her other skills did not always match her soaring oratory. As part of the suffragettes' campaign of militancy Emmeline Pankhurst recommended smashing the windows of the powerful. Unfortunately, during an afternoon of hilarious practice in Ethel Smyth's garden, Emmeline Pankhurst failed to hit the target once. She had to leave the stone throwing to others.[8]

The achievements of the Votes for Women campaign and the Women's Liberation Movement were hard-won. Emmeline Pankhurst was repeatedly jailed and frequently on hunger strike. However, perhaps because of her celebrity, she was never forcibly fed. Other suffragettes fared worse. The process was so gruesome that, after being forcibly fed for a fortnight, most prisoners were in a state of collapse. There are terrible stories of hardship. Emmeline's daughter, Sylvia, was forcibly fed twice a day for five weeks. Constance Lytton had her health destroyed in prison and, like many others, she never fully recovered. Voting rights for women were earned by pain and suffering.

Members of the Women's Liberation Movement did not have to endure prison and few were arrested but they had to take more than their share of abuse. Most of the press made little attempt to understand the movement's motives. Instead of reporting the policies they preferred to libel the women. Supporters of the movement were portrayed as hairy, man-hating harridans with no sense of humour and no chance of attracting a man. It was a ridiculous, inaccurate and unworthy calumny but, in the way of such insults, it still hangs round the necks of female activists like a lead necklace.

Completing the Revolution

The suffrage campaigners believed, and the Women's Liberation Movement hoped, that their victories would be followed by further progress towards a world where the needs of women would be given the same importance as the needs of men. It did not happen. Success was followed by disappointment. In each case the revolution stalled; in the late 1920s as a result of the Great Depression; in the 1980s with rising unemployment following Margaret Thatcher's accession to power.

The work of the campaigners was never completed.

The question at the heart of this book is whether the time has come for a new liberation campaign and a third leap forward.

The need for improvement is very great. Violence against women is common in Britain. Each year, the number of rapes runs into scores of thousands and hundreds of thousands of women are assaulted in their own homes. Another terrible statistic: on average, two women are murdered each week by their partners. Too many women have to accept verbal and physical abuse as a normal part of their lives. Young women at many universities have had their student years ruined by the fast developing lad culture of disrespect for women.

Discrimination against women is much less obvious than the blatant injustice that was prevalent a generation ago, but women still face an accumulation of disadvantages. Perhaps they are not told of the best job opportunities, perhaps they get on the short list but never quite get the job and perhaps their best ideas are disregarded until a man says something similar, and takes the credit.

Women tend to occupy the worst paid jobs in our society and have little legal protection. Because most women are obliging, their compliance is taken for granted and their complaints are very often ignored. Even women with great talent and ambition find it difficult to navigate their way through to the top in a world that has been very obviously fashioned by men for the convenience of men.

Women in the finance sector, whom we quote in Chapter 7, have been taught by experience exactly how twenty-first century discrimination operates – below the radar and usually denied.

> 'They tell us this place is a meritocracy but men are taken more seriously and always seem to get the best opportunities and the best jobs.'[9]

And when women have children the discrimination gets noticeably worse.

Some of this unfairness can be put right by enforcing the rights that are already on the statute book – for equal pay and for protection against discrimination. Making sure that more women are in positions of power in our companies and important institutions would also help. So would ensuring that the House of Commons contains as many women MPs as men. But these reforms, while valuable, will not – on their own – produce the new and better world that most women want.

Equality with men was the cry of the Votes for Women campaigners and it found an echo in the demands of the Women's Liberation Movement. Achieving equality is necessary but many female activists through the ages have realised that equality with men is not enough. Because of the social and political failures of our society, many men lead cramped and depressing lives. There is no advantage in joining them in their misery. A new liberation campaign should have a loftier purpose. Women should not limit their ambition to what men have: they should focus on what women need.

Setting this higher and perhaps even utopian purpose means that it is not just the symptoms of inequality and discrimination that must be dealt with. As Veronica Jarvis Tichenor writes,

> 'To strike at the heart of the gender structure, we must… aggressively disrupt and reconstruct assumptions that lie at the very core of who we think we are'.[10]

These assumptions about gender roles are often unhelpful but they buttress our sense of identity and are difficult to eliminate. Men are leaders and women are followers; men are self-confident and women are diffident; men are rational and women are emotional; women are good with babies and men are good with cars; women do the cooking and men go off to do something more important. Both sexes are trapped in stereotypes that limit our aspirations and make us fearful of change.

Doubts and Reluctance

According to the famous story in the Anglo-Saxon Chronicle, King Alfred fell asleep when he was left in charge of baking the cakes and let them burn. Although Alfred was no misogynist, there remains a small suspicion that he neglected his duty because he felt that baking was not a man's responsibility.

Most men nowadays would probably attend to the cakes, or at least set a timer to prevent them burning. Indeed most men now profess a commitment to equality between the sexes but the number who give genuine support, let alone help to instigate the steps leading to change, remains depressingly small. And to be fair, in this book we stress the fact that, although help and support from men is welcome and much needed, women have to take charge of the campaign for their own liberation.

It is therefore somewhat dispiriting to find that there still appears to be a residual resistance in women themselves to challenge inequality. It is never easy to summon the energy to fight against such heavy odds. The pioneers who led or were involved in the two great women's campaigns of the past century found the strength and inner resources to persevere against taunts, insults, physical abuse and innumerable inexcusable setbacks. However the truth is that the jibes did not only emanate from those in power, but were thrown at them by the general public, by other women and even by their own families. Have we women in the twenty-first century lost some of that resilience or is something else holding us back?

There is a great deal of current publicity surrounding sexual and gender identity and this is a complicating factor, but the reluctance to engage with the struggle for equality is also connected with who women think they are in a broader social arena. Having been told from an early age that the main battles are over and that if they try hard enough they can rule the world, young women are under enormous pressure not to fail and even when they succeed what they find is often not to their liking.

the battle is not over

So the temptation for some women may be to take over from Alfred and follow Nigella Lawson back into the kitchen.

Feminism

What inspired the Votes for Women campaigners and the supporters of the Women's Liberation Movement was that deep belief in the rights and entitlement of women, which we call feminism.

Jude Kelly, Artistic Director of London's South Bank Centre says,

> 'I'm convinced that feminism needs to be a big, bold, baggy overcoat that can accommodate each fully rounded female.'[11]

It is hard to disagree with such an inclusive statement but many women still find the coat to be uncomfortably restrictive. The concept of feminism as a liberating force is still misunderstood and mistrusted. Attitudes vary from acceptance of the word as a beacon signalling an empowering sense of freedom from past shackles to doubts and fears about humourless harridans challenging the very notion of womanhood.

Throughout this book we endeavour to rehabilitate and reclaim feminism.

The feminism we espouse is straightforward and should be uncontroversial. Brenda Hale, who is now president of the Supreme Court, put it this way when we met her:

> 'A feminist is someone who believes women are equal to men in terms of potential and entitlement.'[12]

It is a wise and simple description requiring no further explanation. The problem arises when we try to make this belief a reality. Equality and improvement do not come about just because we state their inherent fairness. Being a feminist may imply the need for action. Not everyone is eager to campaign but supporting those who are prepared to fight on our behalf is a necessary contribution that every woman can make.

In *I Call Myself a Feminist: A View from 25 Women under Thirty* published by Virago in 2015 Martha Mosse says,

> 'Feminism is fairness.'[13]

Kate Nash writes:

> "I personally think our generation has sat back a bit, because we could... I feel like it's our responsibility together to start

making a noise, taking action. We need to have a more 'fight it' attitude, get angry, make some waves, be loud."[14]

Sustained equality between the sexes is long overdue. We owe it to Millicent Fawcett, Emmeline Pankhurst, Sheila Rowbotham, Lynne Segal, Harriet Harman and many more to fulfil their feminist aspirations.

A campaign to rehabilitate feminism, overturn the cultural norms that sustain male supremacy and create a society that gives as much weight to the needs of women as to the needs of men, cannot reasonably be described as a process of reform. It amounts to a revolution.

In later chapters we speculate on what that revolution might involve. It must have a strong political element but it would be very optimistic to imagine that such a revolution might be driven by politicians. During the last twenty years most politicians appear to have lost confidence in their ability to make fundamental changes in our society. They will have to be pressed hard by women campaigners, who in turn will need the help and support of other enlightened and progressive forces in our society.

Role of the Arts

Music, words – on the page or in the theatre – paintings, sculpture and dance help us to express emotions vital to our intellectual and emotional growth and wellbeing. Through the arts we can challenge stereotyping and disrupt the notion of a static, unchanging world.

The arts can help us to query long-held and often unquestioned assumptions about the way we conduct our lives. Separate from the political establishment itself, they can prompt us to think about the effect of politics in our daily existence. They have the power to encourage us to dismantle cultural norms.

During the 1970s, for example, at the height of the Apartheid era in South Africa, the Royal Court Theatre in London staged plays like 'The Island' and 'Siswe Banzi is Dead' by the South African playwright, Athol Fugard, criticising that heinous regime. The principal actors John Kani and Winston Ntshona were black. Many of us already had strong feelings about apartheid but Fugard's plays provoked a personally felt visceral shock in the audience. What we were reading and hearing about in the media was brought to life through drama.

The arts have the potential to open the minds of the people of Britain to the possibility of creating a society where the needs of women are just as important as the needs of men.

Being consumers rather than practitioners of the arts ourselves, we interviewed several people whose intimate connection with the arts gives them the right to speak with some authority.

As professional singer Elizabeth Roberts told us that

> 'The arts reflect back to us what is and also what could be.'[15]

In a society where the entitlement to equal rights and opportunities is taken seriously, we need to invest in and promote the arts. They help us to imagine a better future.

Lessons of History

We expected our study on the Votes for Women campaign and the Women's Liberation Movement to lift our spirits and so it did. The suffragists and the Women's Liberation Movement showed us how to confront injustice and how to be victorious.

We were surprised at the number of practical lessons provided by those past campaigns. There is a famous picture of suffragettes chaining themselves to railings but that was only one of a stream of publicity ideas that kept their cause constantly in the news and their opponents forever on the defensive. On a summer afternoon they hired a balloon and dropped several thousand leaflets from the sky over London. On another afternoon a suffragette sidled into Lambeth Palace to lobby the Archbishop of Canterbury. Somewhat nonplussed, he offered her tea.

The Women's Liberation Movement had wide ambitions. The movement certainly wanted the government to introduce reforms but they saw their main purpose as creating a grass roots community of women, with scores of support groups in towns and cities across Britain. The movement was also an important self-help organisation. As we recount in Chapter 4, members of the movement opened over sixty women's centres: protected spaces where women could find refuge, support and stimulation.

Of course, Britain of the twenty-first century is notably different from the Britain that existed before the First World War or in the 1970s but the qualities needed to challenge injustice and to win are the same as they were in the past. A modern campaign will need the resilience of Millicent Fawcett's suffrage societies, the eye-catching excitement of Emmeline Pankhurst's Suffragettes and the revolutionary vision that inspired the Women's Liberation Movement.

In the last chapter of this book we suggest how a new liberation campaign might be developed. The lessons from our history provide bedrock principles. Appeal to all women; be democratic and inclusive; be relentless in achieving success; always remember that while reforms are useful, what women really need is a fundamental change in the way society is organised.

Most important of all, a new liberation campaign must be an organisation of women, led by women, with its policy and priorities determined by women. Men should be encouraged to support but, as campaigners from Millicent Fawcett to Harriet Harman have insisted, only women can know what women need and it is only women who will find the stamina to carry their cause through to success.

There is no advantage in trying to start afresh; we should build on what we have. Many women are already members of campaigning organisations. Our concern is that, while these groups do good work, they have not yet found a way to mobilise their collective strength in a way that puts maximum pressure on government and on the other power centres in our society.

But the biggest lesson of all is that a new liberation campaign must have an appetite for success. It must convince its members that victory is not only possible but, with enthusiasm and relentless campaigning, victory will be assured. G. D. Anderson stresses the strength of womanhood:

> 'Women are already strong. It's about changing the way the world perceives their strength.'[16]

Moments of Joy

It is tempting to describe such a stupendous endeavour only in terms of selfless dedication and unflinching determination. No doubt a lot of hard work will be necessary but the Votes for

Women campaign and the Women's Liberation Movement taught another lesson that Lynne Segal repeated to us:

> 'There is great collective joy in working with other like-minded women.'

During both of the earlier campaigns, the women pioneers found a sisterhood that lifted the spirits and was valued almost as highly as the great victories themselves. In our next chapter, we describe two days of hope, of shared happiness and of collective joy. A new liberation campaign will have moments just like these.

2

Days of Hope

Votes for Women Demonstration
Hyde Park on Midsummer's Day, 1908

As the first fanfare of bugles sounded, the enormous crowd quietened for a moment. Then they saw the small figure of Emmeline Pankhurst moving to the front of the platform, and a uniquely feminine cry of joy swept across Hyde Park. 'Votes for Women', and then again

> 'Votes for Women' and a third time, even louder, 'Votes for Women'.[1]

There were nineteen other platforms and scores of other speakers but that elegant woman, with the extraordinary carrying voice, was the one they had all come to see and, if they could press close enough, to hear. Half a million people looked up at the leader of the suffragettes, knowing that history was being made.

Thousands of suffragettes in white gowns, with sashes, favours and ribbons in the newly chosen colours of purple and green and white, the straw hats of the men and the prettily trimmed hats of so many women. Less like a crowd, Emmeline Pankhurst declared, and more like 'a vast garden of flowers'.[2]

All of Britain had been invited. A quarter of a million tickets had been handed out. Massive posters were put up in 70 towns and every borough of London. Maps showing the routes of the seven processions were fly-posted on every vacant wall. Pavements were chalked with time and place. Everywhere the invitation was the same: 'Come to Hyde Park on Midsummer's day'.

The careful planning included a thread of humour. Flora Drummond, the 'General' of the suffragettes, as she loved to be called, hired a launch to steam up the Thames. She stopped opposite the terrace of the Houses of Parliament where insiders say that 'MPs entertained their lady friends to tea'.[3] In her loud clear voice Flora Drummond invited them all.

'Come to the Park on Sunday' she urged.

And to reassure the faint-hearted who might be worried by the suffragettes' reputation for militancy, she added,

'The police will protect you. There will be no arrests!'[4]

One MP was sufficiently alarmed to summon a police launch. In a glimpse of things to come, the police arrived too late to stop the fun or capture the suffragette.

It is not known how many MPs (and how many of their ladies) accepted the ''General's' waspish invitation but the suffragettes had many well-known supporters in the crowd. George Bernard Shaw and his wife, Mrs H. G. Wells, Mrs Thomas Hardy, the writer Israel Zangwill, and Keir Hardie, the Leader of the Labour Party, all led the processions into the Park. But on that day, Sylvia, Emmeline Pankhurst's daughter, said it was not individuals but the size of the multitude that mattered.

'Self was forgotten; personality seemed minute, the movement so big, so splendid.'[5]

The speeches set out the justice of the cause, exposed the hypocrisy
of the government and rejoiced in the feeling that the women's suffrage campaign was unstoppable. Conversions were made: onlook-
ers became supporters and supporters became enthusiasts. The belief
spread through the Park that victory must be very close. Before the
end, the demonstration began to feel more like a celebration.

At 5 o'clock, the bugles sounded again and the official proceedings were over. But the sun still shone, the bands still played and
many hours passed before the crowd went home. It had been both
a demonstration and a gala event.

The crowd enjoyed themselves greatly but, at its heart, the Hyde
Park demonstration was a statement of political strength. It had
been organised to meet a challenge from Herbert Gladstone, the
Home Secretary. Herbert was the son of William Gladstone, pillar
of nineteenth century liberalism and a prime minister who had
betrayed the suffrage campaigners a generation earlier. Now the
son showed the same disrespect as the father.

The Home Secretary contrasted what he thought were the feeble
efforts of the women with, as he contended, the more robust efforts
of the men who had demanded the vote in previous decades. Then
he revealed the extent of his ignorance.

'The men', he said, 'had assembled in their tens of thousands all over the country… Of course it is not to be
expected that women can assemble in such masses, but
power belongs to the masses…'[6]

Emmeline Pankhurst picked up Gladstone's shabby little gaunt-
let and the Hyde Park demonstration was organised. In size, it

dwarfed any demonstration that had been held in support of votes for men. *The Times* said that the suffragettes,

> "had counted on an audience of 250,000. That expectation was certainly fulfilled; probably it was doubled; it would be difficult to contradict anyone who asserted it was trebled. Like the distance and the number of the stars, the facts are beyond the threshold of perception".[7]

The Daily Express took a more historical view.

> 'The Women Suffragists provided London with one of the most wonderful and astonishing sights that has ever been seen since the days of Boadicea....'

And then in a comment that must have caused Emmeline Pankhurst to smile and should have caused Herbert Gladstone to hang his head, *The Daily Express* added:

> 'Men who saw the great (William) Gladstone meeting years ago said that, compared with yesterday's multitude, it was as nothing.'[8]

Before the final bugle call was sounded, the great crowd in Hyde Park on that midsummer's day passed a resolution. It demanded that women be accorded the same voting rights as men. Christabel, Emmeline Pankhurst's oldest daughter, immediately arranged for the resolution to be sent by special messenger to the Prime Minister, Herbert Asquith.

Surely Asquith could not ignore the wishes of such a multitude.

But he did. In a response which read like a studied insult, he said that he had no plans to introduce legislation to extend voting rights to women.

Nine days later a further demonstration in Parliament Square was broken up by over five thousand police, many of them mounted. Disgusted by Asquith's intransigence and the violence of the police, Mary Leigh and Edith New went to Downing Street and threw stones through the windows of No 10. It was the first act of damage committed by the suffragettes. The two women contacted Emmeline Pankhurst and said that they would understand if she repudiated their actions. She refused to do so.

Mary Leigh and Edith New were each sentenced to two months in prison. Emmeline Pankhurst visited them in the cells.[9]

After the peace, excitement and joy of Hyde Park, the Votes for Women campaign had entered a much darker phase.

Women's Liberation Demonstration
Central London: 6th March 1971

A Recollection by Eva Tutchell

'I don't think anyone realised we were starting a movement',[10] said Sheila Rowbotham and neither did I, until I emerged from Hyde Park tube Station and heard thousands of women's voices laughing, talking, singing, shouting slogans.

The noise hit me. Women were everywhere holding banners with a variety of demands and slogans.

> 'Women hold up half the sky'
>
> 'Equal pay NOW'
>
> 'Free abortion on demand – Who does your body belong to?'
>
> 'Equality: the time is NOW'
>
> 'Equal Pay is not enough – we want the MOON!'

A banner demanding equal pay was thrust into my hand and I found myself swept along, marching with no hesitation towards Trafalgar Square. What struck me and remains with me nearly half a century later, was the warmth of the women to one another (including me – instant comradeship was on offer), the humour and the determination on their faces. It was a practical lesson in political solidarity.

The journalist Jill Tweedie was there:

> "Long and short and thin and fat, quiet, middle aged ladies in careful make up, bare-faced girls with voices loud as crows, Maoists, liberals, socialists, lesbians, students, professionals, manual workers, spinsters, wives, widows, mothers.
>
> 'One two three four – we want a bloody sight more!'."[11]

On that snowy March day in 1971, knowing no-one, feeling nervous and still defining myself as a housewife (albeit politically active) at home with young children, I decided to join that women's liberation march in London. All I knew was that it was about equal pay and abortion rights, and that I supported both. I was intrigued to find out what a march of women would feel like.

Political activism for me (in the Labour Party) was still controlled by men. They were the main speakers at rallies and demonstrations.

I found myself walking with two women holding two large banners connected by a washing line with a stocking, bra, apron, suspenders, and a huge tailor's dummy of a woman hanging from it. The two marching alongside me had met through a small local women's group, which was still finding its purpose but already becoming aware of the comfort of a new spirit of sisterhood.

It was freezing cold but nothing could dampen our enthusiasm and energy.

As we marched along, women bystanders were urged to join us. Several did and told us their own stories on the way. Some were concerned about their isolation as 'housewives' at home, others talked about their lack of promotion possibilities at work. One woman spoke vehemently about her demotion when she returned to her job after having children. These were all private conversations from and to complete strangers as we made our way to Trafalgar Square, but no doubt replicated along the long line of vociferous, demonstrating women.

Unlike the Hyde Park demonstration of 1908 where the marchers wore white with sashes and favours of purple, white and green, we were wearing a multicoloured array of coats, boots and scarves. I was wearing an Afghan coat of the sort very popular at the time, bought cheaply at a market stall and which gave off a somewhat unpleasant whiff of unspecified dead animal when it got wet – which it certainly did as we trudged through the snowy sludge.

The purpose of the demonstration was to present a petition to the Prime Minister at 10 Downing Street with the four demands formulated the year before at the first Women's Liberation Conference which had been held at Ruskin College (of which more in Chapter 4).

1. Equal Pay
2. Equal Educational Opportunities
3. 24-hour nurseries
4. Abortion on demand.

The plinth in Trafalgar Square was occupied by women making impassioned, cogent speeches and it gave me a thrill to hear strong female voices ring out, one after the other – arguing for a more equal and liberated future.

I remember admiring their courage just to stand behind a microphone addressing such a large and varied audience.

There was impromptu street theatre, provoking much laughter as we recognised the universal stories and situations, mostly to do with domesticity, which were so familiar to us.

Such demands with the accompanying demonstration did not come out of the ether. The same enthusiasm and determination had been present at the 1908 Hyde Park demonstration in support of women's suffrage. There were echoes of that previous march in the confident female voices echoing around Trafalgar Square boldly asserting their rights.

On 15 January of that year, three months before the 1971 demonstration, Mary Stott, veteran woman columnist in *The Guardian* had written:

> 'A mass demonstration is planned for March 6th. Has the loosely knit Women's Liberation Movement the resources, financial, organisation, practical to mount a really effective mass demonstration?'[12]

We proved that we most definitely had, and for many of us who were there and took part it proved a turning point.

I went home uplifted and determined to play my part in this new and slightly scary but exciting movement.

At first I was not sure what to do but after describing my experience to a friend, Jo Delaney, like me a Labour Party member, we decided to set up and run a women's section in our local Labour Party, which would meet in the afternoons so that women with children could come, prams and all, and talk about politics, mainly but not only issues of relevance to women.

Twenty tentative women arrived at our first meeting, many with young children. We had no real agenda on that occasion and the discussions were rambling but uninhibited.

Were we on our way to the Moon?

3

Winning Votes for Women

The campaign began in surprising fashion.

While in parliament on a summer's day in 1866, John Stuart Mill, MP and political philosopher, was told that two women were waiting for him in Westminster Hall. Mill hurried out to see them and was surprised to find them empty-handed. 'Where is the Petition?' he asked with some concern. The two women took him to the apple seller's stall and explained that they had hidden it under the apple-cart to keep it safe from prying eyes.

The petition under the apple cart called on parliament to grant votes to women. Emily Davies and Elizabeth Garrett, two of the women who had collected the signatures, had brought it to the Commons in a Hansom cab. Mill was anxious that they might only have collected about a hundred names, but when he saw the size of the petition, he was delighted, exclaiming,

'Ah, I can brandish this with effect.'[1]

A few days later, on 7 June 1866, Mill laid the petition before parliament and started the national campaign for women's voting rights[2] that was to last for over fifty years. It was fitting that

Mill should present that important petition because his writing
and speeches made him the intellectual mainspring of the suffrage campaign, developing cogent arguments and challenging the
trite man-made assumptions of Victorian Britain. His support for
equality had been inspired by his beloved wife, Harriet Taylor. In
turn, Mill inspired the leaders of the votes for women campaign
and, through them, two generations of women activists.

In the following year, the government brought forward a Reform
Bill designed to double the number of male voters. But women
would be excluded. In the debate, Mill moved an amendment to
give women the same rights as men. He argued that women were
worthy citizens and should not be denied the vote because of their
sex, which he called, 'an entirely irrelevant consideration'.

Mill's speech[3] won a warm response in the House of Commons
but the government would have none of it. Mill's amendment was
defeated by 196 votes to 73 and the vote in parliamentary elections remained a male prerogative.

Mill's amendment called for women to have the same voting
rights as men. This became the defining purpose of the women's
suffrage campaign and, in spite of strong pressure, remained
unchanged for half a century. In hindsight, it might seem surprising that the demand was so limited. Until 1918 many men
did not have the vote, and 'the same voting rights as men' meant
that many women, like many men, would be denied the franchise.
This limitation was accepted by the campaigners because the
right to vote was never an end in itself. The women, who fought
governments for so long, suffering ridicule, contempt, abuse and
pain, had a more compelling vision. Their aim was equality. Millicent Fawcett, who led the largest women's suffrage organisation
for nearly thirty years, saw the right to vote as an essential step

towards a society where women had 'equal laws (and) enlarged
opportunities'.[4] Emmeline Pankhurst, leader of the suffragettes,
called the vote 'a desperate necessity'[5] to transform the power and
status of women.

Inferior

That improvement was sorely needed. During the nineteenth century women were regarded at best as second-class citizens and,
in some respects, as scarcely citizens at all. Women had few legal
rights and many men expressed outrage if it were suggested that
women were entitled to the protection of the law. Millicent Fawcett tells of a discussion in 1870 with a Liberal supporting farmer
about a clause in a Government Bill that would require a husband to ask his wife before he spent her money. The farmer was
incredulous.

> 'Am I to understand you, ma'am, that if this Bill passes and
> my wife have... £100 left to her, I should have to ask her
> for it?'[6]

The notion that women necessarily led lives that were more
restricted than men was central to the culture of the nineteenth
century. In her autobiography,[7] Emmeline Pankhurst recalls that
her parents discussed her brothers' education as 'a matter of real
importance', whereas her education and the education of her sisters were scarcely discussed at all. She was puzzled to be told that
her duty in life would be to make the home attractive, whereas her
brothers had no such obligation. A confirmation of her inferior
status came one night as she lay in bed pretending to be asleep.
Her father bent over her, 'shielding the candle flame with his big
hand', and said, somewhat sadly, 'What a pity she wasn't born
a lad.'[8]

Double standards existed everywhere, including in the 'domestic sphere' where women were supposed to have a special role. The Infant Custody Act afforded mothers access to their children only up to the age of seven; thereafter the father had sole custody. The 1857 Divorce Act allowed a man to divorce his wife after a single infidelity, but a woman could not divorce her husband for infidelity unless cruelty was also proven. As late as 1906, a new law placed most of the responsibility for child neglect onto mothers. A poor woman named Annie Woolmore, who was helped by the suffragettes, had been sent to prison for not keeping her home clean even though she was sick, had no water in the house and her unemployed husband testified that she 'starved herself to feed the kids'.[9] Most judges believed that the law existed to safeguard the rights of men, and that the intended role of a woman was to be placid and supportive.

An Injurious Anomaly

The 1869 Reform Act was a sharp disappointment to the growing number of women who thought that they should have the right to vote. Many local suffrage societies were formed and more women were drawn into support. Florence Nightingale gave the campaign encouragement by joining the Manchester Society. One supporter described how,

> 'the tour of meetings, consisting of six or seven in a fortnight', was a great success. The 'novelty of hearing women speakers... (ensured that)... the doors were thronged with people unable to obtain seats'.[10]

Campaigners hoped that these indications of greater activity would persuade Benjamin Disraeli, who became Prime Minister in 1874, to grant the vote to women. There was good reason for optimism. In the year before taking office, Disraeli had declared that denying the vote to women was,

> 'an injurious anomaly (which I) trust to see removed by wisdom of Parliament'.[11]

But once in power, Disraeli did nothing to remove that anomaly. This pattern of politicians talking sweetly in support of votes for women while in opposition but adopting a different stance once in government was to be repeated many times during the next fifty years. In due course the anger caused by this duplicity fuelled support for a different kind of suffrage campaign, based not just on petitions and constitutional argument but on militancy and direct action.

After the failure of the government to act, the suffrage societies set about creating their own majority in parliament by calling on individual MPs to pledge their support. It was successful, but it took a very long time. Not until 1897 did a Bill promising votes for women gain a majority in the Commons. It was moved by the aptly named Ferdinand Faithfull Begg and was carried by 228 votes to 157.

What happened next revealed a bigger problem. Begg's Bill was a Private Members' Bill with no guarantee of sufficient parliamentary time to pass through all the required stages. So it fell. Indeed a small coterie of anti-suffragists, often led by the obnoxious Henry Labouchère, who combined venomous opposition to votes for women with vicious homophobia and an even more rabid anti-Semitism, took delight in obstructing Bills supporting women's suffrage. On one occasion Labouchère and his group spoke for hours about a trivial Bill dealing with 'verminous persons' to ensure that no time was left to debate women's suffrage.[12] The filibuster was accompanied by much ribald self-congratulation. The lesson was that a Bill promising votes for women would not pass into law unless it received government support.

Throwing Women Overboard

The extent of that difficulty – of winning support from a government of either major party – was demonstrated in the struggle
with William Gladstone's Liberal Government which took office
in 1880. While in Opposition, Gladstone had made a speech that,
although embellished in characteristic manner by high-flown
phrases and rhetorical flourishes, was taken to express support for
votes for women.

> "The law does less than justice to women ... and... if
> it should be found possible to arrange a safe and well-
> adjusted alteration of the law as to political power, the
> man who may attain that objective... will, in my opinion
> be a real benefactor to his country".[13]

Many women in the suffrage societies drew the reasonable conclusion that Gladstone, himself, might decide to be that 'real benefactor'.
But they were disappointed. Disraeli had betrayed the supporters
of women's suffrage and now Gladstone, that self-declared man of
principle and saviour of fallen women, proceeded to do the same.

In the Election campaign Gladstone had promised the vote to agricultural labourers. Knowing that a Bill was being drafted to honour this
pledge, the women's suffrage societies ran a vigorous campaign urging the government to include votes for women. Their greatest success
was in persuading the Parliamentary Reform Conference, comprising
over 2,000 delegates from all over the country and with John Morley,
Gladstone's great ally, in the chair, to call on the government to 'confer
the franchise on women' on the same basis as men.

The new Bill was awaited with much excitement but when it came
before the House of Commons there were two unpleasant surprises:
the Bill did not mention women's suffrage and the Prime Minister
declared that he was totally against any move to amend the Bill to

include votes for women. When such an amendment was tabled by William Woodall, a fellow Liberal, Gladstone intervened to declare, 'I offer it the strongest opposition in my power.' His opposition was so fierce that he frightened a hundred or more Liberal MPs, who had hitherto supported votes for women, to change sides and vote against the amendment. It was lost by a large majority.

Gladstone justified his decision by arguing that the Bill was facing opposition in the House of Lords and contained as much as 'the vessel could safely carry'. The government used this nautical metaphor repeatedly throughout the debates, insisting that, 'women's suffrage would outweigh the ship'. Millicent Fawcett's tart response[14] was to note that Gladstone's action in 'throwing the women overboard' was in sharp contrast to the heroic traditions of seamen who are 'always prompted in moments of danger to save the women first'.

Gladstone really did have to battle against the House of Lords to get his Reform Bill into law. However, by his selective use of government power, the agricultural labourers secured the vote while the women of Britain did not. Emmeline Pankhurst, living contentedly with her husband and young family, pondered the contrast. Writing much later she explained that, in her opinion, the agricultural labourers had won the franchise:

'by burning hay ricks, rioting, and otherwise demonstrating their strength in the only way that English politicians understand'.

Emmeline Pankhurst admitted that in 1884 she was too young to learn the appropriate lessons from the debacle. However she added that, over the years,

'I acquired the experience and wisdom to know how to wring concessions from ... Government'.[15]

The next two decades were years of dispiriting frustration for the supporters of women's suffrage. Thousands of signatures were gathered for petitions but the petitions were all rejected. There was still the occasional glimpse of hope. The Isle of Man gave women the vote in all elections and the Trades Union Congress supported the principle that women should have the same voting rights as men. But the overriding feeling was that the moment of greatest opportunity had passed. The focus of political debate had shifted and other matters were absorbing the time and energy of the men in parliament. Gladstone tried to persuade both houses of parliament to accept home rule for Ireland and the Liberal Party split apart on the issue. As a result, the Conservatives were in power for two decades with scarcely a break.

Lord Salisbury, the Conservative leader, was the last Prime Minister to sit in the House of Lords. A distant patrician figure, he was somewhat disconnected from the everyday life of people in Britain. Urged by his doctors to take more exercise, he rode a tricycle with a footman in attendance to push him up the hills. Heavily focused on foreign and colonial matters, he regarded the suffrage campaign as a nuisance and all domestic politics as something of a distraction.

The Antis

In 1889, there was a further disheartening development. Over a hundred women, some well-known and mostly titled, signed an open letter opposing votes for women. The letter was published in a fashionable magazine and attracted considerable attention. It insisted that men and women have different roles in society:

> 'The "struggle of debate and legislation" belongs to men
> and "women's direct participation is made impossible either

by disabilities of sex, or by strong formations of custom
and habit resting ultimately on physical difference....'[16]

The letter signalled the beginning of a counter-attack that was sustained for more than twenty years. At first the Antis, as they were called, were an informal group. However as the struggle became more intense, a Women's Anti-Suffrage Society was set up with the novelist Mrs Humphrey Ward as its leader.

In hindsight, it is easy to dismiss the importance of the Antis. They were never very well organised. One of the Antis admitted, with charming frankness, that

'it was our fate... to attract all the ultra-feminine and lady-like incompetents'.[17]

Many of the arguments used by the Antis seem insubstantial and the leaders of the Women's Suffrage Societies took pleasure in exposing the contradictions between their statements and their actions. Mrs Ward insisted that, 'the political ignorance of women... is imposed by nature'[18] and that women are not suited to the hurly burly of politics. However, as Millicent Fawcett pointed out, this did not stop Mrs Ward from campaigning vigorously to help her son win a parliamentary seat.[19]

It is not clear how many women supported the Antis but not all of their sympathisers were from the establishment. Queen Victoria was strongly against votes for women but so too was Beatrice Potter, better known as Beatrice Webb, one of the founders of the London School of Economics and author of a famous Royal Commission Minority Report, which set out the founding principles of Britain's welfare state. Beatrice Webb did not abandon her opposition to women's suffrage for nearly twenty years and her belated explanation, that she had not personally suffered discrimination because she enjoyed rarity value as a female economist, has always seemed beside the point.

The Antis were most successful when they made women feel guilty. One postcard distributed by the Antis shows a baby in great distress. The poem on the back explains:

> "Mummy is a suffragette
>
> And I am no one's pet
>
> Oh! Why am I left all alone
>
> To cry and suffer yet".[20]

Mrs Ward wanted the Antis to be more assertive: she organised training courses to teach the Antis how to campaign as effectively as the suffragists. But this enthusiasm failed to take account of the feelings of her supporters. Most believed that campaigning was unfeminine and the idea of adopting the same aggressive approach as the suffragists made them feel very uncomfortable. As a result, the Antis stayed on the side-lines, sometimes vocal but never as forceful as Mrs Ward intended.

Helping Not Voting

The political parties found a better way of mobilising female support. They set up special organisations for women and gave them the task of assisting candidates at election times. Significantly, neither the Primrose League nor the Women's Liberal Federation had much difficulty in recruiting women even though both organisations were firmly based on the principle that the role of women was to help and not to vote. Mrs Gladstone, wife of the Liberal leader and the first president of the Women's Liberal Federation, was honest enough to say that the aim of the Federation was, 'to help our husbands'.[21]

In asking women to be supportive of their menfolk, the Primrose League and Women's Liberal Federation were working with the grain of the times. Victorian and Edwardian women were frequently told by men that their subordinate place in society was in accordance with their nature. From the cradle, girls were taught that, provided they married and provided they accepted a domestic role as mother and homemaker, they had fulfilled their destiny. Many girls were taught little else. Education of girls was patchy at best until the 1870 Act and, thereafter, was heavily conditioned by contemporary culture. Exceptional women occasionally broke through the barriers of prejudice but most women had no opportunity to go to university or enter a profession or set up a business. A domestic life awaited them, confined them and sometimes frustrated them but, like it or not, this future was inevitable and, according to men, entirely natural.

John Stuart Mill recognised that, if women were to win the vote, these assumptions had to be challenged and he did so with brilliance and humanity. In his famous essay *The Subjection of Women*, Mill rejects the popular belief that it is in women's nature to be subordinate to men. No one can know the true nature of women, he argues, because the behaviour of women has been long constrained by laws, rules and customs. Mill insists that women only consent to their subordinate position because they lack the confidence to fight their masters. Because a position of subordination is all that women have ever known, it appears normal, unchangeable and, in its familiarity, even comfortable. Mill describes an additional constraint. In the nineteenth century, women were taught that they could only find fulfilment through the relationship with men. Any challenge to male superiority and, in particular, any challenge to her husband or her father would put a woman at risk of the loss of her emotional security as well as the loss of social status, home and children.

Mill's essay was published in 1869, very early in the suffrage campaign.[22] It is an extraordinary document, at least fifty years ahead of its time, and it gave strength and confidence to both Millicent Fawcett and Emmeline Pankhurst. But few men agreed with Mill's analysis. This was a period when women were praised in sentimental terms for their elegance, their beauty and the refinement of their manners, qualities that were held to represent the essence of womanhood. But, alongside these compliments, men would often warn that strongly held opinions, forceful argument and intellectual prowess were incompatible with the idealised vision of female virtue that men sought in a wife. When pressed by Samuel Smith MP to explain why women's suffrage was not in his Reform Bill, Gladstone confessed to the fear that, if women voted in parliamentary elections, it would,

> 'trespass upon their delicacy, their purity, their refinement, the elevation of their whole nature'.[23]

Other men had more down-to-earth objections. Lord Cromer, who led the male section of the Antis, objected to a change in the status of women because,

> 'it would be subversive of peace in our homes'.[24]

The question which many men voiced, often with genuine puzzlement, was why women whom they idealised would want to enter the acrimonious and traditionally male preserve of politics. The answer, frequently suggested, was that 'real women' – delicate, refined and married – were satisfied with their lot and it was only a rebarbative minority who were campaigning for change. It was even alleged that these noisy activists behaved in such an unwomanly manner because they lacked the beauteous qualities of their sex and could not attract a man. A famous cartoon of the time pictures five miserable women under the rubric, 'Suffragettes who have never been kissed.'[25] This slur was frequently repeated. Emmeline Pankhurst answered the allegation directly. Her own home life and relations were, 'as nearly as ideal as possible' and,

lest anyone should miss the implication, she adds that her first *why?*
child was born a year after her marriage, her second after another
eighteen months and that a further two children followed.[26]

The WSPU *Women's Social and Political Union*

After 1905, and more particularly in the six years before the First
World War, Emmeline Pankhurst became the best-known votes for
women campaigner in Britain. She had served a long apprentice-
ship. Living first in Manchester and then in London, she combined
public service with a deep involvement in politics. Her husband
was a socialist, republican and agnostic, winning friends with his
charm but making enemies with the causes he promoted.

Emmeline Pankhurst supported her husband in his radical politics, welcomed the progressive politicians and thinkers from across
Europe who congregated at their home, joined the Independent
Labour Party (ILP) alongside her husband and was arrested in a
demonstration to safeguard the right to hold public meetings.[27] But
in 1898, her beloved husband died, leaving her heartbroken and
short of money. For three years she withdrew from politics and concentrated on supporting her four children. When she became active
again she wanted to use the ILP to reinvigorate the suffrage campaign. However, with characteristic impatience and egged on by her
eldest daughter, Christabel, who had formed a strong attachment
to two leading suffragists, she decided that ILP was spending too
much time on other issues. On 10 October 1903 she called together
a little gathering at her house in Nelson Street, Manchester, and the
Women's Social and Political Union (WSPU) was established.

Several of Emmeline Pankhurst's friends who formed that first
small membership of WSPU also came from the ILP and at first
there was cooperation between the two organisations. Keir

Hardie, leader of the ILP, remained a loyal ally of the Pankhursts and was particularly close to Sylvia, Emmeline's second daughter. But a breach was inevitable. Like members of other suffrage societies, Emmeline Pankhurst believed that the aim of the campaign should be to secure for women the same voting rights as men. Members of the ILP pointed out that, even if the campaign succeeded, most working class women, like most working class men, would still be without the vote. A common taunt was that WSPU was ignoring the poor and was really only seeking 'Votes for Ladies'! For a time Hardie was able to avoid a split but eventually the Labour Party declared itself unambiguously in support of votes for all adults, men and women, rich and poor.

Emmeline Pankhurst was incandescent. She believed that the demand for universal suffrage was a step too far and would be used by Liberal ministers to oppose any reform of the voting laws. And in the short term she was right. But the breach meant that leading women on the left of politics stood aside from the suffrage campaigns. Mary Macarthur, who founded the National Federation of Women Workers, thought that it was far more important to organise women into trade unions and improve their working conditions than to secure the vote for a minority of affluent women. Margaret Bondfield, who later became the first woman cabinet minister, was accused by Sylvia Pankhurst of being 'uninterested in the question'[28] of votes for women. This was an unworthy slur. Margaret Bondfield had no doubts about the importance of the vote. Indeed, she argued that women needed the vote 'to produce a profound psychological change in the attitude of men to women and of women to society'.[29] But, like Mary Macarthur, she believed that the necessary change would only come about if all women, and not just the well-off, had the right to vote.

Although the WSPU had the same limited objective as other suffrage societies, it differed from them in almost every other respect.

For years, Emmeline Pankhurst had supported the Manchester Society, but she thought that its leader, Lydia Becker, was too inclined to compromise and too ready to accept the empty promises of politicians. There was also a sharp contrast in behaviour and method. Lydia Becker, like Millicent Fawcett and most leaders of the long-standing suffrage societies, believed that votes for women could be won by sober argument and persistent lobbying. Emmeline Pankhurst had tried that and had suffered continual frustration as she watched politicians procrastinate and dissemble. She was convinced that the only way to influence government was by militant action.

Women's suffrage societies were traditionally set up like friendly societies. The members paid a subscription, a committee would be elected to decide policy, the minute book and the accounts would be open for inspection and the society would proceed by consensus. These democratic niceties did not impress Emmeline Pankhurst. The model in her head was not of a well-meaning friendly society but what she called a 'suffrage army in the field'.[30] Her aim for the WSPU was to have no constitution, no governing body, no business meetings and no election of officers. And discipline would be rigid. A woman could join for a shilling (5p) but had to sign 'a declaration of loyal adherence' to the policy of the WSPU and promise never to work for any political party until votes for women had been won. WSPU members were the foot soldiers of the suffrage army and were expected to obey orders.

Emmeline Pankhurst's determination to avoid democratic decision making and to take more power for herself caused many tensions in the WSPU. First a group of committed organisers who objected to the lack of democracy left to form the Women's Freedom League. Five years later, there was a split with long-standing allies over the decision to move to a new level of militancy. And in

1913, Emmeline Pankhurst's second daughter, Sylvia, was expelled for leading the semi-autonomous East London's Federation of Suffragettes. By that stage, Emmeline Pankhurst had achieved her aim and there was not even the merest pretence of democracy in WSPU. All important decisions were taken by Emmeline or, increasingly, by Christabel, her eldest daughter.

Emmeline Pankhurst was often called an autocrat and a dictator. She answered the criticism directly.

> 'Autocratic? Quite so. But, you may object, a suffrage organisation ought to be democratic. Well the members of the WSPU do not agree with you. We do not believe in the effectiveness of the ordinary suffrage association.'[31]

Fawcett and Pankhurst

This ice cold single-mindedness brought a new and often uncomfortable aspect to the votes for women campaign. Since Lydia Becker's death in 1890, Millicent Fawcett had become president of the National Union of Women's Suffrage Societies and the country's leading suffragist. Like Emmeline Pankhurst, Millicent Fawcett had been brought up in a middle-class family. Both were married to men with radical views. But whereas Emmeline Pankhurst was by nature an outsider, Millicent Fawcett was part of the political and social establishment. Her husband, Henry, who had been blinded in an accident, was a leading Liberal MP and was serving in Gladstone's cabinet when he died of pleurisy.

While Emmeline Pankhurst saw the right to vote as the only route to female emancipation and regarded every other campaign as a distraction, Millicent Fawcett took up a range of causes to advance the rights of women. She supported her sister, Elizabeth Garrett, in the campaign to open the medical profession to women. She wrote an acclaimed book on political economy. She helped to found a Cambridge College for women and led an official delegation to inquire into the conditions of women in prison camps in South Africa. Her personality was that well-judged combination of femininity and sharpness of wit, which many intelligent Victorian women seemed able to deploy. While always appearing lady-like, Millicent Fawcett could be ruthless in debate. Yet the warmth of her personality meant that Millicent Fawcett was loved in a way that Emmeline Pankhurst never was and never sought to be. Emmeline Pankhurst was a woman apart, idolised by her followers but feared by the establishment.

Circumstances sometimes forced Millicent Fawcett and Emmeline Pankhurst to act together and some supporters hoped that they would eventually combine their efforts. That was never possible. Millicent Fawcett advocated 'quiet argument' and 'constitutional methods' while Emmeline Pankhurst supported militancy. Cooperation also required a certain generosity of spirit. Millicent Fawcett could usually manage that but Emmeline Pankhurst found it much more difficult. Although Millicent Fawcett was eventually disenchanted by the violent actions of the WSPU, in the early years she paid tribute to the campaigning of the Pankhursts and their followers.

> 'They succeeded in drawing a far larger amount of public attention to claims of women to representation than had ever been given to the subject before.'[32]

On more than one occasion Millicent Fawcett organised celebration dinners for members of WSPU when they were released from prison. By contrast, Emmeline Pankhurst's lengthy autobiography never mentions Millicent Fawcett by name and almost every reference to the suffrage societies which Millicent Fawcett led is accompanied by contemptuous criticism.

Emmeline Pankhurst's determination to be in unrivalled control also killed the possibility of cooperation between WSPU and the so-called radical suffragists, mainly members of working class societies based in Lancashire, with many members who knew the Pankhursts well. The radical suffragists had fought a strong campaign in the years before WSPU became active, producing an enormous petition signed by thousands of textile workers and acting as an effective link with the trade unions and the ILP.[33] But Emmeline Pankhurst's lack of interest in their activities and Christabel's increasing dislike of associating with working class women meant that most members of this important group shifted their focus back to trade union activities. An important opportunity to broaden support for the suffragist cause had been lost.

Militancy

After 1903, there were two campaigns supporting votes for women, very different in tone, behaviour and methods. Their adherents went by different names. Members of the constitutional suffrage societies continued to call themselves suffragists, but members of the WSPU were soon called suffragettes.[34] The suffrage societies had thousands of members and significant resources but, at the outset, the WSPU was so small that Sylvia Pankhurst admitted that it was regarded as no more than, 'a family party'.[35] Committed to militancy, the WSPU also took time to translate that bold intention into action. When Christabel Pankhurst interrupted a meeting addressed by Winston Churchill and tried to move an amendment in support of women's suffrage, she got scant attention in the hall and the chairman politely ruled her out of order. Christabel conceded that 'little was heard and nothing remembered'[36] of that protest.

Eighteen months later, Christabel Pankhurst was better prepared. The Liberals were expected to win the coming General

Election and the target meeting was packed with Liberal supporters. Christabel arrived with Annie Kenney, an Oldham mill
worker who had become her devoted admirer, and with a large
banner calling for votes for women. They waited until the end of
the meeting and then, as Christabel unfurled the banner, Annie
Kenney demanded to know whether an incoming Liberal Government would give voting rights to women. When no answer
came, Christabel intervened and the meeting was soon in uproar.
The two suffragettes were ushered into a side room and, in a
moment of high comedy, given a lecture on lady-like behaviour. What happened next is not altogether clear but both were
charged with assaulting police officers. From the dock, Christabel Pankhurst admitted the assault but produced an inventive
plea in mitigation.

> 'I was not aware that the individuals assaulted were police
> officers. I thought they were Liberals.[37]

Both defendants were fined, both refused to pay and both were
taken to Strangeways gaol. The protest had an impact. On their
release, Christabel and Annie Kenney were feted by sympathisers. The Trade Union Council booked the Free Trade Hall and the
two ex-prisoners addressed a packed meeting. According to Hannah Mitchell, a leading suffragette based in Manchester, the affair
was a talking point throughout the North of England. Christabel
Pankhurst had learnt very quickly how to attract attention and
win supporters to the suffragette cause.

The militancy built relentlessly. Suffrage campaigners intervened
in every bye-election and stalked cabinet ministers at every election rally. Suffragettes lay in wait outside parliament or near the
Pal Mall clubs and chased the politicians as they rushed for their
taxis. The jostling of cabinet ministers became so intense that ministers had to be permanently guarded. When ministers decided that
persons attending political meetings must be vetted, suffragettes

slid into the hall before the doors opened and burst forth when the politicians arrived. Two campaigners hid in the rafters of a hall in Louth for nearly twenty-four hours in order to confront David Lloyd George.[38]

The suffragettes also became adept at organising local meetings. They would ring hand-bells, chalk the time and place of the meeting on pavements and often include a hint that a famous person would speak. A crowd would gather, pass a resolution demanding votes for women and demand the endorsement of local politicians. The pressure was relentless and tested the nerve of every government supporter.

Emmeline Pankhurst wanted to move the centre of WSPU's operations to London. Keir Hardie introduced her to Mrs Pethick-Lawrence, an affluent woman of progressive views. Mrs Pethick-Lawrence became the WSPU's treasurer; she and her husband funded the move to London, allowed WSPU to set up an office in their property in Clement's Inn and provided enough money for WSPU to employ organisers and support staff. Teresa Billington, one of the newly appointed organisers, wrote that, 'the change that came in mid-summer 1906 was a matter of wonder and delight'.[39] She went to work in Scotland, Annie Kenney was despatched to the West Country and Christabel Pankhurst worked in London. For the next six years the Pethick Lawrences supplied Emmeline Pankhurst and the WSPU with the resources to build what Teresa Billington called, 'an efficient organisation'. WSPU had become much more than 'a family party'.

A Liberal Government was soon in power. The new Prime Minister, Henry Campbell Bannerman, was a decent man and had some sympathy for the suffragist cause but his difficulties were severe. His health was failing. He took office as head of a minority government expecting an ambush from the Conservatives. To secure his position he needed to win an early election but three of his most senior Liberal colleagues were plotting to replace him. In the event he won the election and managed to see off the plotters but the struggles exhausted him. When the government gave no indication of any intention to legislate for female suffrage, the WSPU staged a sit-down protest on the steps outside Campbell Bannerman's house. Weary and under pressure, he finally gave a commitment to meet representatives of all the campaigning groups.

The deputation that met the prime minister claimed to represent over a quarter of a million women, with textile operatives sitting alongside women graduates, temperance campaigners, socialists and liberals. To make the historical point, the campaigners' case was opened by Emily Davies who had brought the petition to John Stuart Mill forty years earlier. The arguments were well marshalled by the suffragists and, in the closing speech, Emmeline Pankhurst hinted at future militancy. But the meeting ended in anti-climax. Campbell Bannerman's advice was to be patient. It was a message that disappointed Millicent Fawcett and further convinced Emmeline Pankhurst of the unreliability of politicians. The WSPU contingent marched to Trafalgar Square and held a meeting condemning the government's position. 'Patience can be carried to excess', was Keir Hardie's comment.[40]

Two Demonstrations

The government's programme for the new session was due to be announced on 12 February 1907 and the National Union of Suffrage Societies organised a demonstration on the previous day. The weather was so bad that the event became known as the Mud March. It was led by Millicent Fawcett, her sister Elizabeth Garrett Anderson, Lady Balfour and the Countess of Carlisle with many carriages and motor cars in the procession as well as very many women trudging on 'bravely through the mud'. At the rally in Exeter Hall, the writer Israel Zangwill made a famous speech.

> "Our case is so simple that it is like having to prove that one and one are two. Indeed that is precisely what the opposition denies. It says that one and one are not two; that in politics one man and one woman are only one, and man is that one."[41]

The demonstration was well reported and regarded as a great success. The following day the government announced its legislative programme and, as predicted, there were no plans to extend the vote to women. The reaction of the WSPU was different in tone and intent from the demonstration organised by the National Union of Women's Suffrage Societies. Emmeline Pankhurst summoned what she called a Women's Parliament in Caxton Hall. The meeting was angry and indignant. A deputation was elected to take a resolution demanding votes for women to the House of Commons.

Before the women reached Parliament Square, the procession was faced by a solid line of police. When the women pressed forward a corps of mounted police rode at the procession, scattering the women. The procession re-formed and the women were scattered again. The brutal battle went on for hours. Over a dozen women managed to get into parliament and tried to hold a meeting. They were arrested. Many more were arrested in Parliament Square. Over fifty women and two men appeared before the magistrates the following morning. All refused to pay a fine and all were imprisoned.

The WSPU demonstration gained much more publicity than the Mud March and most of the publicity was supportive. In general, the press deplored the aggressive behaviour of the police and the government suffered a deal of criticism. Those three days in February revealed much about the nature of the campaign and about the government's response. The National Union was shown to be very well supported at many levels in society but not much feared by the politicians. The WSPU had shown that militancy could attract more publicity and, instead of alienating public opinion, as many had expected, could sometimes win support. The government was also beginning to appreciate the difficulty of finding an appropriate response to a militant campaign carried out by determined women.

Herbert
Asquith

Campbell Bannerman's vacillation was frustrating but within three years he was dead and the suffrage campaigners faced a more formidable obstacle. Herbert Asquith, the new Prime Minister, was against votes for women in principle and so, very vociferously, was his wife. Asquith expressed strong doubts about the capacity of women to understand public affairs and was contemptuous of the work of the suffrage campaigners.

During one debate Asquith disagreed with the truism that 'women are the female of the species' and insisted that they came from a species that is distinct and inferior to men, just as a rabbit comes from a distinct and inferior species. George Bernard Shaw was one of the few men who protested at this odious comparison. He wrote in the *Times* that it was impossible to support a Prime Minister who, 'places one's mother on the same footing as a rabbit'.[42]

Asquith was determined that women would not get the vote while he was Prime Minister and he was prepared to use all the powers of government and all his ingenuity, including double-dealing and trickery, to defeat the campaigners. He took an early opportunity to spell out his position. At some stage, he said, the government would introduce a Reform Bill but it would not include votes for women. When pressed, Asquith grudgingly acknowledged that the

Bill might be amended to include women but it was clear that he would not welcome such an amendment.

With Asquith in Downing Street there was little hope of concession or compromise. People sometimes wonder why the confrontation between the votes for women campaigners and the government became so much nastier in the years immediately before the First World War. One answer is the militancy of the Pankhursts and the WSPU. A better answer is the behaviour of Herbert Asquith.

What came next was unexpected. Herbert Gladstone, the Home Secretary, suggested, to general surprise, that the women campaigners had not exerted enough pressure to be taken seriously. Making a comparison with the demonstrations before the Great Reform Bill of 1832, he explained that men had won the vote at that time by assembling,

> 'in their tens of thousands all over the country... it is not to be expected that women can assemble in such masses, but power belongs to masses....'[43]

Whatever the home secretary hoped to achieve by these remarks, Emmeline Pankhurst took them as a challenge. The WSPU organised the enormous Hyde Park demonstration that was described in Chapter 2. The masses assembled, the demonstration was a remarkable success and the demonstrators waited for the government's response. It came from the Prime Minister. In a moment of contrived anti-climax, Asquith merely reiterated government policy. At some stage, he said, there would be a new Reform Bill but it would not mention votes for women. However it might be possible for it to be amended. He gave no timetable and no certainty: so much for the power of the masses when those masses happened to be women.

The response was rapid and predictable. The WSPU called on its supporters to demonstrate outside the House of Commons and they turned up in their thousands. A deputation asked to see Asquith but he gave no reply. Some of the crowd tried to get into parliament but were held back by police. When the police lines broke, mounted police were brought in to disperse the crowd. Twenty women were arrested. They refused to pay fines and were imprisoned in Holloway. Mary Leigh and Edith New were sentenced for breaking the windows of 10 Downing Street. This was the first instance of deliberate damage to property. It represented a further step in WSPU's campaign of militancy.

Prison

On the opening day of the new session, the WSPU planned what was called a 'rush' of parliament. Before it took place, the law intervened. Emmeline and Christabel Pankhurst and Flora Drummond were summoned for planning an illegal act. This was not a clever move. The trial provided WSPU with a great opportunity for publicity. Uncomfortable revelations emerged about the involvement of government ministers in the legal process and, most newsworthy of all, two cabinet ministers appeared in the witness box. The magistrate found the three women guilty. They refused to be bound over to keep the peace and were sentenced to several months in prison. Emmeline Pankhurst managed to capture further publicity by using a phrase in court that was often repeated during the years of struggle.

> 'We are here not because we are law-breakers; we are here in our efforts to become law-makers.'[44]

During the next five years the suffragettes were noisy, antagonistic and aggressive. To the dismay of many of its supporters, the Liberal government's response was more impetuous than strategic. This was a period of great political turbulence and the government mostly had its mind on other problems. Lloyd George's budget to provide unemployment insurance and pensions put the government in direct conflict with the House of Lords and was the cause of two years of hard-fought political battles. Wave after wave of industrial disputes prompted Lloyd George to say that rebellion was spreading across the country, 'like foot and mouth disease'. Ulster was in uproar as Edward Carson raised an army to defeat the government's policy of home rule for Ireland. And by increasing its military fleet, Germany had become a formidable threat to Britain's naval supremacy.

Faced with such challenges, a more thoughtful government, with a more flexible prime minister, might have reached a settlement with the women so that it could concentrate on its more intractable problems. Instead, the government chose to regard the suffrage campaign as unjustified, malicious and best dealt with through the courts. It was a foolish mistake. Militancy was met with retribution and the ever-increasing severity of the sentences provoked political outrage and more militancy.

The imprisonment of the Pankhursts and Flora Drummond led to a new demand from WSPU. While in Holloway, Emmeline Pankhurst insisted that suffragettes should be regarded as political prisoners. Some rights were conceded but the principle was not. The spiral of conflict took an extra turn. Each time a WSPU member was imprisoned, the demand was made for political prisoner status. When that was refused, the prisoner went on hunger strike.

This new tactic threw the authorities into confusion. The government knew that if a suffragette died, the political consequences would be dire. The authorities tried to tempt the prisoners with delicious food. Sylvia Pankhurst says she was offered, 'chops and steak, jellies and fruit'.[45] Predictably, this rarely worked, so the authorities started releasing hunger strikers when it seemed that their health was being seriously damaged. This policy suited the WSPU well enough but it made the government look weak and out of control. During the summer of 1909, the government thought about an alternative policy and eventually decided that prisoners on hunger strike should be forcibly fed.

Forcible Feeding

Prison authorities had no experience of forcible feeding and what might have seemed in theory like a logical response to a refusal to eat was soon revealed in all its brutish reality. Sylvia Pankhurst was forcibly fed during her many imprisonments, on one occasion for a total of five weeks. She described the excruciating experience:

> "Six wardresses... 'flung me on my back on the bed and held me down firmly by shoulders and wrists, hips, knees and ankles. A man's hands were striving to pull my lips apart... a steel instrument pressed my gums, cutting into the flesh... They were trying to get the tube down my throat. They got it down I suppose, though (by then) I was unconscious of anything then save a mad revolt of struggling... I vomited as the tube came up... I was left sobbing convulsively.

> Morning and evening the same struggle... My gums were always sore and bleeding with other bits of loose jagged flesh... sometimes the tube was coughed up three or four times before they got it down. ... often I fainted once or twice after the feeding...."[46]

The truth about forcible feeding soon became public knowledge. According to Millicent Fawcett, the courage of the hunger strikers,

> 'made a very deep impression on the public and touched the imagination of the whole country'.[47]

The policy caused uproar in the medical profession. Immediately after the first forcible feeding in Birmingham, over a hundred local doctors wrote to the prime minister calling the action, 'unwise and inhumane'.[48] Critical articles appeared in the *Lancet*. The government was losing the propaganda battle.

Conciliation Bill

Frustrated by the government's intransigence, Lord Lytton, brother of a militant campaigner, and Henry Brailsford, a radical journalist who supported Millicent Fawcett's National Union, formed a Conciliation Committee to draft a Bill that would command cross-party support. The Committee contained representatives from all the main parties and there were hints that the government, which after the election was in a minority, might be looking for a solution. Optimism ran so high that Emmeline Pankhurst declared a suspension of militancy. The Conciliation Committee drafted a Bill, all suffrage societies accepted it and the WSPU held a grand demonstration at the Albert Hall. Emmeline Pankhurst was convinced that, 'the time is ripe for a suffrage bill'.[49]

Emmeline Pankhurst's optimism was widely shared but was misplaced. In a series of disgraceful episodes, the government used parliamentary trickery to stop two Conciliation Bills from becoming law. The first Conciliation Bill was passed with a big majority but Asquith, Churchill and Lloyd George spoke against it and, in spite of making reassuring noises, Asquith managed to sabotage the committee stage so that the Bill ran out of time before the end of the parliamentary session.

Considerable pressure was put on the government to return to the Bill in the autumn session. A petition with over a quarter of a million signatures was collected and Millicent Fawcett estimated that over 4,000 meetings were held. But the session lasted for barely a week before a General Election was called. The Conciliation Bill was not considered and the supporters of Votes for Women felt betrayed.

Black Friday

The result was Black Friday. WSPU members met at Caxton Hall and began to move in small groups to lobby the government. Emmeline Pankhurst's group managed to reach the entrance to parliament but a formidable corps of police blocked the path of the other demonstrators. According to eye-witnesses, the police drove the women back, punching them, kicking them and throwing them to the ground. Nevertheless, helped by what Emmeline Pankhurst called a 'friendly' crowd, more of the women began to get close to parliament. [50] At this point, mounted police were called in but the women still refused to withdraw. There were heavy casualties and the suffragettes set up a medical station in Caxton Hall to treat wounds and broken bones. At last, after six hours it became clear that the police attacks would not clear Parliament Square. Then, and only then, did the police start making arrests.

There was much evidence of violence and many women reported that their breasts were squeezed and the police had made obscene suggestions. Henry Brailsford collected a host of witness statements. One young woman was marched to the police station with her skirts held over her head. Mary Earl swore a statement describing her treatment:

> '...the police were most brutal and indecent. They deliberately tore my undergarments, using the most foul language... They seized me by the hair and forced me up the steps on my knees... I was then flung into the crowd'.[51]

It seemed that the police had been brought from Whitechapel with orders to teach the women a lesson and not to bring the demonstration to an end by making arrests. Churchill, the Home Secretary, rejected calls for an enquiry and denied that the police were following his orders. According to him, the decision to make few arrests had been made by his predecessor.

The police were heavily criticised and were also ridiculed. Mounted police had failed to clear the square and there was a particular humiliation prepared for them by Evelina Haverfield. She was an excellent horsewoman and her empathy with the animals was so great that she was able to coax the horses out of the police lines and, according to some reports, even get them to lie down while the police riders struggled to regain control.[52] The police had behaved like bullies and the watching crowd enjoyed their discomfiture as the suffragettes fought back and Evelina Haverfield worked her magic.

The suffragettes were angry at the violence and sought revenge. Two days after Black Friday, Asquith was jostled in Downing Street and a stone was thrown through the window of his taxi. He seemed very frightened. But that was an isolated incident. The expected wave of militancy did not come.

Emmeline Pankhurst is often described as impatient and intransigent, but at this time she behaved with great restraint. Instead of abandoning the conciliation process, she called a new truce and joined the other suffrage societies in supporting the Conciliation Committee's new Bill, which offered the vote to women householders. What convinced Emmeline Pankhurst was the promise made by Asquith in a letter to Lord Lytton, Chairman of the Conciliation Committee. The prime minister wrote that the new Conciliation Bill would be given facilities to complete all its stages in the Commons, adding that his promise would be honoured, 'not only in the letter but in the spirit'.

Treachery

With such a written assurance it is little wonder that the suffrage societies were convinced of Asquith's good intentions. But the trickery continued. When the Commons reassembled in October, Asquith made a shock announcement. The government would bring in a Bill granting universal suffrage. But only to men: the Bill would have to be amended to include the limited suffrage for women in the Conciliation Bill. There was no prospect of equality: if the amended Bill passed, all men would get the vote but only some women. Asquith had created a situation where the women would be left behind once again.

WSPU ended the truce. Windows were smashed in public buildings, in the homes of cabinet ministers, in Banks and in West End shops. A passionate suffragette, Emily Wilding Davison, was convicted of trying to set fire to a post box, the first incident of arson in the WSPU campaign. She told the court that she was protesting against government treachery.

Worse treachery was to follow. After the government introduced its manhood suffrage Bill and amendments granting limited suffrage to women were tabled, another 'bombshell' was dropped. The Speaker ruled that the amendments would make such a fundamental change to the Bill that the amended Bill could not be allowed to proceed. As a result, the Bill was withdrawn and the attempt to secure even limited suffrage for women failed.

In the row that followed, Asquith was accused of orchestrating the whole wretched affair. Did he expect such a ruling by the Speaker or was he, a lawyer and experienced parliamentarian, as surprised as he claimed? The evidence is inconclusive but the outcome certainly served his purpose. He lost nothing by withdrawing the manhood suffrage Bill, which had little support in the Liberal Party, the intervention of the speaker allowed him to escape from his promises to Lord Lytton and, much to his evident satisfaction, there would be no votes for women. Lloyd George referred to this episode as the 'torpedoing' of the Conciliation Bill. It was a revealing remark and did nothing to suggest that the government had clean hands.

WSPU embarked on a determined campaign of window smashing. Stocks of rocks and flints were maintained at secret locations and well-dressed women would hide the missiles in their clothing until the target buildings were reached. The suffragettes became expert at causing a great deal of damage before police arrived. Misinformation about dates and locations was fed to the police. Techniques improved. Sylvia Pankhurst discovered that a hammer had to be used on certain plate glass as flints simply slid off. The damage was infuriating, inconvenient and expensive. Shopkeepers demanded government action.

The government response was to charge the leaders of the WSPU with conspiracy to commit damage. Emmeline Pankhurst, Mr and Mrs Pethick Lawrence and 'Pansy' Tuke, the WSPU Secretary, were arrested. The WSPU office was ransacked and the printer of the WSPU journal was threatened. Christabel Pankhurst was not at the office that day. When she heard of the raid, she fled to Paris. With her mother in and out of prison and suffering a collapse in her health, Christabel increasingly took on the role of the WSPU leader – in exile but determined to be very much in control.

The case against the WSPU Secretary was dropped but Emmeline Pankhurst and Mr and Mrs Pethick-Lawrence were found guilty. In spite of a plea for leniency from the jury they were sentenced to nine months imprisonment. It is not clear what the government expected to gain from the prosecution, but the outcome was a torrent of protests from home and abroad and three more truculent prisoners on hunger strike. Before a week was out, the prisoners were granted the rights of political prisoners but the protests continued, led in parliament by Keir Hardie and George Lansbury.[53] The press criticised the bullying of the printer and the censorship of the suffragettes' journal. Attempts to forcibly feed the two women were abandoned and they were soon released. Frederick Pethick-Lawrence, on the other hand, was forcibly fed twice a day for a fortnight before being released in a state of collapse.

Destruction

On her release, Emmeline Pankhurst rushed to Paris to see Christabel and they agreed that WSPU should take more militant action. The instructions to the suffragettes were to use arson and bombs to destroy property. Prime targets were golf courses, sports pavilions, unoccupied houses, piers and hayricks. Art galleries and museums were attacked and national treasures were damaged. The Rokeby Venus in the National Gallery was slashed and several other important paintings were damaged in London, Manchester and Birmingham. Pillar boxes were filled with dye or varnish or set on fire. Houses owned by politicians and other prominent persons were burned. The Theatre Royal in Dublin suffered an arson attack. The Grandstand at Ayr Racecourse was burnt to the ground. A bomb was set off at Oxted station. Bombs were exploded in Westminster Abbey, St. John's Westminster and St. Martin's in the Fields. Two ancient churches in the Midlands were destroyed.

Some commentators have suggested that this campaign of destruction amounted to terrorism. If so, it was terrorism of a particularly limited kind. The campaign was directed at property; no person was killed or badly injured. Indeed, over the years the government was so short of victims that it had made a disproportionate fuss about the injury to the ankle of one politician who had been accosted by suffragettes and stumbled while rushing for his taxi.

A more pertinent question is whether the escalation of violence was necessary or desirable. The immediate reaction was unfavourable. The acts of destruction were condemned in the press and were unpopular with many of the public, particularly when the targets had no obvious connection to votes for women. Even more dispiriting was the effect on the WSPU. The Pethick-Lawrences, so recently allies, friends and cell-mates of Emmeline Pankhurst, decided to accept exclusion from WSPU rather than support the increase in violence. Other suffragettes also left and formed a new organisation. Even Sylvia Pankhurst thought that the new policy was mistaken.[54]

Throughout the votes for women campaign, Emmeline Pankhurst had justified the militancy of WSPU because it 'made women's suffrage a matter of news'. No doubt this was true when WSPU was first formed but by 1913, after eight years of vigorous and ingenious campaigning, the suffragettes were well equipped to gain publicity without arson and bombs.

The boycotting of the census had produced stories across the country. The cutting of telegraph lines was high profile. The chaining of suffragettes to screens in the Houses of Parliament provoked the Westminster authorities into much newsworthy nonsense. There was the delightful idea that suffragettes might package and post themselves to intransigent politicians. Then there was the use of the balloon to distribute leaflets,[55] the placing of WSPU flags on the greens of the Balmoral golf course, the demand under ancient law for the right to petition the King, the comparison between the harsh treatment of women demanding the vote and the appeasement of Sir Edward Carson who was planning treason in Ulster and, of course, Annie Kenney's peaceful invasion of Lambeth Palace to lobby the Archbishop of Canterbury.[56] There was no shortage of stories to fill the newspapers.

In her speeches Emmeline Pankhurst insisted that the new violence was necessary to force the government into concessions. Millicent

Fawcett thought that a different outcome was more likely. The use of arson and bombs directed at a host of apparently random targets would give Asquith a fresh opportunity to claim that women did not have the required judgement and maturity to take part in parliamentary elections. Fortunately for the cause of women's suffrage, the government chose, at this moment of high opportunity, to exercise some restraint. The reason for that somewhat surprising decision was the power of Millicent Fawcett's own organisation.

A Shield

Some of the most prominent women in the land were members of suffrage societies in Millicent Fawcett's National Union. These included the wives, sisters and daughters of MPs and peers. This influential membership meant that politicians who attacked the suffragists would be well advised to act with great care. When Winston Churchill ignored the requirement for restraint, he attracted a level of opprobrium that was a warning to others. After a demonstration in Downing Street, Churchill saw a well-dressed woman standing nearby. He told a policeman to 'drive that woman away'. That woman was Mrs Cobden Sanderson, a friend of Churchill's wife and Churchill himself had dined at her house. Mrs Cobden Sanderson was shocked at her treatment and the general view was that Churchill had behaved disgracefully. A few days later, Hugh Franklin – a young man related to a member of the government – attempted to horsewhip Churchill for his insulting behaviour.[57]

Millicent Fawcett and her supporters could not help Emmeline Pankhurst and WSPU members to escape prison and hundreds of suffragettes suffered desperately. However, the influence of the National Union of Women's Suffrage Societies acted as a shield that protected the cause of women's suffrage from the worst political consequences of the escalation of violence. It is tempting to describe the votes for women campaign after 1908 just in terms of the actions of the suffragettes but that would be massively to understate the influence of Millicent Fawcett and the National Union.

The WSPU gave excitement and momentum to the campaign but the constitutional Suffrage Societies gave it breadth, respectability and a measure of protection.[58] Without the National Union and without Millicent Fawcett's determination to hold the moral high ground, Asquith might well have used the campaign of fire and bombs not just to attack the perpetrators but to mount a new assault on the cause itself.

Christabel

Emmeline and Christabel Pankhurst were both parties to the decision to escalate violence but in reality that meeting in Paris marked the transfer of power from a mother enfeebled by prison and hunger strikes to a daughter who was fit, fierce and obsessive. Emmeline Pankhurst was single-minded but had shown that she could also be pragmatic. There was none of that flexibility in Christabel. She kept contact with events in Britain through Annie Kenney, her besotted admirer, who each week took the boat to France and suffered hideous sea-sickness to keep her appointment with destiny.[59] Christabel's response to every piece of news was to order an increase in militancy. Sometimes her instructions were startling. Sylvia Pankhurst says that she was sent a message telling her to 'burn down Nottingham Castle', apparently in an attempt to emulate the action of the campaigners of the 1830s.[60]

According to Sylvia, Christabel also began to reposition the suffragettes. The WSPU had always stood aside from party politics; it opposed the Liberals not on ideological grounds but because they formed the government that was denying the vote to women.

Now, much to the distress of the left-wing Sylvia, Christabel showed signs of favouring the Conservatives. Sylvia also noticed that Christabel was rejecting any possibility of cooperating with men, even long-standing supporters like Henry Brailsford. She was also becoming very selective about the women whom she wanted in WSPU. Christabel insisted that Sylvia's East London Federation of working women should leave WSPU. When pressed for a reason, Sylvia recalls Christabel saying that working women were, 'the weakest portion of the sex'. What Christabel wanted was, 'picked women; the very strongest and the most intelligent'.[61]

Much of this criticism comes from Sylvia and she is not always an accurate reporter of her sister's behaviour. However, the evidence supports her account. Sylvia and the East London Federation of working women were expelled from WSPU without good reason and, at this time, Christabel published a booklet entitled, 'The Great Scourge and How to End it'. In this she asserted, without supporting evidence that over three-quarters of the men in Britain had venereal disease and that most ailments afflicting women, including childlessness, resulted from contact with these infected men. Christabel adopted a new slogan: 'Votes for Women and Chastity for Men'. Christabel's booklet was well received in certain church circles.

The government knew of the divisions in the votes for women campaign but could find no way to benefit from them. Ministers felt trapped between the relentless constitutional pressure of the National Union and the increasingly outrageous militancy of the suffragettes. There was much soul-searching about the best way forward. Four options were listed in a House of Commons debate. The suffragette prisoners could be allowed to die, they could be transported, they could be treated as lunatics or they could be given the vote. None of these options was attractive to the government. Instead Reginald McKenna, the Home Secretary, proposed a new policy to tackle hunger strikers.[62]

Cat and Mouse Act

McKenna's initiative was the Prisoners' Temporary Discharge for Ill-Health Bill. This would allow hunger-strikers to be released for short periods to recover their health. They would then be imprisoned again and, if they went back on hunger strike, the process would keep being repeated until they had completed their full sentence. For obvious reasons, the new law became known as 'the Cat and Mouse Act'.

At first the Act attracted support, particularly because people assumed that it would mean an end to forcible feeding. But the government soon faced difficulties. Tracking down the prisoners who had been temporarily released proved difficult: the 'mice' kept hiding and wearing disguises and using decoys. The pattern of release and re-imprisonment also meant that it would take many years for some prisoners to complete relatively short sentences. The example of Emmeline Pankhurst was compelling. She was now back in prison after WSPU had taken responsibility for blowing up Lloyd George's house on Walton Heath. The Daily Mail calculated that under the Cat and Mouse Act her thirty-six months of penal servitude would not be completed for twenty years. And for some extraordinary reason the authorities also continued to use forcible feeding, although not in the case of Emmeline Pankhurst, their most high-profile hunger striker. Government policy looked incoherent.

Emily Wilding Davison

When he was considering the options for government policy, the Home Secretary said that 40 or 50 women would be prepared to die for their cause.[63] A few months later, Emily Wilding Davison threw herself at the King's horse during the Epsom Derby and

died of her injuries. She was carrying a WSPU flag and WSPU colours were sewn into her coat. It has never been clear whether she
intended to kill herself or whether she was trying to attach the flag
to the King's horse. She had attempted suicide in the past, but she
left no note for her family and the close friend who was with her
at Epsom said she gave no hint that she was thinking of killing
herself. Yet anyone who has stood by the rail at a racecourse and
seen the speed and power of the horses can be in no doubt of the
likely consequences of running into their path. Perhaps the truth
is that Emily Davison did not much care about the risk to herself.
Advancing the cause had always been the sole aim of her life as a
fervent suffragette.

The funeral procession was large and dignified. The mourners,
some in black and some in white, carried purple irises, crim-
son peonies and the green of laurel leaves. Emmeline Pankhurst
planned to attend the funeral but she was arrested and taken back
into custody immediately she left her flat. Apart from this act of
pettiness, the government made no response to Emily Davison's
death. But the awful event seemed to add to the cloud of weari-
ness that enveloped the cabinet. The only flicker of energy came
from McKenna. The WSPU offices were raided, their printer was
hounded and there was even talk of legal action against WSPU
donors. But the police action did not stop WSPU. Acts of destruction increased during the latter part of 1913 and the first half of
1914. By that measure WSPU was as strong as ever.

Yet in the months before the outbreak of war in August 1914 there
were indications that the power balance was changing inside and
outside the suffrage movement. After years of ambiguity about its
political position, the National Union of Women's Suffrage Societies
had entered into an alliance with the Labour Party. The suffragettes,
including the Pethick-Lawrences, who had left WSPU over the escalation of violence, had formed the United Suffragists which seemed

likely to become a new strategic force in the campaign. The expulsion of Sylvia Pankhurst, an avowed socialist, and her organisation of working women in the East London Federation had narrowed the class and political range of WSPU membership. Most important of all, an increasing number of the British establishment – in the church, the professions, the arts and in commerce – wanted the conflict ended. Whatever their personal political positions, they knew that the matter would only be settled if women secured the vote.

Feeding this appetite for a settlement was the increasing recognition that the votes for women issue had been mishandled. In parliament and across society the government's mistakes were recalled and condemned: not just the broken promises, the violence of the police and the brutality of forcible feeding, but a host of smaller misjudgements that stayed in the mind and damaged the government's reputation.

Lady Constance Lytton's experience was often quoted. When, along with other suffragettes she first went to prison, she gave her full name and title and was well treated, receiving good medical support. However she noticed that other suffragette prisoners fared much worse. So she disguised herself as a seamstress and, when she was next arrested, gave her name as Jane Warton. 'Jane' was forcibly fed and her health was permanently damaged. Her courageous ploy revealed what many had suspected: when the Home Secretary said that all prisoners were treated equally, he was telling a blatant lie. Lord Lytton wrote to the newspapers and made sure that his sister's story was well known and remembered.

East London Deputation

The government needed to make a decisive move to limit political damage. But when the move came, in June 1914, it seemed to arise accidentally, without planning or forethought. Sylvia Pankhurst had been recalled to prison after a battle with the police in Victoria Park. Once released on licence she proposed that the East London Federation send a deputation to lobby Asquith. In a change of approach, members of the federation decided to abandon support for the limited suffrage of the Conciliation Bills and argue for universal female suffrage; a significant change in the political demand. Sylvia requested a meeting and Asquith refused. She wrote again and he refused again. After a procession to parliament, Sylvia was sent back to prison. The East London Federation sent another letter and received a third refusal. However when Sylvia was released, she rushed to the Commons to press for the meeting. Weakened by another hunger strike she looked a pathetic figure. But she would not leave and, after much lobbying, Hardie, Lansbury and Henry Nevinson persuaded Asquith to meet a deputation of six from the East London Federation on the following Saturday.[64]

Sylvia Pankhurst drafted the statement to be read to Asquith but decided not to attend the meeting. This was good judgement because Asquith disliked her intensely. The six working women in the deputation had been chosen by a mass meeting and were led by Mrs Savoy, a brush-maker who called herself Mrs Hughes for the day because her husband 'did not want to see his name in the papers'.[65] After the opening statement, Mrs Savoy startled the meeting by putting a parcel on the table. Much to the prime minister's relief the parcel contained nothing more sinister than a brush and Mrs Savoy used it to show how she earned her living. She was paid a penny farthing for a completed brush, which took nearly two hours to make. Each of the women described how they lived, the struggle to make ends meet and the terrible fear of the workhouse. Their message was that conditions for women in the East End would only be improved if women had a part in choosing their representatives in parliament. Asquith seemed impressed. He summed up their case fairly and said he would give it, 'very careful and mature consideration'.[66]

The deputation believed him, the suffrage campaigners rejoiced and the press reported a breakthrough.

We shall never know whether that extraordinary meeting on 20 June 1914 was, as Sylvia Pankhurst called it, 'Asquith's first step towards surrender'.[67] Eight days later Gavrilo Princip, a 19-year-old Bosnian, assassinated Archduke Franz Ferdinand, heir presumptive to the Austro-Hungarian throne. The obligations written into the two great alliances that divided Europe were activated and in August the Great War began.

War

Events moved rapidly and often in unexpected directions. The government announced an amnesty for suffragette prisoners. WSPU called an end to militancy and Emmeline Pankhurst and Christabel devoted their time to recruiting men for the armed services. Christabel led a campaign to present young men in civilian clothes with white feathers. Prompted by Millicent Fawcett, the National Union turned itself into a Women's Active Service Corps in support of the war effort. Not all suffragists were happy with these developments. The National Union split over its attitude to the war. The East London Federation and the United Suffragists gave their energies not to the war effort but to the relief of suffering. Sylvia adopted the slogan, 'Women should stand for peace' and was publicly repudiated by her mother and sister.[68]

The final breakthrough came as another surprise. General Elections had not been suspended during the war and the war committees of both major parties, heavily supported by the press, demanded that all soldiers should have the vote. Unexpectedly Asquith intervened to say that, if that was agreed, women should be included.

"When the process of industrial reconstruction has to
be set on foot, have not the women a special claim to be
heard on the many questions that will arise directly affecting their interest and possibly meaning for them a large
displacement of labour? ... I cannot deny that claim".

He seemed sincere but Emmeline Pankhurst accused him of introducing the issue of the women's vote in order to avoid giving the
vote to soldiers.[69] It was a bizarre comment that revealed how far
her priorities had changed.

A Speaker's Conference was set up to report on electoral reform.
It recommended universal suffrage for adult men with special
arrangements for young soldiers but concluded that votes for
women should be introduced on a much more limited basis. The
final government proposal was that women should only have the
vote if they were householders or the wives of householders or
were graduates voting in a university constituency. The worst discrimination was in respect of age. All men over 21 would have
the vote but, even if women had the required qualifications, they
would not be able to vote until they were 30.

The Act

A rear-guard action was waged by the United Suffragists and the
East London Federation, now re-formed as the Women's Suffrage
Federation. Mrs Pethick-Lawrence said the discrimination was the
result of some 'grotesque working of the political mind'.[70] Nevertheless most suffrage societies, including the WSPU, noted that
the terms were better than those in the old Conciliation Bills and,
with surprisingly little argument, accepted the government's proposal. The Bill received the Royal Assent on 6 February 1918, and
women voted in the General Election on 14 December 1918. Over

8 million women had been enfranchised but the cherished principle of equality with men had not been achieved.

In later chapters we examine the legacy of the suffrage campaign, its many lessons and how they might be used in future campaigns. Florence Nightingale's prediction that the suffrage campaign was 'the last and greatest battle' was not fulfilled. It was 50 years before the next major campaign, the Women's Liberation Movement, set about transforming the status and role of women in British society. That is our next chapter in the struggle for women's rights.

4

The Women's Liberation Movement

Between 27 February and 1 March 1970, a Women's Liberation Conference was held at Ruskin College, Oxford. The organisers were expecting 50 participants: 500 women turned up, some bringing husbands, children, friends and sleeping bags.

According to Michelene Wandor in *Once a Feminist'* (1990),[1], the women attending this first women's liberation conference in England came from a wide variety of backgrounds and experiences and with varying motives and expectations.

> "I wanted to put women back into history." (Sheila Rowbotham – the main instigator of the conference)[2]

> "I had been on a course run by Juliet Mitchell on The Role of women." (Audrey Battersby)[3]

> "A friend took me. I was the only real hausfrau there." (Marlene Hobsbawm)[4]

> "I wanted to inject the trade union background into socialist feminism later." (Audrey Wise, later a MP)[5]

The historian Catherine Hall described the conference as, 'a lot of people at the same time talking about the same things.[6]

What were those 'same things' and what had happened that made that weekend in 1970 such a propitious time to hold this conference?

The campaign for women's suffrage and its legacy – women becoming participating citizens after universal suffrage was finally gained in 1928 – had a more long-lasting and more far-reaching effect than is perhaps recognised.

For the majority of the population in Britain, life after World War 1 was hard: unemployment leading to poverty and insecurity in a highly stratified society. The commonly accepted picture of 1920s 'flappers' having a good time illustrates the lives of only a tiny minority although, through the 1920s and into the 1930s, as Carol Dyhouse says in *Girl Trouble: Panic and Progress in the history of young women* (2014) because of the dearth of men of marriageable age young women had to earn their living. 'Cheap mass produced clothing and cosmetics enabled working class girls to look good,' she writes, with an accompanying photograph of factory girls in Walthamstow modelling carnival hats.

Many women who had taken on traditionally male roles during the war were back in the home or in unskilled work on low wages. Contraception was still not freely available and many women had more children than they could afford. In the professions, married women were not allowed to work.

After the Second World War, life for women in the 1950s, although often drab, was different. Women who had, like their predecessors, worked in munitions factories or on the land returned to domestic duties. However, for working class women, life was substantially less poverty-stricken than it had been for their counterparts in the 1920s. Work was available in factories, in offices and at lower levels in public services.

The boast of many men was, 'I earn enough money for my wife not to have to go out to work.'

In the 1950s, many middle-class women seemed to lead lives of comparative ease. Back in the home, their days consisted of getting the children to school, cleaning (with some new gadgets) and cooking while listening to programmes on the BBC Light Programme like *Housewives Choice*. The name needs no further explanation. *Mrs Dale's Diary*, which was broadcast daily between 1948 and 1969, were the musings and homilies of the rather smug wife of a country GP. *Two Way Family Favourites*, was played every Sunday lunchtime, presented by Cliff Michelmore and Jean Metcalfe. This was a record request programme in which women at home asked for records to be played for men on national service abroad. The image was of a family, minus the man, gathered round the radio over lunch. More 'risky' was 'naughty' Wilfred Pickles whose weekly show *Have a Go* (1946–1967) was based on his tours around the country where he and his wife Mabel visited village halls asking 'ordinary folk' about their memories. One of the most popular items was when people were asked for their most embarrassing moment and this quite often included some slightly titillating story. More than once it involved women's knickers dropping down.

Hollywood films with happy endings fed more romantic fantasies. Doris Day exemplified the sanctity of the safe girl next door. The dancing and singing in the film *Seven Brides for Seven Brothers* were joyful and brilliantly executed although the obvious message was somewhat questionable. Mills and Boon and other popular fiction could be borrowed from Boots Lending Library. Laura, in the 1948 film *Brief Encounter*, is on her way there when she meets the doctor with whom she nearly has an affair. She returns to the safety of her home and husband and in the last scene of the film she is sitting darning a sock with a 'mushroom' inside it. Her life's adventure is over.

However, Betty Friedan in her ground-breaking book *The Feminine Mystique* (1963), warned that beneath this cosy, unruffled exterior was a growing dissatisfaction and resentment only partially alleviated by Valium.

Women in the USA and Britain who read her book, recognised an identifiable common malaise and became increasingly restless.

The 1960s was a period of political and social unrest in Europe and, by the latter part of that decade, demonstrations against injustice were evidence of a reaction to fake satisfaction. University students protested against a sterile curriculum in England and France. Student leader Daniel Cohn Bendit became a household name. In the USA, the Civil Rights Movement began in earnest and there were demonstrations against the war in Vietnam. The Prague Spring in Czechoslovakia turned to Winter and progress halted. In Britain, an increasing lack of confidence in government and other institutions, coupled with anger at low wages, resulted in protests and strikes in the workplace.

The 1968 strike by women machinists for equal pay at Ford's in Dagenham became a symbol for the rights of women elsewhere in society. Women across the classes responded to the political upheaval, questioning their general status.

The Beginnings of the Women's Liberation Movement

In the USA, Betty Friedan had become frustrated by the slow progress towards women's equality despite the success of her book and had helped to form and lead The National Organisation for Women in 1966. In 1968, the first national gathering of the Women's Liberation Movement took place in Chicago and the well-known protest against the Miss America Competition was arranged. Women threw symbols of their oppression – bras, suspenders, pots, pans, mops, curlers into a trash can outside the competition venue. This simple demonstration got huge publicity and, although no bra was ever burnt, members of the women's movement were instantly labelled 'bra burners' by opponents of women's rights. And that pejorative myth still persists.

Both those organisations owed their existence to the Civil Rights movement in the USA and women who had been active in the Civil Rights movement brought their ideas and tactics with them.

Meanwhile, in Britain, Barbara Castle was appointed Minister of Transport in 1965, the first female Minister of State. Germaine Greer's *The Female Eunuch* was published in 1970. Unusually for a feminist writer, Germaine Greer's style is irreverent, funny and often intentionally coarse. Her main accusation is that men hate women and that women are unaware of the extent of that hatred even though this affects the way they see women themselves, especially sexually. Instead of pretending they are content, women should insist on their own sexual enjoyment. She also tells women to be braver about claiming the rights to which they are entitled.

In the same year though less well known, Robin Morgan's anthology *Sisterhood is Powerful* as well as Kate Millet's provocative *Sexual Politics* were published, read and discussed. Small informal groups of women had begun to meet as a result of reading books such as these as well as a revival of Simone de Beauvoir's *The Second sex,* first published in France by Gallimard in 1949.

Women in the Trade Union movement and political parties were challenging the male imposed ways of running things.

The Ruskin Conference

It was against this background that the Ruskin Conference took place.

Some of the participants at the conference were political activists: from Maoists, Leninists and members of International Socialists and the International Marxist Group to members of the Labour Party. Others had confined their activity to protest movements such as CND and anti-apartheid. Yet others came with vague but persistent feelings of dissatisfaction with their own lives or frustration with the way women generally were viewed and treated.

The idea of holding a women's conference came from Sheila Rowbotham, a student at Ruskin and a member of their history workshop. Her suggestion at a workshop seminar that there should be a workshop meeting about women's history was met with derisive laughter by the men and this spurred her on. 'A few of us met in a tiny student's bedroom and decided to call the conference.'

> 'Women have been lying low for so long', she wrote during
> that period, 'that most of us cannot imagine how to get up'.[7]

On the first day there were papers and discussions on the family, motherhood, delinquency, equal pay and more. On the Sunday the discussions took a more political slant, with papers on 'Women and the Revolution' and 'Political Perspectives on Women's struggles'. The closing session was called 'Where are we going?'

The conference concluded with four demands:

1. Equal pay
2. Equal educational opportunities for women
3. 24-hour nurseries
4. Abortion on demand.

It had been a boisterous weekend. Some women came away elated with a feeling that something had been achieved:

> 'I think I was generally and uncritically excited by almost every single thing', said Sue O'Sullivan.[8]

Others were unhappy about what they saw as intolerant interference from political groups on the left. Indeed, according to Lois Graessle,[9]

> 'the Marxist-Leninists were most forthcoming to volunteer to take minutes then rewrote them to suit their view of history'.

Despite these differences between those who came to hear their nascent views confirmed and to seek friendship and those who were impatient for change and had clear notions of how to achieve their ends, the conference succeeded in bringing together diverse groups and individuals with some agreed common aims.

Lois Graessle also remembers,

> 'how people got together and what was going on underneath, not what was being spoken about…'.[10]

Jo Delaney, active campaigner in the Women's Movement and the Labour Party during the late 1960s and 1970s says,

> 'The changes we wanted to see seemed both massive and revolutionary but at the same time so obvious and so reasonable – and we had the appetite!'[11]

The newly published women's magazine *Shrew* (1971) printed its own version of the conference, attempting to combat what they saw as the misrepresentation in the mainstream Press. *Spare Rib* magazine was published for the first time in 1973 to give voice to women's concerns and causes and built up a steady distribution. In 1979, the rather more academic *Feminist Review* began regular publication.

The redoubtable Carmen Callil founded Virago books in 1973 saying that what was needed was a, 'publisher that spoke directly to 50% of the population – women'. She was joined as founder director by Ursula Owen in 1974, who described the necessity of a feminist imprint as 'seizing the means of cultural production'. For many of us walking into their beautiful bookshop in Covent Garden to be faced with all the green spines of books written by women some new, some forgotten was an exhilarating experience.

I remember once finding Dora Russell sitting among the shelves and immediately bought a copy of her book *The Tamarisk Tree* so that she could sign it, despite already having a copy at home. The books in The Silver Moon Bookshop in Charing Cross Road (another women's bookshop) were always so plentiful that they almost seemed to spill out onto the road and inside we squeezed past one another to find what we wanted. Unfortunately neither of these outlets exists any more, having been priced out by exorbitant business rates. However, Gay's the Word was founded in 1979 and is still located in Bloomsbury.

Some of the four demands from the Ruskin Conference have since been partially met. Less tangible are the achievements of the resulting Women's Liberation Movement. Its influence lasted about twelve years (1968–1980) during which time many women began to question the purpose of their existence and, realising that they were being held back by discrimination, began to express their concerns.

> 'The women's liberation movement paved the way from silence to expression', says Dale Spender.[12]

They discovered solidarity through sisterhood and not only found but raised their collective voices.

Miriam David describes feminism,

'as a set of ideas and values (which) has been a collaborative and cooperative adventure'.[13]

An example of such an 'adventure' occurred in November 1970. Emulating the success of their American sisters, feminists in Britain sabotaged the Miss World contest hosted by Bob Hope in the Albert Hall. Sally Alexander[14] tells of the exhilaration of dressing up in high heels and posh dresses to mingle with the audience, excitedly aware of the disruption they would cause. They carried flour in little packets of paper in their handbags, ready to throw onto the stage. At the pre-arranged signal of a football rattle, pockets of women all over the hall got up and rushed towards the terrified Bob Hope who ran backstage. They protested loudly about the denigration of women represented by beauty pageants, scattering little flour bombs as they leaped onto the stage only to be carried out by their arms and legs by the police.

> 'It was a spectacular consciousness raising event', says Sally Alexander. 'The publicity was enormous.'

What was the Purpose of the Women's Liberation Movement in Britain?

Small groups of women started to come together. Some met to enjoy the liberation of not being dominated by men. Others formed conscious raising groups. Women's sections sprang up in the Labour Party and in the trade unions. Women formed strong bonds of friendship. Mrs and Miss were replaced by Ms.

Women were becoming aware of the sources of their oppression, their lack of prominence and power in society. They realised the need to challenge the male structures that held them back. More insidious, but if anything more pervasive and harder to tackle, were the feelings of endemic inferiority and powerlessness which rendered most of them silent.

> 'I spent a long time listening to other people – mainly men. Like most women I remained silent'.

This is how Sheila Rowbotham, the well-known feminist historian and academic who helped to start the Women's Liberation Movement in Britain, described herself in 1962. A prolific author writing about women's issues, she has influenced our thinking on gender for over 45 years.[15]

Lynne Segal agrees.

> 'It wasn't just that women felt frightened to protest publicly but that most of us found it difficult to speak publicly at all… We were used to being dominated by men. It was hard not to want to be.'[16]

Like Sheila Rowbotham, Lynne Segal is an academic, a professor of psychology and gender studies at Birkbeck College, London. Originally from Australia, she has lived in London since 1970 and has been a tireless activist and lifelong campaigner for women's rights.

Sally Alexander writes,

> 'I was completely silent in every meeting with trade unionists. I felt completely excluded.'[17]

Another active feminist from the 1960s, Sally Alexander is a professor at Goldsmith's University and founder of the *History Workshop Journal*.

Given their subsequent fame as feminist writers and campaigners, it is hard now to envisage the struggle even women such as these had in order to summon the courage to give voice to their doubts.

On a personal level, not only did I (Eva) not speak at meetings myself, it never occurred to me that I might have something worth hearing to say. I was happy to service committees in the local Labour Party and arranged some successful occasions but did not open my mouth until I was brought up short one evening by Joy Mostyn, an influential local party member in her fifties. It was after a well-attended meeting in 1972 that I had organised, with a government minister as the main speaker:

> 'Eva my dear', she said, 'Well done. That was a very good turn-out but you have a voice too and I think it's about time we heard it, don't you?'

A wake up call which forced me to contribute at the next meeting. Every woman needs a Joy Mostyn.

A disinclination to question and resist domestic inequality because of the possibly disturbing effects on relationships, coupled with the fear of the consequences of questioning discriminatory practices at work started to be overcome through the sharing of common experiences with other women. They were able to rely on one another for support and even small successes were reported and celebrated, which reinforced commitment in a recognised struggle.

Housewives and Housework

In 1939, Margery Spring Rice, niece of Millicent Fawcett and Elizabeth Garrett Anderson, published *Working Class Wives* which

> 'stripped the veil of indifference and ignorance which concealed the hardships of millions of women from their more prosperous sisters'.[18]

A total of 1,250 women responded to a questionnaire about their daily lives. The National Health Service was not introduced until 1948, so despite the work of Infant Welfare Centres, Health Visitors

and District Nurses, *Working Class Wives* is a shocking chronicle
of women enduring the birth of six or seven children, often more,
rising at 6:30 am and on their feet for much of the day until 11.00
at night. The enquiry was set up because of concerns about the
health of these women, who spent what they called their 'leisure
moments' in the day 'shopping, taking the baby out, sewing, tidy-
ing cupboards, repapering a room(sic) and gardening'. And yet it
is not the hard work that they resent, their main complaint is 'the
dreadful monotony'. As one woman from Cardiff says,

> 'It gets a little dreary.'

Visiting their doctors was often unproductive (and cost money).
The 43-year-old wife of a miner in Rotherham recounts having
severe pains in the lower part of her back which was so painful
that she went to her doctor, who told her that "all women got back
ache round about 40, so why worry?' 'So I don't', she says.

Hannah Gavron's *The Captive Wife: Conflicts of Housebound Mothers* published nearly thirty years later, in 1966, is a sociological survey
based on interviews in the mid-1960s with equal numbers of working
and middle-class housewives living in London. Life was much easier
for all these women than that of those surveyed by Margery Spring
Rice, but there are some surprising similarities.

One of the most striking findings in Hannah Gavron's research
is how comparable were the experiences of the women she interviewed in both social groups. Many of them admitted to intense
loneliness, doubts about their ability to be a good mother, and
both groups voiced their worry about leaving children to be cared
for by anyone else when they were young.

> 'I don't want to leave the children with just anyone though
> I can't say they are very exciting company', said a post-
> man's wife.

A teacher's wife agrees:

> 'Of course I must be with them all the time, though I must confess that sometimes I *long* to get away.'

The Newsons in their report of 1963(*Infant care in the urban community*) described this period in the life of middle-class housewives as a 'time of frustration and despondency', although most of them did have some form of help. Hannah Gavron's interviews show us that working class housewives are no less depressed.

> 'I was so lonely in those early years, living in furnished rooms', said the wife of a builder's mate.[19]

However, if we add 'bad housing, lack of play facilities, lack of nursery schools, reduced contact with extended family' endured by working class mothers and later, as the slums of the East End were cleared and young families were re-housed in tower blocks, it becomes clear that, despite the feelings of isolation that they had in common, middle-class women were still better off than their working class counterparts.

Surprisingly a number of both middle-class and working class husbands were strongly opposed to their wives working.

> 'He won't hear of me working and he's quite stubborn about it' says a groundsman's wife.

In fact 40% of the working class women interviewed made this complaint as did 27% of the middle class.

Many of Ann Oakley's conclusions in *The Sociology of Housework* published in 1974 concur with Hannah Gavron's. Ann Oakley's study aimed to 'conceptualise housework as work, rather than simply an aspect of the feminine role in marriage'. Again it is dissatisfaction with housework itself that predominates. As with

Margery Spring Rice's findings, monotony is a common experience, as is loneliness. Ann Oakley goes on to discuss,

> 'the low status of the housewife role and the low prestige and trivialisation of housework implied in the phrase just a housewife'.

The other common factor, despite more recent 'labour saving' devices, is the long hours. Seventy-seven hours a week on average.

A telling observation made by Ann Oakley is the need that many housewives have to set themselves standards and routines to which they strive to adhere in order to obtain some measure of control and satisfaction.

Reading these accounts of loneliness and drudgery, it is easy to see how Selma James's 'wages for housework' campaign had popular appeal. The very name 'housewife' seems to suggest that women are as attached to their house as to their husband, but for most women housework is an endless, thankless set of chores. What Selma James demanded was money from the state for this unwaged work in the home. This sounds like a sensible idea but many women rejected it because it simply pushed them firmly back in the home, being paid for work they resented. Ann Oakley poses the dilemma thus: 'the value of being your own master (sic) in charge of your own time and work' and yet as her research demonstrated,

> 'housework is the most disliked aspect of being a housewife'.[20]

There was also the problem of Selma James' personal unpopularity. Her ubiquitous presence at every conference and campaign meeting during the 1970s, loudly demanding to be heard, caused hackles to rise. Jill Tweedie begins a *Guardian* interview with her in 1976 with,

1870s

'To many women in the women's movement, The Wages for Housework campaigners come over like Jehovah's Witnesses... they harangue conferences... burn with a strange fever...'[21]

Bea Campbell is even more scathing, describing her as, 'schismatic, sectarian, polarising: Selma got on women's nerves'.[22]

For Selma James the issue is about class, which she felt the women's movement in Britain chose to ignore. She had spent years working a double day in a factory and as a housewife.

'Too many women in the Movement simply didn't know anything about the world.'[23]

The Women's Liberation Movement has often been accused of being too middle class. We will return to this complex problem later.

Sisterhood

In the 1950s and early 1960s women saw themselves as competitors for men's affection and favours. They were brought up to please men in the way they dressed and behaved. Other women were rivals. Dale Spender describes 'the need to be pleasing, accommodating and ego-enhancing to boys'.[24] Jill Tweedie despairs of the continuing need for women to be 'nice'[25] Shulamith Firestone says, 'I had to train myself out of that phony smile'.[26]

These comments came centuries after Mary Wollstonecraft had warned in 1789 that

'the concept of femininity is cultural'[27]

and even earlier (1680) Aphra Behn had written,

'men want to listen to women who are modest'.[28]

Susan Brownmiller calls this behaviour,

> 'a desperate strategy of appeasement'.[29]

Appearance continues to be a real problem for women. Former family court judge, Susanna Jones told us about a women's conference she attended in 1976 where she was one of the few women wearing a skirt or make up. One way that some women wanted to express their freedom from male imposed norms about how women should look was to wear trousers and dungarees, heavy boots and other items that essentially hid their femininity. Some stopped shaving their armpits and legs. A small group of women at that particular conference seemed to be taking this a stage further and not only dressed but behaved like very aggressive men. They were deliberately intimidating.

On the whole women no longer feel the need for such displays of masculinity but the fact remains that many women are still engaged in a daily struggle with how they think they look. The battle against the tyranny of the fashion to be ever thinner, fitter, almost androgynous goes on. It is corrosive and diminishes self-esteem. In *Sisterhood is Powerful* (1970), Zoe Moss issues this heartfelt plea:

> 'My daughter already buys cream to rub into her skin. I want to beg her not to begin worrying, not to let in the dreadful daily gnawing.'[30]

To be constantly on guard against other women was tiring as well as detrimental to forming relationships. To be part of a group with no men present seemed slightly worrying, if not daring, but it helped to release pent up feelings and allowed women to talk and one of the main and lasting benefits of the Women's Liberation Movement (even for those who never participated in it) is the strong support provided by sisterhood.

'First and foremost we found each other' says Eva Figes. 'Different schools of feminism all stressed the necessity of the solidarity of sisterhood.'[31]

Chimamanda Ngozi Adichie:

'Here's to the possibilities of friendship and connection and understanding.'[32]

According to Lynne Segal, in *Why Feminism?* (1999), many 1970s feminists have recalled,

'the imaginative leap when they first began to turn outwards to other women'.

Sheila Rowbotham says,

'The managing of women's liberation was not a generalised antagonism to men but a positive assertion of new relationships between women, sisterhood.'[33]

Janice G. Raymond called it 'a companionship of equals'.[34]

For Robin Morgan,

'This is not a movement one "joins." There are no rigid structures or membership cards... It is frightening. It is very exhilarating.'[35]

It is difficult for those born and brought up after the 1970s to conceive of the mistrust below the surface that women had previously had for one another.

Germaine Greer writing in 1970 is quite clear:

'Women have no idea how much men hate them.'[36]

Most of us would recoil from such strong sentiments but, being the less powerful group in society, women have found it hard to resist internalising this negative view of themselves and reproducing it by being suspicious of one another.

Ann Oakley explains:

> 'Women were brought up not to like each other much.'[37]

Meeting in Small Groups: Shunning Hierarchy

The Women's Liberation Movement consisted largely of small groups of women meeting in private houses to talk with no men present. This generated the atmosphere to enable them to disclose their individual feelings of inadequacy and powerlessness in a male-dominated world. Such admissions took courage. For some women they were exposing previously unspoken resentments, which they assumed they had been alone in enduring. Some worried about the implied disloyalty to their husbands in talking about these issues.

Whatever their initial reservations, however, those meetings proved to women that they could trust their own sex. Strong bonds between group members developed into sisterhood and later solidarity.

> 'We had to learn to love ourselves and other women so we could trust one another without falling back on men... so we met in small groups and circles'.[38]

Inevitably, problems arose. Janice Raymond expresses what many women meeting in groups were searching for: 'We want a feminist politics based on friendship'[39] and for the majority this seemed to be a desirable goal. The confidence gained from speaking out led them to finding ways to cooperate and to question and dismantle practices that were holding women back.

Lynne Segal in *Beyond the Fragments* describes the work of women's centres that were set up in the north London Borough where she lived. Here they planned and campaigned, undeterred by constant obstacles and difficulties. They were energised by the power that came initially from finding and admitting their common grievances and then working collectively to challenge what had seemed like immutable structures in local politics. They helped to make not only their own lives but those of others easier.

In conversation with Lynne Segal, she told us that this kind of local activity was happening all over the country in the 1970s and newspapers were written and circulated by local feminist groups.

Much of the activity was led by women outside mainstream political parties who gained experience and strength from the peace movement and action against racism.

They demanded that family allowances were increased and paid directly to women, they campaigned for more nurseries and won, they got involved with the Wages for Housework campaign, they made sure that women's health (mental as well as physical) could be discussed freely in women's centres. Cultural events were organised and enjoyed. The Working Women's Charter ultimately failed to materialise but lessons learnt from championing even an unsuccessful cause were useful in future campaigns.

Lynne Segal is adamant that the activity around violence and coercion, which grew in the late 1970, was connected to levels of misery in their lives. And this is still true today.

She quotes Sheila Rowbotham's 'visions of a better life', which we were striving towards then but which has now disappeared.

Miriam David talks about the success of the 'collective, collaborative and cooperative'[40] nature of such actions and laments their passing. Talking, making decisions and carrying them out successfully changed the way these women saw themselves. Such outcomes cannot be dismissed and should be given genuine recognition.

But revolutions, even quiet ones, cannot be expected to run smoothly.

The Pitfalls of Structureless Campaigns

One of the overriding tenets of the conscious raising groups is that they should have no formal structure, no leaders and no hierarchy.

Looking back, I remember the awkward silences of the first local consciousness raising group I attended in the early 1970s. Nobody wanted to be accused of taking charge, so minutes went by when nothing was said. 'Mysterious silences', Sheila Rowbotham calls them.[41] Who should take the initiative and start talking? There was palpable relief when one woman finally took the plunge and off we went. For a short while. Then we realised that the conversation seemed to be dominated by one or two of the more vociferous women and we came to a stop again. This cycle was repeated and ultimately there were positive gains but it did not feel comfortable to begin with. Maybe such hiccups have to be expected when embarking a new way of doing things despite what Janice Raymond calls 'the dogmatism of tolerance'[42] and Jill Tweedie's unhappiness with 'too much democracy'[43] in the women's movement. Sheila Rowbotham says,

> 'sisterhood can become a coercive consensus which makes it emotionally difficult to say what they mean'.[44]

Trying very hard not to disagree clearly creates its own unspoken problems.

Jo Delaney's experience of the lack of structure in meetings was very frustrating and ultimately damaging.

'... Many meetings were completely unstructured; the most intimidating personalities or loudest voices dominated, and because discussion was difficult, disagreement could morph into dissent and dissent into factions.'[45]

Janice Raymond found the lack of structure equally frustrating.

'Without structure radicalism will be frantic, bursting with energy and short-lived.'[46]

To some extent she is right, but those 'bursts of energy' ignited a flame, however flickering, that fuelled and continues to fuel progress.

There is no doubt that the conscious raising groups enabled women to question aspects of their private lives and this could prove risky. Some marriages foundered when put under such forensic spotlight. Women left their husbands and found themselves living and raising children on their own. Some had already had concerns about their sexuality and were able to come out as lesbians. There were positive sides to these disturbances: women knew that they could rely on one another for support.

Communes were set up in which women (and a few men) lived and thrived together in households, sharing not only emotional highs and lows but the more mundane domestic burdens. The exhilaration of living and working, in what seemed a more liberated state, was a powerful indicator that commonly accepted social structures could be challenged. Most communes were fairly short-lived, but having taken such brave steps to question the most fundamental and basic rules of how people conducted their personal lives, the men and women involved generally acknowledge that they learned some valuable lessons about themselves. The experience taught them about greater equality in decision making.

Notwithstanding setbacks, through the Women's Liberation Movement, women learnt to articulate their grievances in a safe environment and this gave them the confidence to trust one another. An awareness of individual and collective inequality was growing. Women understood that systems needed to be challenged and changed and they said so. They knew that equality never happens by accident and that they had to work together to achieve their aims. This felt both risky and exciting but the more they dared to face adversity together the more courageous they became.

By 1975, there were 1500 women's groups in Britain. Some were inward-looking, finding new personal identities by confiding previously unstated concerns. Others were overtly political. Members of fringe groups like International Marxists or Leninists met to discuss and practise a stated political agenda. Some groups deliberately and openly challenged conventional lifestyles, forming non-hierarchical communes. Other women became uncomfortable with their given sexual identity and boldly declared their intention to change how they had hitherto been categorised.

Roxanne Dunbar asserts,

> 'We are developing necessary skills to react collectively and politically rather than privately and personally.'[47]

Years later, in *Lean in* (2013) Sheryl Sandberg tells us that,

> 'the discussion may be difficult but the positives are many. We cannot change what we are unaware of, but once we are aware, we cannot help but change'.

Women were talking. They continue to talk.

> 'We shifted the terms of the debate', says Catherine Hall.[48]

What did the Women's Liberation Movement Achieve and What is its Legacy?

We certainly wanted visible proof that we were being taken seriously. The Equal Pay Act had been passed in 1970. Five years after that came the Sex Discrimination Act. Without pressure from women's movements, Acts such as these would never have been passed. Women now had explicit legal backing if they felt that they were being treated unjustly at work but trying to prove that work is of 'equal value' is difficult and accusations of discrimination rely on one person's word against another's. Unless instances of discrimination are blatant, it is not easy to make a case that sounds convincing. Taking employers to court was and remains a lonely and risky enterprise and even if her case is upheld a woman is liable to face obstacles to promotion in the future.[49]

Interviewers are no longer allowed to ask whether a woman has children and if so what her childcare arrangements are. The effect of this, though apparently laudable, rather than liberating women, often renders children invisible. If both men and women were able to discuss the care of their children freely, then organisations could accommodate and facilitate in ways which would alleviate the pressure on parents in work to lie or hide concerns when they arise. It can be done. Staff working for the Trade Union Congress have told us that both women and men with dependants are encouraged to work flexibly with no hidden disapproval or penalties. The impetus for this kind of legislation is benign, and was a result of women fighting for equality. However it still only required a surface change of behaviour without the necessary fundamental shift in attitudes.

These are examples of partial success in tackling situations which would not even have been considered unless women had understood the need to confront them and the effort involved should not be undervalued.

The four demands resulting from the Ruskin Conference (equal pay, equal education and employment opportunities, free contraception and abortion on demand, 24-hour nurseries) did not appear out of the ether. They reflect genuine, often previously voiced concerns, deliberated over many years by women of every social class. Spending a weekend at Ruskin talking to other women at a conference run by women for women encouraged participants to take the brave step of turning complaints into requests that could not be brushed aside.

Expressing demands collectively is empowering and was a new experience for many women. Taking action as a group gives confidence to individuals: we learnt that we were not alone; that our grievances were real and had roots in a society designed and dominated by men.

In order to make real gains women had to act politically. However strongly felt, and despite the sentiments and support underpinning women's groups, change has never been driven by worthy emotions alone. Belonging to a recognised political party helped. Operating through structures where it was accepted that resolutions were passed and debated at conferences gave women a platform. They were able to reach a wider audience, sometimes fighting an uphill battle, but acting together and with the hope that being heard by people with influence would end in genuine beneficial results.

At the same time, it has to be admitted that some women with strong political allegiances also actively prevented progress. Lynne Segal writes,

> 'Women in left groups were more experienced in centrally organised politics. This always causes tensions in the women's movement.' As an example, when paid help was needed at her local women's centre, 'there seemed to be a contradiction between our emphasis on self-help and collective activity and the idea of state funding'.[50]

There was resistance from local Communist, Socialist Worker Party and International Marxist Group members and the idea was eventually dropped.

In conversation with Sheila Rowbotham, she told us about the kind of occurrence that happens when people act without thinking carefully enough about the consequences. She was present at a national women's conference in 1972, which was taking place in Skegness at the same time as a miners' gala. It was discovered that the miners were going to be entertained by a striptease artist. A group of radical feminists decided that they would disrupt the striptease. A little later, while Sheila was showing a film about the night cleaners' strike, the door flew open and she was interrupted by the returning radical feminists shouting, 'They're brutalising the sisters.' Unsurprisingly the angry miners had ejected them from the striptease.

> 'If only they had stood outside as a picket line, the miners might have thought twice about crossing the line', sighed Sheila.

In Bolton in the mid-1970, Susanna Jones told us that she helped with a Saturday morning clinic run by volunteers from her local women's group. A successful rota system operated to make sure that any woman could drop in for free pregnancy tests. Unfortunately some members of far left groups who joined the women's group did not appear to value this work and the impression they gave was that those doing it were middle-class do-gooders. Despite their championship of the working class, those same activists had little interest in attracting more working class women into the group and seemed to have little understanding of the urgent matters that affected their daily lives, such as unwanted pregnancies.

> 'Quite honestly', said Susanna, 'working class women probably had better things to do than listen to endless discussions about the situation in Nicaragua'.

In the end she left the group because of these women, the final straw being when one of them suggested to Susanna that she was a 'cultural feminist' – only involved because feminism seemed to be trendy. Others left the group, probably for the same or similar reasons.

Susanna is not alone in describing such experiences. Several writers from that period tell of the oppressive dogmatism of reiterated truisms regurgitated by women with inflexible views. They always seemed so certain that they were right. 'I could never be quite so sure', was the refreshingly candid reaction of Sheila Rowbotham.[51]

Domestic Violence

Physical abuse has been a constant theme in women's writings. Erin Pizzey set up the first women's refuge in Chiswick in 1972. Until then, there was little or no public knowledge of the extent of the hidden violence suffered by women of all classes. She brought out into the open what was going on behind closed doors and she went through a torrent of undeserved opprobrium for disclosing this unspoken area of daily life. It disturbed people and made them feel uncomfortable but a consequence of the publicity she generated was the Domestic Violence and Matrimonial Proceedings Act in 1976, designed to protect women and children from violent men.

The women's centres that had sprung up in the 1970s helped women to confide what they were going through at home. And in some conscious-raising groups, women felt able to talk about distress caused by insensitive partners in matters of sex. The private nature of such concerns and the effect on relationships at home inevitably made women wary of speaking about this subject but it was and remains a constant source of unhappiness for some.

Recently Laura Bates[52] and Kat Banyard[53] have made us aware of the prevalence of sexual abuse.

For many younger activists this has become their main focus. We will return to this theme in a later chapter when we look to future campaigns.

What was Missing from the Women's Liberation Movement?

The Women's Liberation Movement is frequently accused of being middle class and not including working class and black and Asian women. There is no doubt that both these accusations are true. This was a movement led and followed by mainly white middle-class women. They were the ones who made the decisions, instigated campaigns and generally spoke for others.

There were exceptions: May Hobbs led the Night Cleaners' Campaign between 1970 and 1972. The Cleaners' Action group was set up in 1970 to fight for decent wages and better conditions of work for women who cleaned the large London office blocks at night.

> 'You're always moaning', she said to them one night, 'so why not do something instead? So we joined the TGWU'.[54]

Some of the more prominent members of the Women's Liberation Movement had ties with the trade union movement so making connections was not difficult. The night cleaners were joined by academics such as Sally Alexander and Sheila Rowbotham who rallied other women to join picket lines, but this was essentially a strike organised by working class women. As one commentator wrote:

> 'Cleaners and feminists picketing, singing and dancing outside the Ministry of Defence made a good story.'[55]

They were backed by several trade unions and when lorry drivers refused to cross picket lines, supplies began to dry up, most crucially the beer for the bar!

As we have seen already, there were local groups in the 1970s that set up and ran over 60 women's centres as well as nurseries and crèches. These benefited all social groups but were short-lived.

We further address the importance of involving working class women in Chapter 6.

Writing about a later Ruskin women's conference held on 18th March 2000, Mary Kennedy says,

> 'There were no black British women present at the conference and the accusation of racism rumbles on.'[56]

The relationship between the Women's Liberation Movement and black women was not taken seriously and has been a cause of tension and distress.

In 1976, Jayaben Desai a worker in the film-processing plant at Grunwick, north London, resigned after being ordered to work overtime and she then instigated a strike among the mainly Asian and female workforce, which went on until 1978. The diminutive Desai was a powerful character, unafraid to challenge her bosses and this gave her fellow workers the necessary courage to strike for so long. The strikers were protesting about working conditions, pay inequality and the institutionalised racism in the company. They were supported by the trade union and wider labour movements and gained huge publicity as 'strikers in saris'. Individual members of the Women's Liberation joined the picket lines outside Grunwick over the two years, but although sympathy was expressed this was not a cause taken up by the women's movement as a whole.

The fact remains that black feminists feel with some justification that they were not represented in the Women's Liberation Movement.

'What exactly do you mean when you say "we"?', asks Hazel Carby at the end of her seminal article *White Women Listen* (1982). A legitimate question and difficult to answer.

She writes about what she calls 'the triple oppression of race, gender and class' suffered by black and Asian women in Britain: gender because they are women in a male-dominated society, race because of prejudice against their skin colour and class because so many of them were and still are in low-paid and low-status jobs. Although later disputed as a concept, particularly by the influential Audrey Lorde, this 'hierarchy of oppression' nevertheless seems to be a useful prism through which to view gender, race and class.

There is the problem of what another writer in *Black Feminism in the United Kingdom*[57] describes as the 'everyday invisibility of black women from mainstream analysis'. Writing in the late 1970s and 1980s, Avtar Brah, Stella Dadzie and Amrit Wilson began to put this right by giving details and insights into the lives of 'minority ethnic' women in Britain, reminding us that this phrase itself covers African, Caribbean and South Asian women speaking different languages, with different cultures and religions.

In *Differences, Diversity, Differentiation: Processes of Racialisation and Gender*[58] Avtar Brah, former professor of sociology at Birkbeck College, warns us against assumptions of 'internal homogeneity in minority ethnic communities'.

> 'African Caribbean communities have mobilised far more around their collective experience of the criminal justice system whereas Asian groups have been much more against violent attacks... on the housing estates where they live.'[59]

The black women's movements in Britain were heavily influenced by sister movements in the USA. These American women took their cue from the former slave and civil rights campaigner Sojourner Truth whose compelling speech made to the Women's Rights Convention in 1851 begins thus:

"That man over there says that women need to be helped into carriages, and lifted over ditches, and to have the best place everywhere. Nobody ever helps me into carriages, or over muddy puddles, or gives me any best place. *And ain't I a woman?* Look at me! Look at my arm! I have ploughed and gathered into barns, and no man could head me. *And ain't I a woman?*"[60]

The black women in America who took part in the Civil Rights Movement of the 1960s found that, 'sexism was rampant there as well as in the black power movement'.[61]

'Intersectionality' has been coined as the word defining 'the place where racial equality and gender equality (or more often inequality) meet'. It is a slightly clumsy word but usefully encapsulates the multiple overlapping discrimination experienced by ethnic minority women and too often ignored by feminist movements.

Black American novelists such as Maya Angelou, Alice Walker and Toni Morrison have always been widely read and celebrated by British feminists but however much we understand and sympathise with the life experiences they describe, white women cannot identify with them as black women do.

One of the most successful organisations run by and for black women is Southall Black Sisters. It was founded in 1979 to assist Asian women to escape from domestic violence, forced marriages and honour killings. In 1992, they secured the release of Kiranjit Ahluwalia, who had killed her husband in 1989, having endured abuse and battering for 10 years. She was sentenced to life imprisonment. Southall Black Sisters campaigned and mobilised public opinion on her behalf through public meetings and demonstrations, joining forces with other women's groups as part of a wider feminist campaign on battered women trapped in marriages.

'Kiranjit became a household name', they wrote, 'and it was a highpoint of feminist activity on violence against women'.[62]

Both in the United States and in Britain black women are more aware of their history and the plight of their male and female ancestors than white women realise. Avtar Brah writes of the 'diaspora formed by the history of slavery, colonialism and imperialism'.[63] Hazel Carby takes this a stage further saying that,

'White women in the British Women's Liberation Movement are extraordinarily reluctant to see themselves in the situation of being oppressors.'[64]

A harsh verdict that cannot be ignored. The best way to answer it is clearly for black and white women to listen and talk as openly as possible and work together to create a more equal partnership.

Avtar Brah again:

'... it is important that we do not compartmentalise oppressions, but instead formulate strategies for challenging all oppressions on the basis of an understanding of how they connect and circulate'.[65]

The difficulties involved in this enterprise had been vividly taken up a decade earlier by Hazel Taylor, a (white) equal opportunities advisor in education who described the dilemma of considering gender, race and class thus:

"In my head, there is a cupboard. It is one of those old-fashioned cupboards with three doors, each leading to a separate small space.... To open all three doors is nearly impossible, as one door knocks another one shut... I, like most of us at times, desperately want not to have to acknowledge too many issues at once, to be able to shut off the uncomfortable pressures..."[66]

But she fiercely opposes this tempting self-indulgence, arguing that whatever the discomfort, the doors of the cupboard must always remain open.

It is possible to feel a degree of optimism. In 2013, a conference was held at Girton College, Cambridge, entitled *A Vindication of the Rights of Black Women*.

A participant on their panel was Hazel Carby, born and educated in Britain, a graduate of Birmingham University, and the writer of that seminal paper in 1982, which was quoted earlier. She is now professor at Yale University. In *Media Diversified: Black British Feminism then and now* (2014) she writes of a student who recently asked her.

> 'Why is feminism still largely seen as a movement for white women and why do some feminists remain unwilling to address issues of white privilege?'

Her reply was

> 'I don't think that all white feminists are failing to address their privilege. I have been mentored and supported by many generous white women scholars over the years, to whom I owe much and it is important to recognise these solidarities.'

Making History: Feminism and Feminists

When women finally gained the right to vote they began to see themselves differently. They were able to take part in the decision-making processes affecting their lives. They rejoiced in this new power. Mary Honeyball in *Parliamentary Pioneers: Labour Women MPs 1918–1945* (2015) paints an inspirational picture of strong, indomitable women who knew their worth and their rights and fought to uphold them. Women like Margaret Bondfield and Ellen Wilkinson were early role models for future generations.

The Women's Liberation Movement benefited from the spirit, tenacity and ingenuity of such forebears who in turn had learnt their tactics and their perseverance from the suffrage movement.

And yet...

The word 'feminism' has provoked extraordinarily anguished debates.

> 'Feminism is usually defined as an active desire to change women's position', writes Rosalind Delmar.[67] Not much to argue with in this definition, one would think and yet she continues, 'the history of the women's movement of the 70s...was marked by bitter, at times virulent, internal disputes over what it is possible or permissible for a feminist to think, say or feel'.

'Massive change proceeds more as a spiral than as a straight line', wrote Gloria Steinem[68] and the word feminism seems to exemplify our tortuous progress through thickets of misunderstandings and misinterpretations. But it is about more than semantics. Maya Angelou declares herself to be a feminist simply because

> 'It'd be stupid not to be on my own side.'[69]

But for eighteen-year-old Yas Necati,[70] although she says, 'I feel like a part of something bigger since I've become a feminist', she continues, 'Feminists were all a lot older, incredibly academic or already dead.'

For many of us, being a feminist involves active campaigning and, to quote Gloria Steinem again, 'Pressing the send button does not make you an activist.'[71] Inertia in the face of unavoidable opposition is understandable but not excusable. We are rarely alone when we challenge sexist practices – remember the power of sisterhood – and it is not necessary to pick what seem like intractable instances to fight against initially.

'Feminism', says Dale Spender, '… is cooperation, diversity and dignity'.[72] It is not complicated and should not be controversial, but for many women it is both. During research for our earlier book, *Man-Made,* the one question that we asked every one of the 115 woman whom we interviewed was whether they regarded themselves as feminists. Many did, but a surprising number had reservations, worried about the false image of feminists as strident, man-hating harridans.

In an interview with twenty-three year old Ashleigh James for this book, she told us that,

> 'young women don't like the word feminist because it is still tarnished by past connections with man-hating and bra burning'.

In *Sex, Gender and Society* (1972) Ann Oakley argues that 'there is still a disparity between belief and practice'.

> 'Arguments long believed in have a tendency to remain suspended in thin air by the slender string of passionate, often irrational conviction.'

She calls on John Stuart Mill:

> '… sex is to all women; a peremptory exclusion from almost all honourable occupations'.[73]

Just over one hundred and fifty years later his words still have resonance. Why do women still put up with inequality? John Stuart Mill understood the subtle disadvantage not often referred to by later commentators – we often fight against the *symptoms* of our oppression rather than the *root causes,* viz,

'It is a political law of nature that those who are under any
power of ancient origin have never begun by complaining
of that power itself, but only of its oppressive exercise.'[74]

There is no suggestion that things have remained stagnant since
1869 or indeed 1972 but 'egalitarian ideology'[75] is not enough.
The Women's Liberation Movement certainly made a difference to
many women's lives. Feminist writers of the 1970s gave us a body
of knowledge and a reference group of women to whom we could
turn for intellectual sustenance. The problems were out in the open
and we actively and collectively strived to right some wrongs. Feminist MPs like Jo Richardson, Shirley Williams, Joan Ruddock and
Harriet Harman followed those early pioneers and have changed
the way women are seen in parliament. Maria Miller MP, until
recently the Chair of the Women and Equalities Committee, which
has cross-party representation, told us that their main concern has
been 'maternity discrimination'. They need our continued support.

What happened to halt progress? Sheila Rowbotham is right when
she says, 'Thatcher shifted the political compass. We were fending
off a veritable onslaught of Tory measures which left us gasping.'

Our energies were dissipated. Inequality was not forgotten but it
seemed easier to concentrate on more visible targets. No apology
is needed for this change of direction but there is more to do.

The Women's Liberation Movement was snuffed out. A new generation of women needs to carry the banner forward.

5

How the Revolutions Stalled

Successful campaigners believe passionately in their cause and are optimistic about the benefits of victory.

Votes for Women campaigners anticipated that winning the parliamentary vote would transform the role and status of women. The Women's Liberation Movement expected that the gains that had been won in the 1970s would clear the way for further progress on the pathway to equality. But, disappointingly, the decades that followed these two successful campaigns were not periods of continuing achievement and enlightenment. At best, progress was patchy and many of the years following each campaign are characterised by stagnation and disillusionment. On each occasion the revolution stalled.

Women in Parliament

Suffrage campaigners believed that the vote would transform the status of women because, women and not men would make the important decisions about matters that affected the lives of women. Millicent Fawcett insisted that women must be decision-makers because,

> 'However benevolent men may be.., they cannot know
> what women want and what suits the necessities of
> women's lives as well as women know these things
> themselves'.[1]

Being decision-makers meant, of course, that women must not only be voters but also be MPs. The suffragists knew how important it was to elect women to parliament. When in April 1918 it seemed that women might not be allowed to stand as parliamentary candidates, the suffragists created uproar and an amendment had to be rushed through parliament into law.

Getting women elected proved much more difficult than the suffragists expected. Seventeen women contested seats in the General Election of December 1918 and there were several formidable candidates. Christabel Pankhurst, Charlotte Despard and Emmeline Pethick-Lawrence were leading lights from the suffrage campaign. The Labour candidate in Stonebridge was Mary Macarthur, the most famous woman trade unionist in Britain. Some of the women candidates won substantial support in the election campaign and Christabel was even tipped by the *Daily Express* to become MP for Smethwick. But, in the event, sixteen of the seventeen lost. The only female victor was Constance Markievicz,[2] a Sinn Fein member who was in prison for her part in the 1916 Easter Rising and never took her seat.

Parliament then took ten years to do what it should have done in 1918. The WSPU had been disbanded and there was a natural dip in energy after the first victory. However, many of the other suffrage societies continued to press for all women to be granted the vote. They noticed a change in the political atmosphere. No dire consequences had followed the Act of 1918 and the idea that women should be permitted to vote on the same basis as men was soon regarded as uncontroversial. Yet women still had to wait until 1928 before Stanley Baldwin's government, with cross-party support and little opposition in the Lords, brought forward a Bill to remedy the unfairness.

Even then, with full adult female suffrage, very few women managed to win enough support from male-dominated political parties to become parliamentary candidates and only a tiny number were elected to the Commons. The first woman to take her seat was Nancy Astor. In her maiden speech she said that becoming an MP had been like Francis Drake's decision to sail out of Plymouth Sound to face the Spanish Armada![3] Nancy Astor and her female colleagues certainly faced formidable odds. In the election of 1929, only 14 women were elected alongside 601 men. And for nearly twenty years the proportions scarcely changed. The number of women in the Commons did not exceed 20 until 1945 and did not exceed 30 until as late as 1987.

The result of this imbalance of gender representation in the House of Commons has been great, far-reaching and depressing. The Commons has been focusing on priorities set by men for centuries and the institution is very slow to change. The tiny number of women MPs has meant that, for most of the last century, matters of concern to women have been very easy for male politicians to brush aside.

The imbalance of representation has a dispiriting effect on feminist campaigns outside parliament. Campaigners need to know that their cause resonates in the Commons Chamber and want to hear their arguments repeated and developed by sympathetic women MPs. Regrettably, with few women in the Commons, this has not happened very often. The advice that has been given to campaigners has frequently been the same as Henry Campbell Bannerman offered to the suffrage deputation that lobbied him so robustly. 'Be patient', he said. And, just like the suffragists who formed that deputation, subsequent campaigners tend to arrive hopeful and enthusiastic but leave demoralised and angry.

None of this should be taken as criticism of the women who have been elected to parliament. They include many of the most dedicated and effective parliamentarians who have ever sat as MPs: women like Margaret Bondfield, Ellen Wilkinson, Irene Ward, Edith Summerskill, Barbara Castle, Margaret Thatcher, Betty Boothroyd and more recently, Shirley Williams, Joan Ruddock, Harriet Harman and Theresa May. Of course not all of these female MPs worked to increase gender equality and that has been part of the problem. With so few women in the Commons, success requires that women maximise their influence by working together for the common cause. That has rarely happened.

Margaret Thatcher was famously contemptuous of feminists and of feminism. She did nothing to increase the number of women MPs and never had more than one other woman in her cabinet. When Gro Brundtland, the female prime minister of Norway, asked her why she had appointed very few women ministers, Margaret Thatcher said that she could not find women who warranted promotion. Gro Brundtland's sharp response was that Margaret Thatcher should try harder.[4]

The UK has a second female prime minister and time will tell whether Theresa May lives up to her declaration that she is a convinced feminist. She has much to do. On the Conservative Benches in the House of Commons, male Tory MPs heavily outnumber their female colleagues. That is the core of the problem. Success in a parliamentary democracy is not just about principle and commitment; it is always about numbers. The big groups have the power and it is the majorities which decide policy. For the last hundred years, there have never been enough women in parliament to sustain the momentum for reform.

Petering Out

The Votes for Women campaign and the Women's Liberation Movement ended very differently. The Women's Liberation Movement came to an end soon after Margaret Thatcher won the General Election of 1979. We discuss the reasons and the consequences later in this chapter. The momentum behind the Votes for Women campaign petered out more slowly. Of course, after such a long and exhausting campaign, the initial victory of 1918 was bound to lead to a decline in activity. Many suffrage societies decide to disband and recruitment of new members slowed down. The National Union of Societies for Equal Citizenship, the successor body to the National Union of Suffrage Societies, called it a period of 'some difficulty'.[5]

The Votes for Women campaigns had been narrowly focused on winning the right to vote and this had been a major reason for their success. However it also meant that not much serious thought had been given to what would happen after the victory had been won. The optimistic expectation that sustained the campaigners was that winning the vote and gaining the right to sit in the Commons would, of itself, lead to a major change in the status of women. However, when so few women became MPs during the 1920s, feminist campaigners had no alternative strategy.

The decline of the WSPU illustrated the problem. As an indication of its political ambitions, WSPU first transformed itself into a political party: The Women's Party. However, once Christabel failed to win the seat in Smethwick, she seems to have given up thoughts of becoming an MP. Little further was heard of the Women's Party and Christabel soon left for America where she became an evangelist for the Second Adventist movement. The suffragette movement, with all its vitality and determination, had run its course.

Women Workers in the War

Perhaps surprisingly, many feminists put their faith in an entirely different process of change. When the First World War began in August 1914, British industry had to be reorganised to support the war effort. Millions of men left civilian work to go into the armed services and the government decided that women should fill the gap. As many women moved into paid employment for the first time there were optimistic forecasts of great and desirable changes in the status of women. Vera Brittain spoke of a 'revolution'. Millicent Fawcett believed that,

> 'the War revolutionised the industrial position of women. It found them serfs and left them free'.[6]

Even Mary Macarthur, who had a better appreciation of what was happening in industry, initially came to a similar conclusion:

> 'The War was changing "the status and position of women,… it is not so much that woman herself has changed as that man's conception of her has changed."'[7]

Unfortunately the truth is more complex and less encouraging. About 1.6 million women entered employment during the four years of war, pushing up the number of women at work to nearly 5 million. This was a very substantial increase in female employment but, perhaps surprisingly, most women of working age remained outside paid employment. Everyone knew a woman engaged on war-work but usually it was what happened to other people. The mobilisation of women was nothing like as comprehensive as wartime propaganda suggested.

There is a popular myth that the new women employees all went to work in munitions factories. In fact only one woman in seven went into munitions and related activities. A similar number went into various parts of the engineering sector. But, by contrast, over a quarter went into commercial and banking employment and a good number went to work in the civil service or in municipal offices. The rest went in relatively small numbers to a host of businesses from hotels to pottery and from hospitals to agriculture. Government propaganda liked to show young women 'doing their bit' in work that was directly associated with the war but this gave a false impression. In fact female employment was spread much wider and was much less concentrated than the government wanted to suggest.

A lot of attention has focused on how women were brought in to replace men in male-dominated workplaces. This process was much less successful than is sometimes suggested. Most of the men and their trade unions feared that substitution would reduce pay levels and that, when the war ended, the men would have no jobs to come home to. Employers, for their part, were unenthusiastic about losing their skilled workers and disliked the idea either of training a new workforce to craft level or of breaking skilled work down into elements that could be carried out by employees with limited training.[8]

The government made a two-pronged attack on these problems. Government agents toured the country meeting employers to extol the virtues of female labour. The process took a long time and was only partly successful. Alongside this charm offensive was a major effort by government ministers to persuade trade unions that men had nothing to fear from female substitution. The key assurance was that the replacement of men by women would only be temporary. Over and over again ministers repeated that at the end of the war, the men would get their jobs back.

The pledge that the introduction of women workers would only last for the duration of the war influenced the views of everyone. The employers were reassured that they did not need to make permanent changes in production methods; male workers were reassured that their jobs were safe; trade unions were able to make temporary arrangements for female substitutes and dilutees without worrying too much about long-term consequences.

The effect on women workers was profound. The insistence by government, employers and trade unions that their employment was only temporary and that, when the war was over, their lives would return to 'normal' discouraged any thoughts that some significant change was taking place in the role or status of women. Moreover, officialdom was keen to stress that the primary role of a woman was not as a worker but as a mother. The Hills Committee of the Ministry of Reconstruction said in 1919 that

> 'The primary function of women in the state must be regarded... (and in particular)... her service in bearing children and the care of infant life and health ... she must be safeguarded as the homemaker for the nation'.[9]

One government welfare officer went further and argued that war work would make women into better mothers.

> 'The future mothers of Britain will through their factory experience be more broad-minded and self-reliant and with a determined spirit gives greater hopes of a splendid future generation.'[10]

Any idea that many women regarded war work as providing emancipation from their domestic role is not supported by the evidence. Some women liked their paid work but there were many complaints. Although equal pay was promised, it was rarely delivered. Increasingly the practice across industry was to establish 'women's rates' at well below the male wage and pay those rates as a matter of course to women workers. Deborah Thom's study of pay levels at Woolwich Arsenal revealed that only crane drivers, clerks and supervisors received equal pay and in each case only after appeal.

Work in munition factories in particular was long, hard and hazardous. The handling of TNT caused what was called toxic jaundice, turning skin yellow and leading to a breakdown in health. Nearly 300 cases and 84 deaths were recorded among women in the last three years of the war but the condition was so widespread – 'they saw our yellow faces and called us canaries', said one munitions worker – that the true figures are almost certainly higher.[11] The danger was never properly acted on by government, management or trade unions. When a group of women refused to handle explosives they were taken to a tribunal and fined.[12] It is little wonder that work in munitions factories was not very popular.

Legacy of the First World War

As the war came to an end, the government began to do what it had promised and started the process of discharging women from the workplaces that were government-controlled. Private companies followed suit as their male workers returned from the front. But many did not return. A many as 750,000 men lost their lives and the restoration of all 'customary trade practices', which everyone expected, was more patchy and intermittent than had been intended. Some changes, particularly outside the engineering industries, were not completely reversed. Women had demonstrated that they could supervise other women, that they could be adept at administrative duties, that they could be effective shop-workers and that they were better at cleaning work than most men. Nevertheless, a great many women lost their jobs and went back to their domestic duties.

The exodus of women which had been started by public policy, was completed by the economic depression that began in 1920.

Both men and women lost their jobs but the greatest effect was on women. The change was so rapid that after only three years of peace, women made up a smaller proportion of the national workforce than before the war had started.

Some commentators have given the impression that women workers were unhappy to be pushed out of their jobs. No doubt there were plenty of disappointed and frustrated women workers who wanted to stay, particularly in popular clerical work, and there were certainly many disputes about the clumsy way in which the process was handled. Nevertheless the reaction of most women seems to have been one of cheerful resignation. Everyone knew that the jobs were only temporary and, when they came to an end, no one was surprised. The work was often hard and the hours were often very long. Married women in particular felt that they had been encouraged to neglect their families. For many women, it was a welcome return to a familiar domesticity.

The war years brought fewer long-term benefits to women than many observers had expected. Vera Brittain's talk of a revolution was misplaced. Millicent Fawcett's prediction that women would gain a new freedom was overstated. Mary Macarthur, who had started the war with high hopes of a great improvement in the status of women, ended it with words of disillusionment:

> 'At this moment the new world looks uncommonly like the old one, rolling along as stupidly and blindly as ever and that all it has got from the war is an extra bitterness or two.'[13]

Nevertheless, there was a legacy. It was no longer possible to question the ability of women to undertake many jobs that had previously been regarded as beyond them. Women had established new opportunities to work outside the traditional 'women's work' within textiles and domestic service. Increasingly it dawned on employers that women workers were not just 'women' but, like men, their intelligence and ability varied considerably: women began to be judged as individuals rather than just by their sex.

The devastation of war also forced an unwelcome social change. Many women were left as widows and the awful death toll meant that there was a considerable shortage of men of marriageable age. Very many women faced the inevitability of being lifelong widows or spinsters. Work and wages took on an even greater importance for women than in pre-war Britain.[14]

Legal Improvements

The valuable part played by women during the war also encouraged a modest change in political attitudes. Women still had to wait a decade to be granted the same voting rights as men but at least parliament spent a little of that time removing some of the legal restrictions that applied to women. Husbands and wives were allowed to inherit property equally, women and men were able to use the same grounds for divorce and, by the Sex Discrimination (Removal) Act, women were granted access to the professions, to the civil service, to juries and to universities. Each of the new laws was introduced by men and faced little opposition. And for good measure, parliament also passed a resolution in favour of equal pay for equal work. Millicent Fawcett viewed the legal changes with great pleasure. For a time it seemed that she had been right all along and that the franchise had ushered in a period of steadily improving rights for women.

However, a close examination of the measures shows that there were other forces at work beside the desire to increase equality. Two of the new laws were attempts to clarify the law on property rights and divorce, both of which had become extremely confused. The third law, with its grand title – the Sex Discrimination (Removal) Act – was driven less by the desire to remedy injustice than by, in this case, the government's determination to avoid a political defeat.

Immediately after the 1918 General Election, Ben Spoor MP had tabled the Emancipation Bill on behalf of the Labour Party. The Bill gave considerable rights to women including the universal right to vote and the right to sit in the House of Lords. Exceptionally for a Private Members Bill, it looked like becoming law. To avoid this embarrassing outcome the government tabled the Sex Discrimination (Removal) Bill, which was rather less precise and gave no extension in voting rights or entry to the Lords. This Bill passed into law and the Emancipation Bill fell.

Nevertheless, in spite of the ambiguous motives of the government, the legal changes were valuable and indicated a concern for women that had not been in evidence for a very long time. On the other hand, the Sex Discrimination (Removal) Act had much less practical effect than its grand title seemed to suggest and the government, having been forced into tabling the Bill, was probably happy with that outcome. The Equal Pay Resolution was also a dead letter. While useful in declaring Britain's support for a just principle, the Resolution was no more successful in raising women's pay than the guarantees given by ministers during the war. As we demonstrate later, while new legal rights are important, it takes more than an Act of Parliament or a Commons Resolution to overturn cultural norms that have been established for generations.

The Long Pause

Emmeline Pankhurst died in 1928 a few days before the Equal Franchise Act received the Royal Assent. Millicent Fawcett died in the following year. She lived to see millions of women voting in a General Election for the first time.

Emmeline Pankhurst's funeral was enormous. Crowds lined the route from Westminster to Brompton Cemetery, wearing,

> 'tri-colour sashes, ... medals, rosettes and ribbons, and the broad arrow badges of those who went to prison for the cause'.[15]

Mary Stott was not an uncritical admirer of Emmeline Pankhurst but she caught the public mood.

> 'When... her death was reported, a bell tolled in my head for the death of a hero'.[16]

The following year, the National Union bade an emotional farewell to Millicent Fawcett:

> 'We knew that she was a great leader of women and a great historical figure... But in addition we loved her, her personality, her appearance, her *self*'.[17]

Millicent Fawcett's memorial service was packed. *Time and Tide* described the magnificent event and added a note of justifiable irony. The memorial service was attended, the magazine reported, by,

> 'Leaders of the three political parties, each of which had at some time opposed or delayed her work.'[18]

Messages from across the world paid tribute to these two extraordinary women. It felt like the end of an era and, in a depressing sense, it was.

The year 1929 was the year when the momentum behind the Votes for Women campaigns finally petered out. Much had been achieved but the era of reform was over. There were no major parliamentary initiatives for a generation and feminist campaigns outside Westminster were fragmented and intermittent. Not until the Women's Liberation Movement emerged in the late 1960s was there any realistic expectation that the injustices that still afflicted women might find an effective remedy.

The newspapers decided to call the first General Election run on the basis of universal suffrage, the 'Flapper Election'. Perhaps this was merely an example of the inclination of the British press to trivialise great events. However it might also indicate that the newspapers recognised that many of their readers had heard enough about women's rights and, in a period of high unemployment, increasing poverty and political upheaval, Britain would rather smile at young people enjoying themselves than listen to campaigners challenging long-held beliefs about the status of men and women.

British society between the wars had a veneer of brittle glamour. The new fashions in clothes were enticing to those with money to spend. A new style of popular music, strongly influenced by American jazz, could be played on the increasing numbers of gramophones. More radios were being sold and perhaps most important of all, cinemas were opening everywhere, showing films with heroic men and beautiful leading ladies. This world of romantic fantasy was fresh and addictive. One young woman in Bolton said that she saw 12 films a week, every week.[19] Against this background of exciting change, claims for greater female equality voiced by former suffragettes could often sound rather old fashioned.

This long pause in the revolution was also the result of uncertainty among the feminists themselves. There was no shortage of campaigners. Many passionate feminists from the Votes for Women campaigns were keen to press for greater equality and women like Dora Russell, Dorothy Jewson and Ellen Wilkinson had the energy and conviction to take the campaign forward. But after the clarity of the suffrage campaigns there was now no agreement on

nal Union of Societies for Equal Citizenship (NUSEC),
ht have provided the forum where a well-supported
e could be agreed, split apart in 1927. The schism was

ostensibly about whether there should be special legislation to protect women at work but the deeper reason was a disagreement about the overall direction of policy. On one side were those, caricatured as the old guard, who pressed for equality with men. On the other side were the 'new' feminists led by Eleanor Rathbone, who had taken over from Millicent Fawcett as president of NUSEC and argued for a wide-ranging policy, based not on what men had but on what women needed. Common cause proved impossible and those giving priority to equality left NUSEC to join the Open Door Council. The repercussions of this division lasted for decades.

Eleanor Rathbone was a political independent but many of the 'new' feminists were in the Labour Party and campaigned for policies that would help working class women. The depression that ran through the 1920s created mass unemployment. It reached a first peak in 1921 and then a second peak in the winter of 1933 when unemployment reached an all-time high. Poverty levels rose and was made worse when the government cut unemployment benefit by 10% and then again when it imposed a family Means Test. This decision became part of the folklore of working class life. The father of one of the authors (John) was made redundant at 22 in a family that needed the money but was denied benefit because one of his step sisters was still in work and earning.

So Much to do

Misery was not evenly spread across the country. Parts of the southeast escaped the worst of the depression but Wales, Scotland and industrial areas in the north of England suffered desperately. Shipyards built about 2 million tons of shipping in 1913. By 1933, the tonnage had fallen by over 90% to about 100 thousand tons. A survey of family incomes in York by Seebohm Rowntree found nearly one in five families was living below the poverty line. In 1933, the BMA published a report listing minimum dietary requirements. In reply the National Unemployed Workers' Movement showed that unemployed families could not afford to buy even the basic foods which the doctors had recommended.

As very often happens, women bore the brunt of family poverty. Some female breadwinners were not entitled to unemployment benefit and those eligible for benefit faced a nasty form of pressure. Benefit would be withdrawn if work was refused. The normal policy was to offer domestic service jobs to unemployed women and they were told that they had to take this unpopular and unregulated work or lose their remaining income. Health care was expensive and unreliable. Maternity death rates continued to rise throughout most of the 1930s. The realities of life were recalled by Catherine Brown.

> "My dad grew up in Manchester in a family of six children which was small compared to some others. They lived in two up two down terraced housing in Hulme, also known as the slums. Disease was rife, TB, polio, etc. claiming the lives of babies and small children. A couple of times a year the families would have to leave their homes for the day so the corporation could come around to de-louse the houses."[20]

There was so much to struggle against and so many vulnerable people to protect. A group of ex-suffragettes campaigned for reform of the Poor Law. Another group argued for free nurseries. Marches and demonstrations were organised against the Means Test. Women joined men in fighting against cuts in wages and benefits. Support was given to the Miners during and after the general strike. Others campaigned for wider availability of contraception and some began to claim the right to abortion.

Most women activists chose their own priority and campaigned for that. As part of the campaign to improve education for women,

Dora Russell started her own school. Eleanor Rathbone led a campaign for family allowances.[21] Ellen Wilkinson was different. She was everywhere and tried to do everything. She looked at the lives of men and was one of the first women to use that oft-repeated phrase,

'What I really need is a wife!'

The struggle for equality did not die. Lady Rhondda, who had failed in her claim to a seat in the House of Lords, set up the Six Point Group with a programme that evolved into a demand for strict equality between men and women. Lady Rhondda also founded *Time and Tide*, the much-loved feminist magazine which was published into the 1950s. However, the Six Point Group never had more than two or three hundred members and, in terms of campaigning activity, was regularly overshadowed by the 'new' feminists. It seemed self-evident that the greatest need of the time was to relieve the hardship that afflicted millions of people. Equality with men seemed a trivial and irrelevant claim when both men and women were suffering dreadfully in Britain during the Depression.

Political developments in Britain and continental Europe also weakened the feminist cause. The Labour Party split when Ramsay MacDonald led a small group of senior Labour Party figures into coalition with the Conservatives. Many Labour MPs, including Ellen Wilkinson, lost their seats in the election that followed. The rise of fascism produced a new and awful challenge not just in Germany, Italy and Spain but on the streets of Britain. A few of the ex-suffragettes were attracted to the charisma of Oswald Mosley and by the strong measures he proposed to end unemployment. Mary Richardson, the suffragette who had famously gone to prison after slashing Velázquez's painting – the Rokeby Venus – in the National Gallery, actually joined Mosley's Party. As the threat of war increased the inclination of most feminists was to campaign for peace and oppose rearmament. Some, like Vera Brittain, held to their pacifism but many, including Dora

Russell, Ellen Wilkinson and Eleanor Rathbone, eventually came to support rearmament against the Nazi threat. It was yet another issue that divided the supporters of the feminist cause.

The Choice

Economic conditions improved slightly during the 1930s, but unemployment and poverty continued to blight whole towns, particularly in the north. Women campaigned through a variety of organisations ranging from the assertive Women's Cooperative Guild to the Citizen's Association, the Six Point Group, the Open Door Council, the Towns-women's Guilds and even the Women's Institute. There was some overlap in objectives but little cohesion. The strongest feeling was of the extent and enormity of the tasks that had to be undertaken. In her essay, *A Room of One's Own*, Virginia Woolf describes the sense of freedom when a woman has a reasonable income and a place that is unequivocally her own. But the essay is not a work of optimism. At one point Virginia Woolf seems to place the moment when women might achieve this freedom far into the next century. Dora Russell was even more pessimistic: she talked about things 'going into reverse'. Little wonder that, in her history of women in Britain, Sheila Rowbotham describes the period as being characterised by 'a mood of doubt'.[22]

The suffragists had a single objective which they pursued unwaveringly until victory. There were disadvantages with this approach but it minimised debate about priorities. In the 1920s and 1930s and again, half a century later, in the 1980s most women activists looked at the distressed state of Britain and decided that there were more urgent problems to be addressed than equality with men. There was nobility in that choice. The suffragists were often criticised for being primarily interested in women who were well-to-do. That taunt cannot be thrown at the feminists who tried to ameliorate the terrible poverty of the inter-war years. They were sometimes belittled for being 'welfare' feminists yet welfare was exactly what many women, and many men, needed.

On 5 October 1936, the Jarrow Crusade of unemployed workers set off on the long march to London.[23] At the front was Ellen Wilkinson, their newly elected MP. In Jarrow, which Ellen Wilkinson said had been murdered by capitalism, 6,000 were on the dole and 23,000 were drawing relief out of a total population of only 35,000. The government offered no help. 'Jarrow must work out its own salvation', said the president of the Board of Trade. So Jarrow did. Along the route of the march, local women and men provided food and board. Some towns laid on a magnificent spread but others could only afford to offer bread and margarine with tea from a bucket. At every stopping place a 'grubby' Ellen Wilkinson, as she described herself, addressed a public meeting. The march attracted world-wide publicity. Every woman in Jarrow supported the march and along the route women cheered as loudly as the men. Ellen Wilkinson knew that humanity is the greatest part of feminism.

The Second World War

Within three years the people of Jarrow were going back to work. This was not, alas, the result of good works by a benevolent government but followed the fateful broadcast made by Neville Chamberlain, the British prime minister, on the morning of 3 September 1939. He reported that Britain had sought an undertaking that Germany would withdraw its troops from Poland. He then uttered the dreadful words:

> 'I have to tell you now that no such undertaking has been received, and that consequently this country is at war with Germany.'

Those workers who had been thrown out of work in Jarrow and in so many other places were now needed to bolster the war effort. The lives of women – and of men – were being transformed by war for the second time in a generation.

The threat to civilians was much greater than in the First World War. Then, the hostilities and the carnage were in France and Belgium: terrible but remote and, for those in Britain, unknowable and unimaginable. In 1940, after the defeat of British forces at Dunkirk, civilians were as vulnerable as those in the services. For many months Britain expected to be invaded and, once that danger had passed, people in towns, cities and even villages faced a nightly bombardment by bombs and rockets.

A much higher proportion of women were mobilised than in 1914–1918. Many volunteered for the armed forces and from 1941 there was conscription. By the end of the war over 64,000 women had joined up in the WRNS, the WAAF or the ATS. Government propaganda was less successful in persuading women into civilian employment but using a mixture of exhortation and legislation Ernest Bevin, the minister of labour, eventually got the work force that he wanted. By the middle of 1943, 90% of single women were in employment and so, contrary to many expectations, were 80% of married women.

The range of work undertaken by women was wider than in the First World War. As expected, many women went into clerical and administrative jobs and to work in shops. They also moved back into the munitions industries and engineering work. A large cohort worked in aircraft factories. Over 80,000 worked in the land army. But many also worked in shipbuilding and chemicals. They moved into transport, working on buses, railways and canals.

More surprisingly, by the end of the war, 25,000 women were working in construction. As a result of rather belated research, it now appears that most of the workers who built Waterloo Bridge in London were women. But unlike the women who worked on code breaking in Bletchley Park, those female builders have remained invisible. The records have been lost so we do not even know their names. They received not a mention when Herbert Morrison, the Deputy Prime Minister, opened the bridge in 1945. He said,

> 'The *men* (our emphasis) who built Waterloo Bridge are fortunate men. They know that, although their names may be forgotten, their work will be a pride and use to London for many generations to come.'[24]

Male Prejudice

Morrison's oversight, or the oversight of the men who briefed him, exposed the tension that was at the core of wartime employment policy. The government wanted women to take up employment and were very happy for cinemas to show newsreels of happy young women doing war work. But the War Cabinet contained not a single woman and very often War Cabinet decisions reflected male prejudice. This powerful group of men accepted that unusual arrangements had to be made in unusual times but buried deep in their psyche was that long-held belief that the natural place for a woman was in the home looking after her family. So the government did not set up training courses that would have allowed women to learn the skills to perform the work that the men had done. Women were kept in supporting roles, like conductors on buses. And the government certainly did not want women to be paid the same wages as men.

The battle over equal pay revealed the attitude of leading members of the War Cabinet. Labour MP Edith Summerskill and two Conservative MPs, Mavis Tate and Thelma Cazalet-Keir, led the campaign to get equal pay included in the Acts that required women to register for war work. However, Ernest Bevin threatened to resign if the commitment was included and Winston Churchill

said that he would make it an issue of confidence for the government unless the women MPs backed down.[25] This was an exercise
of raw power. It did not matter that parliament had passed its
resolution in favour of equal pay over twenty years earlier and it
did not matter that the TUC, of which Bevin had been a leading
member, had supported equal pay for two generations. Prejudice
won the day and the women MPs had to make do with a Royal
Commission. They had every right to be angry. The Royal Commission reported in 1944 and its majority conclusion was that
paying women less than men was justified because women were
less productive than men.

This was a notable setback but the war helped to create a greater
unity among women's organisations. Early in the war, 21 women's
groups met in a conference to discuss wartime policy. Throughout
the war years, cities across Britain held women's parliaments to
press causes as diverse as better support for foster mothers, rent
controls and nursery facilities. But the low number of women in
the Commons – only 12 during the war – remained a continuing
weakness. They met regularly in the Lady Members' Room, which
they renamed, 'the boudoir'.

Pressure from 'the boudoir' and from women's groups outside
parliament persuaded Bevin to set up a Women Power Committee
to advise the government. It was not a success. Edith Summerskill was a member but she and other Labour MPs believed that
the committee gave too much importance to the career prospects
of affluent women and not enough attention to matters of more
pressing concern to Labour supporters, like inadequate council housing and the problems of mothers and children evacuated
from the large towns. Bevin proved generally unhelpful. His attitude was that other matters should have priority in wartime. He
was prepared to support the provision of nurseries because they
allowed more married women to work but he was impatient both

with the wider agenda of the Women Power Committee and with the more down-to-earth arguments of Labour MPs.

The government was much more comfortable when it was extolling the virtues of women as mothers and homemakers. Lots of advice was provided to housewives on how to cope with food shortages by using all sorts of unlikely ingredients like whale meat, doing amazing things with potatoes and working miracles with spam, the composite product that replaced normal meat. Women were told how important they were in winning 'the battle of the Home Front'. In her study of war time propaganda, Susan Carruthers concludes that a major government objective was to recruit the support of women by portraying 'the housewife as hero'.[26]

The Legacy of the Second World War

Ministers spent less time insisting that women's work was temporary than their predecessors had done twenty five years earlier. But the implication that women were merely holding the fort until the men returned was clear in government speeches and, to judge by the evidence from the surveys conducted by the Mass-Observation company, was well understood by most women. But there were complicating circumstances. Many more women were at work than in the First World War and most of them worked for longer, both because the war itself lasted longer and because the demobilisation of the men was phased over a longer period. Many women appeared more settled in their jobs and there was a strong feeling that things could not go back to the way they were. Edith Summerskill saw a change in the balance of power between men and women.

> 'The freedom which women are enjoying today will spell the doom of home life as enjoyed by the male who is lord and master immediately he enters his own front door.'[27]

Although at the end of the war most women went back to their previous life, or something like it, researchers studying the aftermath of war found that many women had indeed been changed by their wartime experiences. They were more confident, more independent and more likely to challenge traditional ideas about the role of women. And female activists saw some of their long-standing demands being met. Family allowances were introduced in 1945 and maternity benefit was introduced in 1948.

The extent of these changes in attitude is still in dispute. Later studies by Penny Summerfield and others show that rather less had changed than had first been assumed. This soon became the new orthodoxy. However, Summerfield herself warns against generalisation. She tells of an occasion when two women interrupted her speech to disagree strongly with her conclusions. They insisted that their lives had been changed fundamentally by the war and so had the lives of many of their friends. The results of the Mass-Observation Surveys have been challenged by some academics but also seem to show a wide range of experience. One woman said that after being,

> 'a cabbage… you feel you've got out of the cage and you're free'.[28]

There is little evidence to show that the governments that took office after the war supported changes in the status of women or even gave much thought to the matter. Clement Attlee came to power in the 1945 Election. His cabinets included only one woman, Ellen Wilkinson, but after she died in office in 1947, there were none. It was a period of exciting political change: the NHS was established, the major utilities were nationalised, India became independent and the Welfare state was created. But there were no significant initiatives by government designed to improve opportunities for women or to increase their power.

William Beveridge, who produced the plan for the Welfare State had very traditional views about gender. In an echo of statements made by powerful men for centuries, he saw women as mothers and homemakers.

> 'In the next thirty years housewives as mothers have vital work to do in ensuring the adequate continuance of the British race and of the British ideal in the world.'[29]

The Labour Government and the Conservative Governments that came after it saw their social role as rebuilding family life after the destructive pressures of war. The family they had in mind would have been easily recognised by the Victorians: a male breadwinner, a female homemaker and well-behaved children. Long after the war was over, politicians continued to laud housewives for their good works in tones that seem patronising to the modern ear. A sign of the times was the way in which Bessie Braddock, Labour MP for Liverpool Exchange, gained a national reputation as the 'housewives' champion'. As far as most politicians were concerned, women were anchored in that role. That had not changed since the first feminist revolution petered out in 1929.

The 1950s were a time of rising prosperity but, as we record in Chapter 4, that decade brought little change in the power and status of women. It was not until the 1960s that the revolutionary spirit was revived, the Women's Liberation Movement emerged, and that very long pause in women's progress to power and equality came to an end.

The Women's Liberation Movement

The Women's Liberation Movement developed an agenda that was far wider than the narrowly focused objective of the suffrage campaigns. The Ruskin Conference called for equal pay, equal education, 24-hour nurseries, free contraception and abortion on demand. The movement also grappled with issues of power, identity and appearance. By challenge and determination it managed to change the way women are treated and regarded. Directly and indirectly it secured important new laws.

There is no mystery surrounding the death of the Women's Liberation Movement. As we acknowledge in Chapter 4, the movement may well have weakened itself by internal conflict but the end came as a result of the election of Margaret Thatcher's Conservative Government in 1979. Britain's first woman Prime Minister felt that women had no need for special laws or special arrangements. They should do what she had done: work hard and make the most of their talents. She might also have added that there was some advantage in marrying a millionaire but, as it happens, she rarely mentioned Denis Thatcher's wealth.

Nonetheless, what brought the Women's Liberation Movement to an end was not Margaret Thatcher's attitude to women but the economic policies that her government introduced. The Conservatives' first budget tightened money supply and restricted public sector pay. Unemployment rose sharply. The 1981 Budget was even more draconian and unemployment went up rapidly until it hit a 50-year high. Almost every day a famous company seemed to be announcing a factory closure and many towns were devastated. For a time it seemed that the government, which was fast becoming the most unpopular in living memory, would have to change course but the Falklands War improved Margaret Thatcher's standing and she won the following election. Thus encouraged, the government continued its policy of tight money and low public spending.

Feminist campaigners faced a similar choice to their predecessors in the 1930s. Do they continue the struggle on behalf of women or do they add their efforts to the work of the many local action groups that were fighting to protect not just women but whole communities? Like their predecessors they opted to defend communities. Much campaigning was needed. As the Conservative Government became more confident, it cut the value of funding to health and education, sold council houses without building affordable replacements, froze pay in the public sector, systematically attacked trade unions and defeated the miners in a year-long battle.

Some victories were won. Even Conservative women joined the battle to prevent the scrapping of child benefit and the proposal to add family credit to the male salary, policies that Margaret Thatcher favoured. The government was also thrown into confusion by the women's Peace Camp, which was set up in 1981 at the Greenham Common cruise missile site. Ministers realised the political impossibility of using police to attack the women as they had with the miners but they could find no alternative tactic which would show up well on the country's television screens. Eviction did not work and the regular government statements that the protest was over were quickly contradicted by journalists who visited the site. The demonstration ended after the last cruise missiles were removed in 1991.

The Revolution Stalls Again

The Women's Liberation Movement aimed to cause a transformation in the way women are regarded and treated. Their work brought many benefits. As we noted in Chapter 4, progress has been made on three of the four demands formulated at the Ruskin Conference. The objectification of women has decreased. The spectacularly awful Miss World Competition no longer has a place in the British calendar. Pictures of naked or half-naked women are no longer displayed on workplace walls. So-called 'Lads Mags' have been banished to the top shelf of magazine displays. Even The *Sun* no longer prints a picture of a bare-breasted woman on page 3 of the newspaper, although it took forty years for The *Sun* to heed the advice that women were giving to the editor.

Unfortunately, there is another side to the story. A reason why 'Lads Mags' are fading from view is that more graphic pornography is readily available on the internet often with violent scenes to attract viewers who have become bored with more conventional sex. Rape is massively underreported because women fear the ordeal of the witness box and the conviction rate remains extraordinarily low. Social media shows that much of the misogyny that cannot easily be expressed in public is still firmly embedded in the brains of thousands of people. We assess the importance of these obstacles to progress in Chapter 8.

Of course there is no way that feminists campaigning in the 1970s could have anticipated how modern technology and particularly the internet would change our lives. Much more disappointing is the way the two great Acts of Parliament, which emerged from the work of the Women's Liberation Movement, failed to deliver the benefits that were expected.

The Equal Pay Act and the Sex Discrimination Act were enormously important declarations of principle. But they were also meant to have considerable practical effect. Equal pay was meant to become a reality. Sex discrimination was meant to be eliminated at work, in education and training, in the provision of goods and services and in the disposal of premises. Some improvements have come about but there is still a large gender pay gap and there are still very many examples of discrimination.

In the forty years and more since the two Acts were passed, we have had to relearn lessons from the 1920s. At that time, it will be recalled, the Commons passed both a Resolution in support of Equal Pay and the Sex Discrimination (Removal) Act. Unfortunately neither made much difference to people at work. As we have seen, the War Cabinet in the Second World War – heavily influenced by Churchill and Bevin – specifically refused to endorse the principle of equal pay and, as a result, pay discrimination continued throughout the war and for very much longer afterwards.

The Sex Discrimination (Removal) Act of 1919 was extremely broad in its scope and although its specific clauses only addressed the civil service, the courts, and the universities, Section 1 made it clear that sex discrimination was to be outlawed everywhere. A few female mayors were elected, most famously Millicent Fawcett's sister in Aldeburgh, but otherwise the Act was a dead letter. Lady Rhondda tried to use the Act to gain a seat in the House of Lords but her claim was rejected. The Act was only used once in the courts: a horse trainer brought a case against the Jockey Club's refusal to grant her a licence. She won but not on the issue of discrimination. Meanwhile each of the areas specifically mentioned in the Act continued their previous practices without much change.

Enforcement

The lessons of the 1920s should have guided those who proposed, supported and drafted the Acts of the 1970s. The earlier initiatives failed because there was no adequate method of enforcement. The two great Acts of the 1970s have disappointed for a similar reason. It is fair to note that the Equal Pay Act and the Sex Discrimination Act actually contained an enforcement mechanism. Unfortunately, that enforcement mechanism proved to be entirely inadequate.

The Acts provide that a woman who believes that she has suffered discrimination can take her case to an Employment Tribunal. To those drafting the Bills this provision must have seemed a model of good sense but the reality has proved very different. Tribunals were meant to provide swift and informal justice but that never happened. In defending a case, employers brief lawyers experienced in cross examination, often from the criminal courts. As a result, a woman applicant will have every aspect of her working life put under the microscope.

In an equal pay case, the aim of the lawyer will be to show that the applicant is not good enough at her job to warrant higher pay. Every past success will be diminished and then brushed aside; every past mistake will be detailed, and magnified. The poor woman is likely to be kept in the witness box for many hours going over every piece of evidence and defending herself in a case which she thought would be about the employer's failures. Even the most strong-minded applicant ends up feeling lonely, isolated and badly bruised.

Tribunal hearings are held in public and the local press is likely to be present. If it is a sex discrimination case, the national media might see the opportunity for a 'human interest' story and come along. The applicant may well find that the details of her claim get scant coverage but any spicy allegation, even if disproved, will be mentioned and might get into the headline. Her clothes and physical appearance will be described and perhaps she will be caught on camera hurrying up the steps to the Tribunal. Win or lose it will be a miserable experience. If the media finds the case worth reporting, it might be horrendous.

Human Rights Barrister Helena Kennedy warns women about the risks of taking discrimination cases:

> 'You might be the victim of your success even if you win the case. Disclosure will make you vulnerable and you will pay the price. You may well be seen as a trouble-maker by future employers. It might well be a pyrrhic victory.'[30]

In our research for our earlier book about women and power, we interviewed several successful women who had suffered discrimination. Most took the same view as Helena Kennedy. Better to keep quiet and move on than take the massive risk of challenging your employer at Tribunal.

The attitude of these accomplished women begins to expose the other side of this sad tale. Employers know that most women will not take cases and, if they do, enough pressure might be exerted on the applicant to get the case withdrawn. If the case is strong, the employer always has the option of settling outside the Tribunal with a confidentiality clause to avoid any embarrassment to the company. Most employers now appreciate that in practice they have much more latitude than the law intended.

How was this mistake made? During the 1970s, there were scarcely two dozen women MPs and nearly half of them were in parties which were not much interested in improving legal rights for women. The woman closest to power was Barbara Castle and she should be given great credit for helping the two Acts onto the statute book. Unfortunately she had to carry almost the entire burden herself. There was only one other woman [31] in cabinet and they were outnumbered ten to one by men. Barbara Castle did an admirable job but, had there been several score more feminists in the Commons to pick over the details of every clause in the two Bills, and a dozen more in the cabinet to make sure that the law would be effectively implemented, the outcome would very likely have been very much better.

Frenzy and Fallow

There have been only two periods in the last hundred years when women have made significant progress towards equality and greater fulfilment. Those two periods of revolution have each been followed by many decades when, at best, the gains have been unimpressive. The task of the rest of this book is to find a way to ensure that the next century is not like the last. We do not want a period of frenzy followed by another forty years of fallow. Next time the revolution must be sustained.

6

Lessons From Our History

The Votes for Women campaigns and the Women's Liberation Movement show us how to confront injustice and, even more important, they show us how to be victorious.

Every campaign has its own context and, of course, Britain in 2018 is notably different from the Britain that existed before the First World War or in the 1970s, but those campaigners under-stood the nature of British society. They recognised the strength of the institutions that hold women back and the power of the cultural norms that maintain inequality. The richness of their experience can be both an inspiration and a guide to modern female activists.

In this chapter we uncover the many lessons from our history. We focus on the need to mobilise women, we suggest how a new campaign might be organised and we show how Britain's culture might be changed to take better account of the needs of women.

We start with the most important lesson of all.

Women Can be Victorious

The Votes for Women campaigners worked hard to secure the vote. After a relentless struggle that lasted five decades, they won through to victory.

The Women's Liberation Movement aimed to change the role and status of women. After twelve years of high activity, they transformed the way women are treated and regarded. Nowadays no one in public life would dare challenge the principle of gender equality.

These were colossal victories against substantial odds. Herbert Asquith, the Prime Minister, had declared that women should never have the vote because they were not fitted to be involved in public affairs. Members of the Women's Liberation Movement were ridiculed in the newspapers and their cause was scorned. Yet by determination and persistent endeavour the campaigners won.

The greatest lesson from the Votes for Women campaign and the Women's Liberation Movement is that by collective action women can win momentous victories.

Mobilising Women

Raising Awareness

Both of the great campaigns were based on the need to raise awareness and mobilise women in support of the cause. The suffrage societies relied on a countywide system of committees with meetings addressed by high-profile women speakers. The Women's Liberation Movement concentrated heavily on local activity, involving women in discussions about the role and identity of women. Then, as now, the campaigners had to work hard to persuade women to look beyond the pressures and demands of their own lives.

'Work, beauty, marriage, mortgage and kids',

is how Laurie Penny[1] sums up the aspirations of most women in the modern world. A bleak picture painted by an idealistic young feminist.

Another young feminist, lawyer Charlotte Proudman, told us that

'Young women are not engaging with feminist issues – they glaze over when I talk'.

How accurate are these accounts of current feelings of young women? Do some believe that the main battles have already been won by the Women's Liberation Movement and, if so, how can these false assumptions be challenged? Even more important, how can young women be mobilised to take on the continuing fight for equality?

Sheila Rowbotham, feminist historian and long-time campaigner for women's rights, reassured us that she does meet young women students who are feeling 'rebellious'. Interestingly, she said that they were often accompanied and supported by young men who seem genuinely concerned but were not trying to dominate the discussions.

How do we raise awareness in the twenty-first century?

To begin with, it is probably necessary for women personally to experience inequality and discrimination at home or at work or in the wider world. They need to recognise that they are suffering injustice, and should name the perpetrators.

It is never easy to question assumptions that are taken for granted about the way the world seems to work. Guilt, dealing with the disapproval of others and deliberately ruffling the outwardly calm exterior of everyday existence takes courage. But, as the two great campaigns of the twentieth century demonstrated, it can be done.

The first thing to remember is that success is more likely when we campaign collectively.

It is clear from previous chapters in this book that there will be resistance from powerful institutions, that campaigns will be long and arduous, that strong leadership is vital and also that many women feel inhibited by what their changed status might look and feel like. Therefore, it is essential that women trust, talk and understand that the next step is to take action together.

New movements tend to start slowly and then gather momentum as they attract publicity. Raising awareness is two pronged: first the individual must feel and acknowledge a grievance and then seek out others whose experiences are similar. The second task is to spread the word by whatever means are available.

The Votes for Women Campaign and the Women's Liberation Movement were successful in accomplishing both of these, using different methods that reflect their different goals and historical contexts.

The suffragists began by relying on petitions. They collected thousands of signatures of support and presented petition after petition to successive government ministers. They were employing the democratic means to an end, which would grant them the equal democratic rights to which they were entitled. Even after having been rebuffed and betrayed on numerous occasions, the constitutional societies continued to petition even while the suffragettes were taking more militant action. They never stopped believing in the power of reasoned persuasion. Women joined their campaigns because they were impressed as much by the strength of their arguments as their visible presence at meetings and rallies.

Maintaining publicity is a vital ingredient in raising awareness. Constant reminders of their cause through propaganda, through the suffragette shops where people could obtain information and ensuring that activities were reported in newspapers all helped to keep the Votes for Women campaign alive in the eyes and ears of the general public. It was taken increasingly seriously. When neighbours and friends become involved it is acceptable to campaign oneself.

The Women's Liberation Movement had a different genesis but raising awareness was a central aspect of its function.

By 1968 all women had been able to vote for 40 years. Equality was now being defined in terms of emotional liberation and independence in relationships as well as seeking equal pay and status at work. A generally unfocussed dissatisfaction was interpreted by feminist writers such as Betty Friedan, Germaine Greer, Ann Oakley, Juliet Mitchell, Sheila Rowbotham, Lynne Segal and many more. They were voraciously read and talked about by women trying to understand the roots of their anger.

Awareness was raised through conversations in small groups and this in turn stimulated a growing movement for equal rights. There was a lot more local activity at this time than is often recognised. Women's centres and nurseries were set up; meetings on welfare were held; members of local women's groups were invited to speak to more traditional organisations like townswomen's guilds, mother and toddler groups and members of the Housewives Register – an organisation set up so that professional women at home with children could meet and talk about more than sleepless nights, teething problems and potty training. The Women's

Liberation Movement was far less regimented than the suffrage campaign and this informality encouraged waverers to ask questions, speak up and then to take part in what Sheila Rowbotham described to us as participatory politics.

Not easy to describe, but an essential part of the Women's Liberation Movement, is the trust that women placed in one another. Meeting in a variety of groupings, whether they had a political focus or were simply a group coming together as women without the presence of men, they had time to think about their individual situations. For many, this led to collective action which in turn gave them the confidence to change habits accumulated over years at home and at work.

Running alongside the personal and perhaps necessarily introspective narratives were, of course, the campaigns for equal pay and anti-discrimination. These campaigns gathered force as women became convinced that the injustices they faced as individuals were common to most other women and they joined in the struggle.

Laura Bates and Kat Banyard have alerted us to widespread violent emotional and physical abuse that is still endured by many women. Through their writings they have raised awareness of unpalatable facts of life in twenty-first century Britain. We will consider their importance in a later chapter but it is worth noting that the uproar caused by Laura Bates happened by accident. In her book *Everyday Sexism*[2] she describes how she started by sharing her own experiences of sexual harassment with friends and family. She was stunned by the number of stories she heard, similar to her own, and shocked to find that these events were almost accepted as 'normal' in women's lives.

She decided to start,

'a very simple website where women could upload their stories'.

She was expecting 50 or 60 women to add their stories. What began as a trickle burgeoned into hundreds within the first week. She should be given great credit for unleashing a veritable torrent of evidence of systematic abuse. This contemporary way of raising awareness of the size of the problem has yet to be followed by successful methods of dealing with it.

Women From All Backgrounds Should Be Involved

The Votes for Women campaign and the Women's Liberation Movement claimed to be speaking on behalf of the women of Britain. Unfortunately, the campaigners' right to make that claim was questioned at the time and has been questioned since.

The source of the criticism is significant. As we discussed in Chapters 3 and 4, men who were comfortable with the status quo were quick to say that each campaign included misguided malcontents who were not entitled to speak on behalf of 'normal' women. However, the uncomfortable truth is that the criticism was also voiced by women who supported gender equality and in most respects were the natural allies of the campaigners.

The core of their criticism is that almost all of the campaigners came from a background of leisured affluence and that their campaigns were designed principally to achieve advantage for women of a similar background rather than for all women. Both the campaigns were criticised for not being sufficiently inclusive, either in their membership or their objectives. These are serious criticisms and we examine them in detail.

It was inevitable that a good number of suffragists and suffragettes would come from affluent families because, in Victorian and Edwardian times, those were the only women with the time and the money to campaign. But, unfortunately, that is no longer a sufficient explanation. Thanks to the valuable research of Jill Liddington and Jill Nelson[3] we now know that it was possible to recruit working class women into the suffrage societies and that a strong working class movement for women's suffrage was built in the North West of England. What happened to that section of the campaign provides us with valuable lessons about inclusivity.

When the young Esther Roper was elected secretary of the Manchester Suffrage Society, she made a direct appeal to women textile workers in Lancashire and Cheshire. Esther Roper was middle class but she appointed two working class women to act as organisers. Her work was given added impetus when she formed a partnership with the poet, Eva Gore Booth, a charismatic woman whom Teresa Billington described as a liquid pool 'of spontaneous combustion'. The textile workers were visited at the factory gates, in local meeting places and in their own homes. Esther Roper struck up a good working relationship with the trade unions, the Women's Cooperative Guild and the ILP. In time, her Manchester Society became the suffrage society for all of the North of England.

Millicent Fawcett supported the society and, with typical canniness, ensured that it had funds and autonomy. The society collected a massive petition signed by thousands of working women. When it was presented to parliament it looked 'like a garden roller in dimensions' and the MP staggered as he carried it to the Commons table. There followed a second petition which included the wool workers of Yorkshire. Delegations of textile workers journeyed to Westminster to lobby the politicians. The society began to develop a working class leadership, mostly including experienced trade unionists like Sarah Reddish, Sarah Dickenson and Selina Cooper supported by Ada Nield Chew, who had led a much publicised protest against factory conditions in Crewe. For a decade and more, these radical suffragists led the most vibrant and successful part of the suffrage movement.

The high point of their influence came with the deputation to the Prime Minister in May 1906. That deputation was made up of four hundred women from all backgrounds and classes, including a large delegation representing 50,000 textile workers. They waved their colourful banners, Sarah Dickenson spoke about life in the textile factories and Eva Gore Booth told the Prime Minister that textile workers should have the vote because they,

> 'are all labouring under the gross disability and industrial disadvantage of an absolute want of political power'.[4]

This enormous demonstration of sisterly unity provided a wonderful opportunity to consolidate broad-based support among women from all backgrounds. That never happened and, although the radical feminists must take part of the blame, a greater responsibility for the failure lies elsewhere.

The main problem faced by the radical suffragists was the disagreement over objectives which had bedevilled the suffrage campaign from the beginning. The suffrage societies were committed to the policy of securing for women the same voting rights as men but, because many men did not have the vote, success in the suffrage campaign would mean that many working women, like many working men, would still be disenfranchised.

The suffrage society was inclined to compromise but Ada Nield Chew wanted a complete change of policy. She declared that support for the limited suffrage should be abandoned and universal suffrage should be adopted as the policy of all suffrage societies.

Christabel Pankhurst chose this moment to intervene on behalf of WSPU. She did not like Ada Nield Chew or her policy of universal suffrage. Christabel Pankhurst's attack was direct and unsisterly. She started a row that became venomous and went on for months, exposing divisions in the suffrage movement and revealing a depth of class-based animosity that was unseemly and damaging.

Christabel Pankhurst was fast developing the view that working women had no place in the suffrage movement. She rationalised this prejudice by arguing that,

> '... the House of Commons, and even its Labour members were more impressed by the demonstrations of the feminine bourgeoisie than of the female proletariat'.[5]

Christabel Pankhurst's snobbishness began to have an increasing effect on WSPU. Old Manchester allies felt out of place in the 'silks and satins' of the London Office[6] and according to Teresa Billington, as soon as the WSPU moved to London,

> '... the working class women were dropped without hesitation'.[7]

That process reached its miserable conclusion when even Christabel's sister, Sylvia, and her small organisation of working class women in East London were expelled from WSPU.

After 1908, WSPU was setting the agenda for the Votes for Women campaign, gaining most publicity and developing a style that was increasingly middle class. Any involvement in industrial or trade union affairs was condemned as a distraction. The North of England suffrage society continued its work but it was no longer close to the centre of the campaign. There were no new campaigns to recruit working class women. A great opportunity to broaden support and widen objectives had been cast aside.

Christabel Pankhurst had got her way. As a result, the objectives and the membership of the Votes for Women campaign were much

narrower than they could have been. When challenged, Christabel
insisted that grievances about inequality and the restricted nature
of women's lives would be resolved once the vote had been won.
However, as we show in Chapter 5, after 1928 the revolution stalled
and for a generation the status of women scarcely changed until the
Women's Liberation Movement became active 40 years later.

The membership of the Women's Liberation Movement was
noticeably different from the membership of the Votes for Women
campaigns. Certainly, many members of the Women's Liberation
Movement were middle class but this was middle class by education rather than by wealth. There were very few of the moneyed
and titled ladies who formed the backbone of some of the suffrage
societies. Millicent Fawcett showed her support for campaigners
who had been to prison by arranging a banquet at the Savoy Hotel.
Members of the Women's Liberation Movement were unlikely to
be found dining in a five star hotel.

The Women's Liberation Movement had none of the snobbery that
damaged the WSPU. A belief in sisterly solidarity was fundamental
to the Women's Liberation Movement and, from the early days,
the inclination to be inclusive was strong. There was also a belief
that it was working class women who suffered the greatest disadvantage in British society. That feeling of solidarity was reinforced
by the involvement of a number of left-wing groups who claimed
an affinity with working people and with the trade unions. It was
both a matter of principle and of practical politics that the movement should seek to include women from all backgrounds.

Unfortunately it did not work out that way. The Women's Liberation Movement never achieved the breadth of membership and
involvement that might have been possible. Part of the reason was
the informality of the movement's structure and decision-making.
The main machinery for coordination was the national conference

and, although nine were organised during the movement's existence, they did not develop plans to broaden membership.

Understandably, many of the local groups were made up, at least initially, of friends and acquaintances. Most local groups welcomed new members and some advertised their meetings but we also heard examples of groups that were comfortable with the way they were and did not want to grow in size or complexity. Many of the leading members of the Women's Liberation Movement were academics. Their knowledge and intelligence was impressive but the nature of the discussion could feel somewhat off-putting to a new member.

It is certainly true that some local groups actively tried to recruit working women but often this was an attempt to gain support for a campaign that had already been determined. Sheila Rowbotham told us how she and a colleague delivered a thousand leaflets on one housing estate inviting women to a meeting. Only one woman turned up. In retrospect it was recognised that it would have been better to talk informally to some of the women concerned about what was important to them and build up from there, rather than start by inviting them to a meeting with people they did not know.

Relations with the trade unions were generally constructive and went some way to broaden the experience and the credibility of the movement. However, the trade unionists preferred to stay within their own organisations, cooperating but not integrating. According to interviews recorded for the British Library Archive, this was largely explained by a difference in perspective. There was a tension between members of the movement who were determined to make a fundamental change in the status of women and trade unionists who wanted to campaign for improvements in pay and conditions. The trade unionists were impatient with 'navel gazing' and some of the academics were unimpressed by what they called 'merely reformist demands' for changes in working conditions.

Nevertheless, as we record in Chapter 4, there were many examples of joint action with the trade unions and, had there been greater national or regional coordination, there might have been more. However, what fundamentally weakened the Women's Liberation Movement were the factions within it. The Marxists, Leninists and Maoists had their own distinct agendas. They felt strongly that the only way to make progress was through concerted political activity. Some of the far left groups used brutal terms to condemn women who did not share their views. Several of the national conferences ended in tears and acrimony with insults hurled and little achieved.

However, the challenge to the movement's claim to be truly representative was not only based on considerations of class. It was also based on ethnicity. Black and Asian women pointed out that the Women's Liberation Movement was almost entirely white, that the interests of women from different racial heritages were not represented and, worse still, they were not understood.

As we explain in Chapter 4, there is no adequate answer to these accusations. During the 1970s, too little thought was given to the separate identities of black or Asian women and there was little understanding that, for them, white women might be regarded as a more serious source of oppression than black or Asian men. Nowadays white women activists from the Women's Liberation Movement do not seek to justify this failure of understanding and what flowed from it. Their view is that it was a weakness which must not be repeated.

Our conclusions are not based on hindsight. The criticism that the Votes for Women campaign and the Women's Liberation Movement were not as representative as they should have been was made very strongly at the time. It weakened them both. Unity based on inclusivity is a powerful organising principle and that lesson should be remembered when the next and, we hope, conclusive liberation campaign is planned.

A Natural Resistance to Change

In 1889, the Women's Anti-Suffrage Society was set up by the novelist Mrs Humphrey Ward. [8] The Antis, as they were called, were less influential than they had hoped, but what lay behind their campaign was significant. They expressed a disquiet about how the women's suffrage campaign might change their own view of a woman's role, her general demeanour including her looks and her place in the home.

Mrs. Ward insisted that women should be delicate homemakers, concentrating on keeping a well-run household. Women should not be troubled by taking part in discussions and making decisions that might ruffle the calm atmosphere which it is their duty to provide for their family. The destabilising effect of women taking on a role outside the home was felt to be a threat.

This is all about power and control and of course it is obvious why men like Lord Cromer, who led the male section of the Antis, found the concept of women's rights threatening. But there are also many women who were (and are) wary of the altered identity they may have to wrestle with if they challenged the traditionally established view of themselves.

The clothes that middle- and upper-class women wore until the 1920s were restrictive: corsets, petticoats, high collars, numerous buttons and long skirts, all preventing easy freedom of movement. In *Femininity*, Susan Brownmiller[9] quotes the announcement by The War Industries Board during the First World War that,

> 'if American Women were released from their armour, 28,000 tons of steel would be freed to build and furnish two battle ships'.

As late as the 1970s many of us sighed with relief when tights (or 'pantyhose' as they were originally called) were invented and we could dispense with fiddly suspenders.

The image of women as frail and fragile creatures unable to share the burden of male physical jobs was particularly ludicrous when one thinks of women working in cotton mills, or attempting to keep their families and homes clean with no modern equipment. Domestic service provided the largest source of employment of working class women until the 1930s. And being 'in service' was hard labour with long hours, carrying coals, water, clothes up and down many flights of stairs. Maids and cooks were still common until the 1950s. None of these women could be described as physically weak but it suited the prevailing myth for their strength to remain invisible.

Few women would object to having the right to own property, having equal rights over their children, signing for their own operations in hospitals and such like but there appears to be a conflict in the power relations at home. In 1989, Airlie Hoschild published *The Second Shift* which lifted the veil on the unequal distribution of labour in the home. No matter how elevated a position a working wife managed to attain as an employee, she remained responsible for nearly three-quarters of domestic duties. Survey after survey tells us that this domestic inequality still persists.

Women complain but to what extent do they exacerbate the situation themselves? Housework itself is mundane but there is something about being the hub of the household that is still attractive. Although some young women may react angrily to this proposition, being the centre of the decision-making and the emotional rock of the family remains seductive. As Catherine Hall says,

> 'At the same time that we were madly criticising men for not taking their responsibilities seriously, we were absolutely claiming the sphere of children and home as ours....'[10]

The job of the modern campaigner is to emulate the activists of the suffrage campaign and the Women's Liberation Movement and show that women deserve a less-restricted and more equal life.

The lesson of the two campaigns is that the inequality that exists in Britain should be exposed. Women should be shown how much the conventions and customs which buttress that unfairness, damage their prospects and deny them fulfilment.

During the 1980s, 'Sensible Footwear', a feminist performing group comprising three young women, challenged the popular conception of what women should wear, and also urged us to consider the language we use every day without thinking. Their presentation, 'Words fail me', made us think about the difference in meaning between Lord and Lady, the sexual nuances of the word mistress entirely absent from master. They questioned why women had (and still have) to fill in forms where they are asked whether they are known as Miss or Mrs while men are all simply Mr. Ms was invented as a handy catch-all titles that did not distinguish between the married or unmarried status but not many women used it and those who did were often mocked.

In the 1970s and 1980s, women began to object to being called 'girls'. No-one would refer to groups of men aged over 30 as 'boys'. It is belittling and emphasises a lack of status. Even when some people began to understand our objection to being called 'girls', they resorted to 'ladies', which again has different and unwanted connotations. It is often used with faux deference. I (Eva) ask why is it so difficult to call us 'women'? The term is neutral, female but without the infantilisation of 'girls' or the implied refinement of 'ladies'. We are all women.

The way we speak, the words we choose to use reflect deep-seated but learnt prejudices formed in a world that favours men. These may seem irrelevant, trivial and unnecessary quibbles to those who refuse to acknowledge that thoughtless language places us firmly in our designated inferior place. It is disheartening when women themselves say that they are wasting their time worrying about such matters.

Petty things happened when we started to ask awkward questions about men's assumed superiority and, unfortunately, conflicting messages came from men and women. I (Eva) remember, as a teacher carrying a load of exercise books along a school corridor with no hands free and meeting a male colleague coming through a door. He let it shut before I could get through saying, 'You feminists can look after yourselves.' But, on the other hand, I also remember more than one occasion when women objected to a door being held open for them by a man saying, 'I'm quite capable of opening a door myself, thank you': courtesy mistaken for oppression.

In the workplace women reaching the top can find it lonely and arid, fitting into structures made by men for the convenience of men. They have the position they strived to achieve but it does not satisfy them. They wonder whether the struggle was worth it. There is no doubt that there are men who find themselves similarly disappointed but it would be unusual to find men who feel that they have sacrificed as much as many successful women, or gone through as many hoops to get there. Success at work validates a man's existence but this is rarely the case for women. Unable to forfeit their happiness any longer, some women leave for an easier life. This should not be the answer. It is the system that needs to be fixed and not the women. That is the lesson of our history.

Nature of the Campaign

Women Must Be In Charge

In her autobiography Hannah Mitchell, who campaigned for Votes for Women across the north of England, talked of the exhilaration felt by women when they realised that the main speakers at suffrage meetings would be women.[11] In Chapter 2, I (Eva) described my own exhilaration when I went on my first women's liberation demonstration.

The principle that women must have charge of their own campaign has echoed through every period of our history. For Millicent Fawcett, it was a matter of common sense. Only women can know what women really need. Hannah Mitchell, believed that only women would bring the necessary passion. Her experience was that men might express sympathy, but only women cared enough to fight.[12]

A hundred years later, Harriet Harman stated the principle directly.

'Women must be the engine of their own liberation.'[13]

Men are welcome to support but a campaign for women must have a membership of women and must be led by women. That has been the nature of every successful campaign. It is the unequivocal message from our history. Women must lead the struggle for their own emancipation.

A Worthwhile Campaign Is Likely To Be Lengthy

The campaign to win the right for women to vote began in 1866 with John Stuart Mill's petition to parliament. It took 50 more years before 8 million women were allowed to vote and another 10 years, until 1928, before universal suffrage was finally won.

Emmeline Pankhurst was driven: urging followers never to surrender and never to give up –and they did not. But at some cost. Setback after setback was countered by determination, resilience and dogged persistence. It is hard for us to gauge the courage that such tenacity relies on. In Chapter 3 we told the grisly stories of women being forcibly fed, sometimes over a period of weeks, and the personal accounts are horrifying. But what kept these and other campaigners going over so many years, was an unshakeable belief in their cause.

Harriet Harman's autobiography *A Women's Work* (2017) gives us example after example of the endurance needed to keep on pressing for even the smallest of concessions. Entering parliament in 1982 as one of a tiny minority of women MPs (she says that at that time 97% of MPs were men) every victory came after lengthy and arduous arguments, persuasive tactics and manoeuvring. Her constant campaigning on behalf of women of all classes paid off. We owe her a great debt for her courageous persistence and what she has achieved, but she herself writes:

> 'We should analyse and be clear about the extent to which inequality persists – and certainly never minimise it. To recognise that we still have such a long way to go is simply to face the facts.'[14]

An Effective Structure

In preparing for a lengthy campaign we should learn the lessons from earlier campaigns about how to maintain momentum. Both Millicent Fawcett's National Union of Women's Suffrage Societies and Emmeline Pankhurst's WSPU recognised that a robust organisational structure is essential, but the two women had very different ideas about how the necessary structure should be designed. There are important lessons to be learnt from a comparison between the two models.

The Women's Liberation Movement's approach was more radical than either of the Votes for Women campaigns. Members of the movement were sceptical about traditional forms of leadership.

They wanted the movement to be firmly based on the principle that all women are equal. As we explained in Chapter 4, the Women's Liberation Movement wanted to achieve a revolutionary change in the way women saw themselves and in the way women were treated. They wanted women to overcome their feelings of inferiority and challenge the male structures that held them back.

The activists in the Women's Liberation Movement insisted that powerful leaders and strong national committees would be of little help in making these substantial changes. More women could be reached and engaged by working through local groups, tackling the problems that women faced in their local communities. Sometimes these locally driven methods looked a little chaotic but they succeeded in reaching women across the country and provided the space where women could think about their role and status.

However, not all of the movement's aims could be achieved by grass roots activity. Problems arose when the movement needed to lobby politicians. Being against sexual discrimination is all very well but politicians want to know how discrimination should be defined and what measures are needed to combat it. Successful lobbying of politicians meant that Women's Liberation Movement needed a system of effective policy making. That means that committees must have a clear structure with an obligation to reach conclusions. And the movement had to choose representatives to explain their policies to the politicians.

Problems arose from the Women's Liberation Movement's attitude to the media. With very good reason, the activists were concerned that they would be misrepresented by journalists. So the activists tended to boycott the mainstream media entirely. The flaws in this policy soon became apparent. Journalists still wrote about the Women's Liberation Movement but, in the absence of hard facts, they indulged their prejudices. This might well have suited the agenda of many national newspapers but it served the Women's Liberation Movement very badly.

To some extent the leadership vacuum was filled by celebrated feminists who came to be seen as informal figureheads of the movement. Germaine Greer's book, *The Female Eunuch*, published in 1970, motivated many women to take part in the Women's Liberation Movement and Germaine Greer appeared frequently on radio and television making the case for reform in sharp and provocative fashion. Rosie Boycott co-founded the feminist magazine *Spare Rib* in 1971 and her writings provided a commentary on the movement's activities. But both Germaine Greer and Rosie Boycott were independent spirits and sometimes attracted attention for views that would not have been supported by many members the Women's Liberation Movement.

The experience of the Women's Liberation Movement demonstrates how difficult it is to design a structure that meets all of the objectives of a campaigning organisation. Nevertheless, our history teaches a number of important lessons. The campaign will not be taken seriously unless its policies have been worked out in detail and have gained general support. An effective campaign will also need properly accredited representatives to talk to politicians, other organizations and to the media.

Democracy

In the modern world, strong leadership is regarded as the solution to almost every problem and it is easy to ascribe the success of the Votes for Women campaign to the strong leadership of Emmeline Pankhurst. She was single-minded and charismatic. She revived the campaign when it seemed to be in the doldrums. Millicent Fawcett paid tribute to the way in which the Pankhursts and the WSPU managed to draw so much public attention to the cause. With her determination and strength Emmeline Pankhurst did much to secure voting rights for women, and she deserves to be remembered as one of the most important Britons of the twentieth century.

Unfortunately, the strong leadership that energised the suffrage campaign is only one side of the story. As we recorded in Chapter 3, Emmeline Pankhurst insisted that WSPU should be run like 'an army in the field'. Her wish to remove every vestige of democratic decision-making from WSPU caused arguments and splits. Teresa Billington, who had been one of the most successful organisers in WSPU, complained that Emmeline Pankhurst was a dictator and she left to form the Women's Freedom League. Emmeline and Frederick Pethick-Lawrence, who had funded WSPU for many years, left after Emmeline Pankhurst refused to listen to their well-founded objections to her decision to encourage the use of bombs and arson.

Emmeline Pankhurst's determination to concentrate power on herself and on her daughter, Christabel, caused many practical difficulties. Emmeline was often in court or in prison and, for the last part of the campaign, Christabel was in hiding in Paris. Both received regular reports but, for much of the time, neither was on hand to take control of events.

The mess that the WSPU made when George Lansbury bravely resigned his parliamentary seat to fight a bye-election on the issue of Votes for Women is a graphic illustration of the problem. The bye-election provided a considerable opportunity to show popular support for women's suffrage. However, Christabel was in France, Emmeline could spend little time in the constituency and the WSPU organiser on the ground felt she did not have the authority to take the urgent decisions that were needed. When the result was declared and Lansbury had lost his seat, the reaction of the WSPU organiser was not that a great opportunity to advance the campaign had been missed. Instead, according to Sylvia Pankhurst, the organiser asked tearfully, 'What will Christabel say?'[15]

The concentration of power meant that the pressure on Emmeline Pankhurst was crushing. The suffragettes' militant campaign effectively lasted nine years. By the end of that time Emmeline was exhausted. Incessant travelling, court appearances, prison and hunger strikes had worn her out and damaged her health. She began to shift power to Christabel but the weaknesses in her daughter's judgement and personality were soon evident. Strong single-minded leadership can bring benefits to a campaign, particularly in the short term. But, if the leader concentrates power so completely on herself that the burden becomes unbearable and, if there is no opportunity to find a worthy successor, the campaign is certain to falter. Concentrated power and autocratic control is not a good model for a future campaign.

Emmeline Pankhurst was very critical of the constitutional suffrage societies led by Millicent Fawcett. Her sense of frustration was understandable but the constitutional suffrage societies, and the National Union that represented them, possessed a quality that WSPU lacked: they had the resilience to be long-lasting. One of the first suffrage societies collected the signatures for the petition that John Stuart Mill presented in 1866 and, unlike WSPU, which was disbanded before victory was achieved,[16] suffrage societies were still campaigning when the Act securing universal suffrage was passed in 1928, over sixty years later.

The more democratic structure of the constitutional suffrage societies brought other advantages. The leadership could be passed from one leader to the next, as had happened when Eleanor Rathbone succeeded Millicent Fawcett, and the organisation could respond to changing times by changing its nature, as had happened in 1919 when the National Union of Women's Suffrage Societies signalled its wider scope by becoming the National Union of Societies for Equal Citizenship. By contrast, WSPU never managed to find an adequate successor to Emmeline Pankhurst and the half-hearted attempt to transform itself into a political party completely failed.

However, organisational structure should not just be determined by practicalities. Feminism abhors the exercise of arbitrary power, and there is a strong moral argument that the founding principles of any feminist campaign should be democratic. Leaders and representatives should be elected. But, the scepticism about traditional ideas of leadership felt by the Women's Liberation Movement is certainly valid. Leaders can become unaccountable, self-obsessed, exhausted or ill. Most overestimate their importance. A new liberation campaign should designate any leader as first among equals, and not regard a leader as some specially endowed individual attended by followers.

Because feminism is suspicious of any concentration of power, the right to make decisions should be shared between different levels in the campaign. There is no sense in setting up some all-powerful and remote national body when the campaign wants to mobilise activity across the country. The Women's Liberation Movement showed that much could be achieved by local groups. The lesson of history is that the national body should plan and coordinate but should not control.

Clear Objectives

If a campaign is going to be taken seriously by the public and by politicians its objectives must be clear and well understood. This was the great advantage of the Votes for Women campaigns.

Everyone knew what the campaign wanted: women to have the vote on the same basis as men. This demand was repeated at every opportunity and remained unchanged for fifty years.

Unfortunately such clarity can sometimes begin to look like rigidity, particularly when the political agenda changes. There is a strong argument that the suffrage campaigns would have grown stronger had the objective been changed to universal suffrage at the time when Asquith started advocating universal suffrage for men. That would have increased support on the left of politics as well as giving the campaigns a much chance to appeal to working class women. Every objective needs to be subject to review and, if necessary, updating.

The Women's Liberation Movement had clear objectives and avoided rigidity during the twelve years from 1968 to 1980 when it was most active. The four demands first agreed at the Ruskin Conference resulted in particular campaigns and, when the demands were met, others took their place.

For the reasons explored in Chapter 5, organised activity after the vote was won in 1928 was patchy rather than sustained. Women had been demanding equal pay for many years but the strike by women Ford workers in Dagenham in 1968 demanding the same skilled rates as the men caught the public's imagination. Barbara Castle backed them and she finally managed to get the Equal Pay Act through in 1970 by holding the Cabinet to ransom.

In her autobiography,[17] Harriet Harman recounts the tale that Barbara Castle told her. Barbara Castle said that her Cabinet colleagues refused to support her on equal pay but were keen to bring forward a Prices and Incomes Policy Bill. She simply said she would not vote for the Bill they wanted unless they backed equal pay. Realising that Barbara Castle was not going to give in, the Cabinet capitulated and the Equal Pay Act was passed.

Equal educational opportunity was the second stated aim. According to Miriam David, the expansion of universities in response to the Robbins Report of 1963 had led to a

> 'major growth in social sciences, and accompanying this phenomenal growth has been the rise of women as students'.[18]

Many of these women became active in the women's movement and, in particular, they challenged the predominance of men in the higher echelons at universities.

The demand for 24-hour nurseries quickly fell by the wayside. As Sheila Rowbotham explains,[19] the idea was to help women who worked unusual hours but the policy seemed to imply that children were to be placed in 'nanny state run nurseries' for 24 hours at a time. I (Eva) have to admit that I never fully understood the purpose of this demand.

I remember marching with a friend in a demonstration in the early 1970s, both of us carrying banners asking for 24-hour nurseries. I turned to her at one stage and asked 'Do you believe in 24-hour nurseries, Jo?' 'No' she said. 'What are we doing here then?' said I. 'Solidarity sister, solidarity', came the reply. She was right, of course. Collective action in support of other women is a powerful lesson in unity.

To have an abortion will never be an easy decision for any woman but the achievement of the fourth Ruskin objective, abortion on demand, has helped very many women. The NHS estimates that one woman in three will have an abortion at some stage in her life. The dangerous practice of back street abortions has finally been relegated to the past.

Landmark Successes

A lengthy campaign can easily go into decline as supporters lose heart. The celebration of successes along the way helps to maintain morale and, if cleverly presented, encourages the impression that the final victory is inevitable.

The disadvantage of a single issue – all or nothing – campaign, as the Votes for Women campaigners found, is that it is very hard to find intermediate successes. The women suffragists celebrated advances in the colonies and in America but those remote achievements found little resonance in Britain. The lesson of history is that a stage-by-stage approach provides more opportunities for morale-raising celebrations than a single issue campaign.

The Women's Liberation Movement could claim many opportunities for celebration: the Equal Pay Act of 1970, the first women's refuge opened in Chiswick in 1971, the progress made by the Night Cleaners as a result of strikes in 1972 and the many successes in 1975, including the Sex Discrimination Act, the Employment Protection Act and the first vote by the General Synod in favour of the ordination of women. The year 1975 also saw the launch of the first UN International Year for Women.

Important victories were won, *Spare Rib* and the Virago Press were launched and women's lives were improved. The disappointment is that, perhaps because of the absence of a National Committee to plan the necessary events, these many successes were not celebrated with the fanfare they deserved.

The lesson of history is compelling: when women win, we should tell the world and keep telling the world until it takes notice.

Publicity

Every worthwhile campaign has to find a way to keep the cause in the forefront of public and political debate.

The WSPU was brilliant at attracting publicity. The WSPU was always visible and always available. Each Sunday the suffragettes held a social event at their premises in London. The WSPU promoted the idea of a women's parliament and held sessions across the country. The ingenuity of the suffragettes was startling. Each month seemed to produce a fresh idea to attract publicity.

Campaigners found ways of infiltrating political gatherings and disrupting them by shouting, ringing bells and brandishing banners that they had smuggled in under their clothing. They became experts at inconveniencing people – particularly the police. One of their strategies was to disseminate false information. In 1911, the suffragettes planned a window smashing foray in London's West End. The news was leaked to the police that it would take place on 4 March and the police geared up for that. In fact it took place three days earlier when the police were completely unprepared.

The demonstrations were beautifully choreographed. Wonderfully inventive banners were carried by marchers who were usually dressed in white or light colours with sashes of purple, white and green. Adopted in 1908 by the WSPU (and displayed to great effect in the Hyde Park demonstration) Emmeline Pethick-Lawrence tells us why those colours were chosen to represent the movement:

> "Purple as everyone knows is the royal colour, it stands for the blood that flows in the veins of every suffragette... white stands for purity in private and public life.... green is the colour of hope and the emblem of spring."[20]

Of course, the suffragettes did not always get it right. The air balloon that distributed leaflets from the sky above London proved difficult to steer and ended up stuck in a tree in Coulsdon.

Unfortunately, much more serious mistakes were also made. The public's attention could be caught by daring action but support turns to condemnation if the activists behave in a dangerous manner. Emmeline Pankhurst understood that distinction: the suffragette campaign was always directed to damage property and never to injure people. Yet in the last eighteen months of the WSPU's campaign, with Emmeline Pankhurst exhausted and Christabel pressing for increased violence, the line that Emmeline had carefully drawn began to be crossed.

Bombing and burning brought many risks and, as the newspapers kept pointing out, there was an ever present possibility that someone would be maimed or killed. Although careful checks were apparently made, it was impossible for the suffragettes to be certain that Lloyd George's house in Walton Heath was empty when they set it on fire. That action and others like it made many political supporters feel anxious and the mood of the public became distinctly hostile. As we argue in Chapter 3, only the reassuring respectability of Millicent Fawcett and the constitutional suffragists saved the cause of Votes for Women from a more serious setback. Militancy is often needed but the events of 1913 show that violence is a dangerous and frequently self-defeating tactic.

The Women's Liberation Movement never contemplated the destructive militancy of the WSPU but, in terms of publicity, it faced a different problem. As we discussed in Chapter 4, the movement challenged the stereotype of women as wives and home-makers, detached from public affairs. It disparaged the notion that women should dress to make themselves attractive to men. It promoted sisterhood among women instead of the customary expectation that women should compete for male attention. These arguments were forcibly expressed and sometimes took graphic form. A few women dressed in men's work clothes to make the point that the obsession with female appearance was misplaced and constraining.

These were necessary arguments but they provided an unsympathetic Press with easy targets. Most of the media decided to ignore the cause of Women's Liberation and just pour scorn on the women. 'Women's Libbers', as they were called – often with a sneer – were portrayed as unattractive man-haters and worse. It was a shameful example of misogynist journalism.

Activists in the movement soon despaired of getting a reasonable hearing in the national media and, to counter the nonsense in the mainstream newspapers, set up their own magazines and local news-sheets. It is not clear whether more could have been done to combat the output from a host of male-dominated newsrooms but, in terms of how the Women's Liberation Movement was perceived, it was an unequal struggle. The message that mostly got through to the public was the spiteful distortion purveyed by most national newspapers.

Did all this matter? After all, the Women's Liberation Movement managed to achieve a great deal in spite of the unpleasant image created by the Press. Fortunately, in a period when Britain was ready to cast aside out-dated attitudes, enough people agreed with the need for reform to keep the government under pressure.

However, a miserable residue of that time remains with us. Many women find it difficult to identify with female activism because they shrink from the unpleasant image created by male prejudice some fifty years ago. That reluctance has an unfortunate effect on the balance of political power. It fortifies the more reactionary forces in British society and reduces the impact of campaigners as they press for reform. One lesson of our history is that, in the next campaign, the hideously false impression of female activism must be expunged.

Changing the System

Existing Power Structures

The Votes for Women campaigners were taught by bitter experience the extent to which Britain was organised to support men and marginalise women. Fifty years later, most activists in the Women's Liberation Movement had learnt that lesson. One or two reforms were not enough: the whole system had to be transformed.

The Women's Liberation Movement was successful in weakening many of the structures that support inequality. But, in raising awareness, the activists had to cope with the difficulty that many of the customs, conventions and attitudes that favour men are rarely noticed because they are so familiar.

Parliament looks and feels like a gentlemen's club: the Commons chamber is laid out in adversarial style with a sword's length gap between government and opposition; the committee rooms are lined with paintings of famous men; the furniture is designed for men with large and robust physiques; the bars stock many different types of beer but have very little seating. This is a place designed by men for the convenience of men.

The supremacy of men is rooted deep in our culture. The notion of leadership that the Women's Liberation Movement rejected is inherently male. The metaphors that are commonly used by leaders come from the war zone or from the sports-field and are best delivered in a deep male voice. Senior managers are expected to work long hours, give the requirements of their job priority over all other obligations and make work-friendly arrangements for the care of their children by, for instance, having a wife.

Our language and our behaviour support these assumptions of male superiority. The person at the head of the boardroom table is the Chair*man*. When in doubt, he will tend to use a male pronoun and will only remember to add 'or she' after a giveaway pause. When he sums up, he will give greatest weight to the men who spoke longest and give less attention to contributions from women, however well argued and perceptive. This scenario is so firmly established as a feature of working life that most women think that is pointless to complain.

For centuries powerful men have regarded these conventions, not as privileges but as the natural order of things. Most men regarded themselves as the leaders and assume that the natural role for women is as assistants and supporters. Those who doubt that conclusion should reflect on what happened when Labour came to power in 1997 with an unprecedented number of women MPs. The women decided to have a group photograph. As they assembled, Tony Blair arrived, uninvited, and put himself right in the centre of the picture. From then on, those successful female politicians were all called 'Blair's babes'. [21]

What particularly infuriates women campaigners is that, throughout the stages of male resistance, men insist that they are acting in women's best interests. Men *know* about the nature of women. They *know* that women are happiest at home looking after their children. They *know* that women are not well suited to the hurly burly of public and political life. While men now accept that a 'few women' may have the talent to do the top jobs, they still *know* that those few will need special assistance. They will need coaching and training. They need to be taught to be better at self-promotion.

They will need to be more assertive. In fact, those favoured women will have to be taught to behave more like men.

The existing system has served men well and they see no reason to support any significant reform. Instead they assert that, if women want to be accepted as insiders, it is women who will have to change to fit the man-made system. Unfortunately, as most female activists soon realise, requiring women to copy men is no pathway to equality. What is needed is to root out the assumptions, the attitudes and the conventions that underpin the power of men. That is a formidable task but unless it is accomplished, women will never achieve equality.

Male Resistance

Most of the women campaigning for voting rights in the last quarter of the nineteenth century assumed that good arguments would be enough to persuade the men in power to support the female cause. They were taught otherwise. The suffragists listened to three British prime ministers making speeches in support of votes for women and expected each of them to take action. None of them did.

The women campaigners learnt that when masculine power is challenged, the men will resist strongly. They also learnt that male resistance passes through several distinct phases. At first the campaign is ignored. Engaging with the campaigners means that the status quo begins to be examined and that is best avoided, particularly when the arguments for change are martialled by the likes of John Stuart Mill or Simone de Beauvoir.

If the campaign persists, men tend to describe it as the work of an unrepresentative minority. As male politicians from Disraeli to

Cameron have insisted, women are held in high esteem as mother, homemaker, handmaiden, housewife and carer.

When patronising compliments fail to quieten the women campaigners, the tone of the male reaction starts to change. Men point out that women will do themselves harm if they demand a change in status. Women cannot have it both ways. If they want equality then they cannot expect men to support them financially. And equality means that women will inevitably lose those chivalrous courtesies that men are expected to offer and women are thought to cherish.

If these lightweight threats fail to end the campaign, the next phase is distinctly nasty. Indeed some women campaigners have been shocked at just how brutal men can become if a challenge to male dominance is sustained. During the suffrage campaign, women were charged by mounted police, imprisoned and forcibly fed.

The insults continued through the Women's Liberation Movement. When campaigners demonstrated against the Miss World competition, the compere – Bob Hope – claimed that they 'must be on some sort of dope'. In reporting the event almost every newspaper sided with Hope and the Miss World organisers.

Both the suffrage campaigners and the Women's Liberation Movement were accused of being bad mothers. This allegation is important because it reveals a great deal. Men working long hours or attending sports events or, even, taking part in political activities are rarely criticised for neglecting their fatherly duties.

Men are determined to get their own way. The story of the campaign for equal pay provides a revealing case study. During the First World War, ministers promised equal pay to women who were doing the same work as men. Few benefited. After the war ended, a Commons Resolution was passed guaranteeing equal pay. Once again, few benefited. Twenty years later, the War Cabinet led by Churchill prevented any equal pay commitment being written into law. An Equal Pay Act was not passed until 1970, fifty years after the original Commons Resolution.

Legal Rights

Unfortunately, the fight for equal pay did not end with the passing of the Equal Pay Act in 1970. A generation later Britain still has a substantial gender pay gap. In 1975, the Sex Discrimination Act was passed and yet many examples of sex discrimination continue to exist in many workplaces and elsewhere. We argue in Chapter 5 that the cause of both failures is inadequate enforcement. And the fact that stronger enforcement is necessary shows how little the men who run British companies and other organisations believe in the importance of the two Acts. Instead of embracing the principle of equality, too many organisations have chosen to ignore or even to circumvent the law.

The implications of this analysis go wider. Many senior business leaders believe that it is inappropriate to use the law to create new or reinforced rights for women. Their argument is that a voluntary approach causes fewer problems and encourages greater compliance. We are deeply sceptical of this argument. Perhaps what the supporters of voluntarism really value is the possibility that a voluntary system gives the opportunity first to water down any proposed reform and then allows the opportunity to implement it slowly and without much rigour.

However, the most telling argument in favour of well-enforced legal right is based on the principle of equality. Men are in control of the policy of most organisations. Voluntarism means that any move towards greater gender equality depends on those men deciding, of their own volition, to award increased opportunities to women. History suggests that women will have a long wait. But, in any event, the approach is wrong. Women are, in effect, being made to wait for powerful men to offer them favours, when equality should be theirs by right.

Political Support

John Stuart Mill's case that women should be regarded as the equal of men was set out in *The Subjection of Women* in 1869. It is a brilliant and convincing essay. If success depended solely on strength of argument, the issue of gender equality would have been settled in that year and there would have been no need for the subsequent efforts of the women suffragists or the Women's Liberation Movement. In the event, Mill's essay had little direct effect on the position of women in Britain. It inspired the Votes for Women campaigners but was disregarded by the establishment; men tended to dismiss Mill's views as eccentric.

The suffrage campaigners in the National Union of Women's Suffrage Societies quickly learnt that to have any realistic chance of overturning prejudice, their arguments had to be backed with political power. So they set about building support in the House of Commons. As we record in Chapter 3, it was a long and painstaking task but they eventually succeeded in persuading a majority of MPs to support their cause. Unfortunately, the campaigners overestimated the power of backbench MPs. Time and time again an MP would table a Private Members' Bill extending voting rights to women only to find that the Bill was obstructed by ministers or talked out by government supporters. The Votes for Women campaign only achieved success when, at long last, the government itself was persuaded to take action.

The Women's Liberation Movement used a different approach. Many of the senior campaigners were part of extensive networks of women's groups and they worked through them. These networks included influential Labour politicians like Jo Richardson. Her work-rate was phenomenal. Tam Dalyell, who knew about diligence, said she attended more meetings than any other MP.[22] Many of those visits were to local women's groups. As a long-standing member of the Labour Party's National Executive she gave great support to anti-discrimination resolutions at all levels in the party.

Organisations in the women's network included the National Council for Civil Liberties and the National Joint Action Campaign Committee for Women's Equal Rights, which brought together trade unionists, activists from the Women's Liberation Movement and sympathetic politicians. Organisations of civil society, notably the trade unions and the human rights campaigns, were recruited as powerful allies and helped to demonstrate that the demand for reform had widespread support. Sympathetic local councils were mobilised. These contacts created a swell of opinion that produced resolutions to constituency party meetings, to the conferences of trade unions, to the Labour Party Annual Conference and to the TUC. Barbara Castle, the most powerful woman in politics, provided publicity, heavyweight support in Cabinet and the skills of a formidable political operator.

The lesson from our history is that a new campaign must aim to build an extensive network of political supporters with the aim of encouraging sympathetic political parties to not only take an interest in women's rights but also to take decisive action.

Women MPs

We argued in Chapter 5 that a major reason why the revolutions stalled after the success of the Vote for Women campaigns, and again after the high point of the Women's Liberation Movement, was that there were too few women MPs in parliament to sustain the momentum of reform and improvement.

It took half a century for the number of women in the Commons to reach 30, and at that stage the women were still outnumbered by more than twenty to one. Entry of women into the House of Lords was not achieved until 1958, nearly forty years after the first woman sat in the House of Commons.

Fortunately, since 1997 the situation has been transformed. There are now 208 female MPs. This is a long way short of parity with men but at least we are increasingly used to seeing and hearing women politicians speaking with the same authority as men on a wide range of subjects. Stella Creasy took on Wonga over their exorbitant rates for pay-day loans and won. Harriet Harman has proved over and over again that a campaigner for women's rights can also be a successful mainstream politician, dealing authoritatively as deputy leader of the Labour Party with every political issue from welfare to defence.

The problem nowadays is more specific. The majority of women MPs are in the Labour Party and the SNP. About 45% of Labour MPs and over 30% of SNP MPs are women. The equivalent Conservative figure is only 21%. This is a significant disparity and has considerable political effects, particularly when the Conservatives are in government.

The lesson of history is that we need a high proportion of women MPs in the Commons. We now need all parties to have a high proportion of women so that the needs of women are represented across the political spectrum.

Equality Does not Happen by Accident

There is a cosy assumption that once an injustice is recognised and condemned, it is inevitable that it will be removed. People assume that we need do nothing or very little to make this happen. Unfortunately, agreeing that something may be wrong is not enough to put it right. Those with the power to effect change must be convinced that they have to act. The most effective way to gather support for reform is through campaigning.

Every campaign has to search for the methods that provide them with the best opportunity to achieve success. In Britain, a branch of the Anti-Apartheid Movement was formed to oppose South Africa's heinous regime. The first stage was to raise awareness. Regular meetings were addressed by British MPs and by people who had suffered under Apartheid. Many demonstrations and vigils were held outside South Africa House in Trafalgar Square, attracting the attention of the general public. Stories were told and re-told, plays by Athol Fugard and others were staged in London. Direct action followed. There were boycotts of South African goods and, during the 1970s, a fresh campaigning method was developed. Peter Hain organised the disruption of sporting fixtures like the Test Matches, the Springbok rugby tour, and tennis tournaments. The Anti-Apartheid Movement used South Africa's obsession with sport to put unexpected but very effective pressure on the regime.

The campaign to secure women's suffrage had one very clear message: votes for women. As we have emphasised, the success of that campaign was due to persistent, vociferous and inventive pressure. As with the Anti-Apartheid Movement, the main element consisted of petitions, meetings, marches, badgering those in power and using any means to gain maximum publicity for the cause. Their strength lay in being relentless: the politicians of the day knew that the campaigners would never go away.

The Women's Liberation Movement grew and prospered more organically. Its aim was to encourage women to recognise and speak out against the unequal status of women. The focus was more personal. Individual women meeting in small groups found the courage to divulge unspoken feelings of injustice. Discovering that what they had assumed was personal was in fact a universal grievance, they acted collectively to demand equal rights and recognition.

These were diverse strategies to suit the needs of each campaign. But the campaigners all knew that wrongs cannot be put right unless attention is drawn to unjust practices and pressure is applied to decision-makers. The lesson of history is that that waiting patiently for justice never works. Deliberate campaigning action has to be taken, often over a lengthy period.

If equality is what women want then women will have to be determined to fight for it.

Equality does not happen by accident.

7

Twenty-First Century Sexism and Inequality

In March 2017, Sunderland football club was in serious trouble. The club was at the bottom of the premiership and was having a terrible season. After a disappointing result against Burnley, David Moyes, the Sunderland manager, was interviewed by BBC reporter Vicki Sparks. Her last question was whether the decision of the club's owner to attend the match had put Moyes under extra pressure. He answered briskly, 'No, none at all'.

On camera, Moyes seemed composed but, once the interview was over, his demeanour changed. He said that Vicki Sparks had been, 'a little bit naughty' with her question about the owner and told her that, 'you might get a slap even though you are a woman' and advised her to be 'careful' next time she came to the football ground.

Unfortunately for Moyes, the cameras were still rolling and his post-interview remarks were recorded. What followed was gruesome and predictable. He held a Press Conference and said that he regretted the remarks. They were made 'in the heat of the moment'. He had apologised to Vicki Sparks and she had accepted his apology. 'That's certainly not the person I am', he insisted, adding that he was a big supporter of women's sport and his daughter had played football as a teenager.

Not everyone was prepared to accept these pleas in mitigation. Women in Football said it was 'deeply disappointed and concerned' by his behaviour. The Shadow Sports Minister called on the Football Association (FA) to take action.[1]

Sporting Sexism

Moyes is one of a long line of men from the sporting world who have been caught making sexist remarks. When Tyson Fury became a world boxing champion, he was asked about sportswomen. He said that, in his opinion, 'a woman's best place is in the kitchen and on her back' and went on to express admiration for the attractive physique of one well-known athlete.[2]

After Marion Bartoli won the Wimbledon Singles title, John Inverdale, the sports commentator, surprised many people by giving his opinion that, 'she is never going to be a looker'. Under pressure to explain, he said that his remarks were 'never intended to be taken seriously'. It was a feeble excuse but his subsequent explanation was worse. He said that he made the remark because he was suffering from hay fever.[3]

As the Chief Executive of football's Premier League, Richard Scudamore is one of the most powerful people in sport. He was greatly embarrassed when the contents of an eighteen-month email exchange with Nicholas West,[4] a senior partner in the law firm DLA Piper, were made public. They ridiculed women, using derogatory sexual terms like 'klunt' and 'gash'. In a reference to one employee, Scudamore advised West to, 'keep her off your shaft'.

In cycling, an independent inquiry had to be held after female riders complained about sexist comments made by senior coach,

Shane Sutton. The inquiry found many failures in the way British Cycling had behaved and said that Sutton should not have been promoted into a management position.[5]

The similarities between these incidents are striking. None of the men were sacked because of their behaviour.[6] Although David Moyes left Sunderland, the reason was not because of his outburst at Vicki Sparks but because the football club had been relegated from the premiership. For his abuse of Vicki Sparks he was eventually fined £33,000 by the FA. David Moyes was believed to be earning more than £3million a year at Sunderland, in which case his fine represents a little over two-day's pay.

In most cases the miscreants simply apologised and the issue faded away. People came forward to support the offenders. Had Scudamore made his 'jokey' remarks in a pub, it was alleged, they would not have occasioned comment. Inverdale's remark was, apparently, just 'banter'. People who objected to Fury's remarks were accused of not understanding the culture of the Travelling Community from which Fury comes. In any case, it was said, Fury's remarks were intended to be humorous. Listeners calling phone-in programmes about the incidents often used the words 'joke' and 'banter' to describe the men's remarks.

There is also a similarity in the way the victims were treated. Scudamore's temporary secretary found the emails in his office account, which she was required to access. She said that she exposed the emails because they were so shocking. In spite of the statements from Scudamore that he regretted sending the emails, she got no support from the organisation for which they both worked.

> 'All they've done is threaten me with legal action over a possible breach of trust.'

Jess Varnish was the first cyclist to criticise the sexism shown by her coach and she had to suffer intense scrutiny and criticism after she made her complaint, particularly when an internal inquiry rejected eight of her nine allegations. It was not until a later independent inquiry uncovered the unpleasant culture in British Cycling that she felt that her complaints were being properly investigated. But even then there was a disappointment. Phrases which would have vindicated Jess Varnish were removed from the draft report and more ambiguous statements were put in their place. She is now challenging the published version.

The BBC was involved in two of the incidents and it does not emerge well. In the Moyes case, it issued an anodyne statement saying that Vicki Sharp's acceptance of the apology from Moyes had 'resolved' the issue. A more thoughtful employer might have realised that Vicki Sharp, whose career as a sports reporter depends on her relationship with senior people in football, had no option but to accept.

In the Bartoli case the BBC took no action against Inverdale, even though he was employed by the BBC. Surprisingly, it did not even spare Marion Bartoli the embarrassment of working with him. Not long after the insult, the BBC sent Inverdale to the French Open to sit alongside Marion Bartoli in the commentators' box. She said that she did not mind, a statement that contains rather more grace than Inverdale deserved.

Private World

These incidents illuminate one element of twenty-first century sexism. Largely as a result of work by the Women's Liberation Movement to redefine acceptable behaviour, sexism is no longer out in the open. Nowadays, the Miss World competition is rarely given prominence by the British media; nude photographs of women are not hung on workplace walls; there is much less of the surreptitious touching and groping that was very common thirty years ago; disparaging remarks about women are heard less often in mixed gatherings. A new orthodoxy of expression has been established. Public figures are more careful about what they say on radio or television. To all outward appearances, Britain has cleaned up its act.

Yet much that is unpleasant is lurking beneath the surface. In the all-male world that men inhabit for a large part of their lives, standards are much lower than most women would like to believe. There are many 'jokes' that disparage women. Men insist that women have limited abilities: they cannot make decisions or read a map or park a car. Men still talk as if they expect women to treat them in a reverential manner: 'she needs to know who is boss'. Men make judgements about women's appearance: some are too drab, some are too fat and some are noted for dressing in a 'sexy' manner. There is an assumption in much all-male conversation that young women are put on this earth for the sexual delight of men.

This private male world is closed to women. And for most of the time, that is the way it stays because, whatever they say in all-male company, men have learnt the new rules. Many men may have found the change irksome, but they quickly discovered that if they spoke the language of equality no particular damage was done to their interests and they even gained some easy credit for being broad-minded and modern. No one really wanted, in the language of the 1980s and 1990s, to be called 'a male chauvinist pig' and, as long as they kept to the new orthodoxy in public, most men managed to avoid criticism.

As we have seen, mistakes are sometimes made and what was intended to be private is made public. When that happens, men know what they have to do. They say sorry, explain that it was only a momentary lapse and, if they are lucky with their audience, insist that they were only joking or indulging in that ill-defined activity that men describe as 'banter'. Most of the time, after a period of embarrassment, they get away with it.

One reason why these men escape serious censure is because most women are very indulgent. Quite a few women spoke up for Moyes, Scudamore and the rest. Most women prefer to believe in the good nature of men, and particularly of men they know. They give men the benefit of the doubt. When I (John) told a very senior academic, who has written extensively on gender issues, what some men say in private, she expressed disbelief.

> 'In my experience not many of these "Neanderthals" exist anymore. You must mix with the wrong people.'

Disengaged

Of course, men who make sexist remarks and laugh at unseemly jokes about women do not regard themselves as Neanderthals. They would not even regard themselves as anti-women. The problem is deeper and more subtle. Most men say they are in favour of equality but the truth is that most of them have hardly ever thought about what it entails.

The sexual revolution started by the Women's Liberation Movement has not caused a seismic shift in male attitudes. It has succeeded in ensuring outward compliance with a new set of more enlightened rules but there has been little debate in male circles about why the new way is right and why the old expressions and practices should be abandoned. The façade is nicely designed but if we look behind, we find a few supporting struts and not much else. It has as much substance as an old-fashioned film set.

Most men are not antagonistic; they are just disengaged. This shows itself in many ways, some quite minor. Although it is well known that the common usage of our language favours the male gender, not many men take the trouble to use gender-neutral terms. Women now chair meetings but, throughout the corporate world, the designation of *Chairman* is used as a matter of course. Women work in the police service but, if it is suggested that we should all say police officer rather than policeman, many men become rather impatient at what they obviously regard as an insignificant quibble.

When I (John) tell male friends and acquaintances that I write about gender issues, the first reaction is one of surprise. They always ask why. I usually say that women are treated very unfairly in Britain and something should be done about it. Many men struggle with that answer. If I quote one or two statistics in support of my claim, I am often told of experiences in their own workplace to demonstrate that women are usually treated fairly or that women bring the difficulties on themselves. They tell me that they know at least one woman in a senior position – and suggest there would be more but, unfortunately, few women apply for promotion. They explain that most senior jobs are full-time – and many women want to work part-time. More recently a clinching argument has been deployed, only half in jest, to show that there is no real problem:

> 'Well, women don't have much to complain about. We
> have a second woman Prime Minister!'

It is fair to note that men have few opportunities to learn much about women's lives and the problems that women face. The rigidity of the current school curriculum means that there is little time to discuss gender issues and, in any event, almost any discussion of politics is discouraged. In our next chapter, we discuss disturbing attitudes in colleges and universities that are reducing the possibility of a relaxed and cooperative relationship between men and women. The segregation of many jobs means that few men work closely with women and the normal pattern of male control means that even fewer men work with women on the basis of equality. At home most male/female partnerships divide the domestic responsibilities so that women undertake the routine tasks, including being the default carer, and men take on specific (manly) duties.[7] There is scarcely any overlap and men often have little insight into what, and how much, their female partners actually do.

Peninah Thomson set up the FTSE Cross Company Mentoring Programme to provide support to talented women building a career. The mentors are very senior executives and are usually male. The aim is to increase the confidence of the women and provide them with an insight into how to achieve success. But there is another and unexpected benefit. Peninah Thomson says that several of the male mentors have told her that the regular discussions with their mentee have given them a greater understanding of the difficulties faced by women in business. During our research, one of the mentors told us,

> 'To be honest, I had no idea of how hard it can be for a woman, even if she is talented and well-motivated. What I learnt made me make a few changes in my own company.'

This male executive clearly wants to help women to be successful. What held him back was not any sort of prejudice but an ignorance of the way in which women are treated in the workplace. That ignorance is shared with very many men.

Several men have told us that their epiphany moment came when they saw how hard things were for their own daughter. One said to us,

> 'I looked back on my career and realised that it was much easier for me. She faces difficulties that I never knew existed.'

Even so, not all fathers understand the nature of the problem. It is natural to wish to smooth a path for one's own daughter but a father should appreciate that, in most cases, the unfairness that she is facing is not unique; it forms part of the workplace experience of almost every woman. The solution is not a series of ad hoc interventions on behalf of daughters lucky enough to have concerned and confident fathers. It is the system that needs changing to ensure that women in general face no greater difficulties than men.

Equality

When men assert a belief in equality, in most cases that claim is honestly made. But ask men what they mean by equality and in many cases the discussion begins to stall. Few realise the extent to which Britain's social arrangements, our employment conditions and our politics give an advantage to men. Most men expect that women will be the main carer for their children and for family dependants but few seem to appreciate that women need sufficient time off work to carry out these duties.

Most men have not given much thought to how discrimination works in the modern world. They support the principles of equal pay, fair recruitment procedures and want women to have an equal opportunity to be considered for promotion. However, if it is suggested that indirect discrimination can be just as damaging as the sort that is direct and obvious, confusion sets in. Caring jobs are vital in a civilised society and involve considerable responsibility but they are very badly paid. Is this because these jobs are mainly done by women? If the answer is yes, as it surely must be, then a society that believes in equality should regard that injustice as just as serious as a more blatant case of discrimination when a woman is denied a job because of her sex.

The fact that the female half of the population is at a significant disadvantage compared with the male half should be a major political

issue. But, although the principle of equality is on the lips of every politician, practical measures to increase gender equality have scarcely
been mentioned in any General Election campaign since the 1970s;
other matters are always given greater prominence. This attitude
happens at grass roots level as well. The writer and activist Sheila
Rowbotham has described how, in political meetings, issues concern-
ing women's rights usually seem to be something of an afterthought.

> 'Everything that relates only to...(women) comes as foot-
> notes to the main text... We come on the agenda some-
> where between "Youth" and "Any other Business"'.[8]

When the discussion is about principles, men are happy to agree
that there is some injustice in the way women are treated but, when
it comes to choosing priorities, they usually decide that there are
other matters which are more pressing and should receive more
urgent attention.

Perception

Unfortunately this cocktail of goodwill and inactivity, diluted with
a splash of ignorance, is very unstable. Women are apt to regard
inactivity as evidence of neglect but, if they protest, men very
quickly move into defensive mode, insisting on their commitment
to equality and behaving as if they have been unfairly attacked.
Surely, the male argument tends to run, women protesters understand that getting the economy right, negotiating new trade deals,
building more houses or whatever else they place at the top of
their political agenda, will benefit women as well as men.

A significant difference in perception begins to emerge. Many
men seem to think that increasing opportunities for women is a
minority issue and should therefore be given less importance than

matters that affect the whole population. Women activists, on the other hand, regard the unequal way in which women are treated as a serious injustice, which should be remedied irrespective of whatever policies are catching the headlines. This is not the first time that a limited male perspective has been challenged. Allowing an injustice against women to continue until other matters are dealt with, is exactly the unworthy approach adopted by the Asquith government over a hundred years ago.

Discomfort and Bitterness

The last element in this analysis is very important, very obvious but rarely mentioned. A significant number of men appear to be uncomfortable in the company of women. Ask most women and they will confirm that, in a mixed gathering, the men tend to congregate and stay together for as long as possible. Women also comment that if a particular group fortuitously happens to contain both men and women, perhaps because they work in the same department, the men tend to conduct a conversation that excludes the participation of the women. Women also notice that if they are placed next to a man and he has no escape, the man will often talk continuously about himself, rarely pausing and never asking a question about the woman's life or interests.

The common feature of all this behaviour is the reluctance to engage even with one woman and certainly not with a group. Indeed many men seem to regard women in numbers as being particularly fearsome. They might try to avoid the experience and, if they cannot, they often show how uncomfortable they feel by making a feeble and revealing joke: 'I am only here as the token male!'

In practice, men have little to worry about. Most women are enormously protective of any man who shows that he needs support.

Both the authors attended a conference on women's rights in Brussels. One of the few male speakers opened with a long story about how he had been the only man at another conference of nearly a hundred women. He said he was terrified at the prospect but the woman who had chaired the conference had been helpful and he had managed to get through the ordeal. Every woman hearing this story could easily decode the message: 'I am very vulnerable so please be kind to me.' And they were. Those women delegates in Brussels made sympathetic noises as he described his predicament and then voted him the best speaker of the conference.

That speaker had found a winning formula: proclaim your weakness and, if you are lucky, a female audience will love you for it. But most men, brought up to value strength and self-sufficiency, are programmed to do exactly the opposite. They tend to avoid meeting women whom they do not know well and, if trapped, try to control the conversation in case they are taken into areas where they might show their discomfort or display their ignorance.

Not surprisingly, some men who behave in this way get a reputation for being rude and arrogant. Women tend to avoid their company and complain to colleagues about their attitude. When the men discover how they are regarded, they are likely to feel angry and indignant. Do they change their behaviour? Very rarely, because making such a change requires a good deal of self-awareness and considerable courage. More likely, they laugh a little too eagerly at sexist jokes and nurture a private desire to get their own back on the women who have criticised them. The vicious circle of misogyny takes another turn.

Misogyny

A disgraceful feature of our society is the way in which social media is used to attack women who have a public profile. Almost any

woman who expresses strong views or exhibits some natural authority becomes a target. Laura Bates has spoken out against the abuse of
women. This is one example of the many threatening tweets she has
received. The capitals are in the original.

> 'YOU BETTER WATCH YOUR BACK...I'M GONNA
> RAPE YOUR ASS AT 8PM AND PUT THE VIDEO ALL
> OVER THE INTERNET'.[9]

The purpose of these attacks is to make the woman feel humiliated, vulnerable and frightened. Judging by our conversations
with women who have been the target of troll attacks, it is very
difficult to shrug them off. Most women who are targeted suffer
considerable anguish.

A popular assumption is that these attacks are launched by sad
men expressing their frustration with the world and their distorted
view of womankind. No doubt many trolls are exactly like that.
However, research by Demos, acting on behalf of Reclaim the
Internet, the campaign set up by Yvette Cooper MP and Stella
Creasy MP, has provided disconcerting information. In an attempt
to find out more about the abusers, Demos tracked the aggressive
use of the words, 'slut' and 'whore' in tweets across the world. The
conclusion was that women are just as likely to tweet these words
aggressively as men.

Demos recognises that its research has significant limitations –
it only analysed the use of Twitter, the information came from all
over the world and not just from Britain and it focuses on just two
words.[10] Nevertheless it shows that women, as well as men, are
prepared to abuse women on the internet. The conclusion reached
by Demos is tentative but important.

> 'These figures suggest that misogyny is being internalised
> and reiterated by women themselves. This use of language

is not, therefore, confined to one discrete online group but rather persists throughout society…'.

If Demos is right, misogyny is embedded in our society and is exhibited by women as well as by men. The Demos survey results are disappointing and uncomfortable for feminists seeking to unite women in common cause.

The extent of misogyny in modern-day Britain may help to explain why there is still an inclination among both men and women to 'blame the victim' as well as the perpetrator when a sexual assault takes place. The notion of shared blame has been discredited many times but the perception persists. The Fawcett Society commissioned a survey[11] which asked

> 'If a woman goes out late at night, wearing a short skirt, gets drunk and is then the victim of a sexual assault, is she … to blame?'

The replies show that more than a third of men and women believe that she is at least partly to blame. Older people are even more judgemental. Half of men and women over the age of 65 think that the victim deserves part or all of the blame.

Any complacency about the security of women (and young men) in our society, should have been swept away by the tsunami of allegations, arrests and convictions that followed the exposure of Sir Jimmy Saville. The investigations shocked Britain but there has been less widespread support for a continuing and thorough investigation than might have been expected. When mistakes were made and some men were wrongly accused, the reaction has not just been a demand that procedures should be improved, as they must be. In some quarters there has been a more radical proposal: that the whole of 'Operation Yewtree' should be closed down.

The crimes committed in the past by former celebrities are called cases of 'historical abuse'. Language is important and this phrase conveys an impression that these vile assaults are part of history and could not happen in the modern world.

An antidote to this optimistic nonsense is contained in Police and Crown Prosecution (CPS) statistics. In the year 2015/2016, the Police in England and Wales recorded 23,851 cases of adults being raped, almost all of them women. In the same year 11,947 cases of rape against children were recorded. Latest figures show that the CPS has also prosecuted nearly 12,000 individuals for sexual assaults other than rape and has taken nearly 13,000 cases of harassment and stalking to court. Recorded rapes, against both adults and children, have doubled in the last four years.

In her book, *Everyday Sexism*, Laura Bates tells the stories of some of the victims. Girls and women report how they were assaulted by relatives, friends, acquaintances and strangers. One young woman wrote,

> 'I was 16. We had spoken on the internet several times before I agreed to meet him, and he persuaded me to go to his home, where he proceeded to rape me and take my virginity ... I have never talked about this before'.

Abuse of Power

The examples of sexism and sexual abuse, which we have quoted, range from the unpleasant to the criminal and the deeply evil. Some caused distress to the victims; others caused untold suffering, damaged bodies and ruined lives. Nevertheless, whatever level of seriousness we allocate to each case, they all prompt the same question: why do these men think that they have the right to abuse women?

The offences are very different but the answer seems to be the same. All the guilty men were much more powerful than their female victims. That power seems to have given them a feeling of entitlement. They evidently believe that, because their victims are less important, their power gives them the right to be disrespectful, to bully, to humiliate or even to expect women to submit to their sexual demands. John Stuart Mill described the process more than a hundred and fifty years ago. 'Men learn self-worship... in common with all privileged people'.[12]

In our society the powerful have many opportunities to exploit the weak and it is not surprising that some men are tempted, like Harvey Weinstein, to use their power and their riches to control, to dominate and for sexual gratification.

In 2005, Donald Trump explained how he was able to take advantage of this imbalance of power. His words were meant to be private but this unpleasant little homily was eventually shared with the world.

> "I'm automatically attracted to beautiful [women] – I just start kissing them. It's like a magnet. Just kiss. I don't even wait. And when you're a star they let you do it. You can do anything ... Grab them by the pussy. You can do anything."[13]

The story was made public during the presidential election and for a few days it seemed that the Trump campaign was doomed. But his poll ratings quickly recovered. Some women dismissed the issue as of little significance. 'I have heard much worse', said one. Trump himself described the words he had used as just 'locker room' talk and reminded his supporters of the actions of President Clinton, a President who had also exploited his power to gain sexual gratification.

Outnumbered

US Presidents are the most powerful men on the planet but it is not necessary to go to the White House to find men who are much more powerful than women. When we wrote our earlier book, *Man-Made*, we were shocked to find how little power is held by women in Britain. Occasionally talented women break through into senior positions but, wherever we looked, those women are massively outnumbered by powerful men.

The excellent reports entitled *Sex and Power*, which were produced for the Equality and Human Rights Commission, track the proportion of women in senior positions in politics, business, the professions, the media, the biggest charities and in the governance of the Arts. Apart from a very few groups like the heads of primary schools, where women outnumber men, or the chairs of magistrates, where women and men are equally represented, the general conclusion was that it is quite normal for women to be outnumbered in positions of power by three or four to one. The reports caused Angela Eagle MP to describe Britain as an 80:20 society, with 80% of the most powerful jobs being held by men and only 20% by women.

Unfortunately there are some positions of power where women have an even smaller representation. One of the worst examples is the Supreme Court. As the highest court in the land, it has enormous power. Lady Brenda Hale[14] is now the President. When we interviewed her in 2014 she expressed disappointment that she was the only woman sitting as a judge in the Supreme Court and that no woman had been appointed to the Court for more than a decade. At long last, in 2017, a second woman, Dame Jill Black, was appointed. However, at the same time, two men were also appointed. The result is that women in the Supreme Court are outnumbered, six to one, by male judges.

Also outrageous is the under-representation of women in executive control of the UK's largest companies. The most powerful people in a company are the chief executive and the finance director. In the 350 biggest companies quoted on the Stock Exchange (the FTSE350) there are 700 such positions. Of those posts, 661 are held by men and only 39 by women. These figures mean that men hold almost 95% of the most powerful jobs in UK business while women hold scarcely more than 5%. That extraordinary imbalance of power is a deplorable example of twenty-first century inequality.[15]

Numbers do not tell the whole story but they should be remembered whenever it is suggested that women are as powerful as men. Britain has a female Prime Minister. When she answers questions in the Commons, we see a number of women MPs sitting on the seats behind her. People looking at the television pictures might imagine that Theresa May's party in parliament is more or less evenly balanced between men and women. That, of course, is what the public is encouraged to think but, as we noted in Chapter 5, the impression is entirely false. In fact, male Conservative MPs outnumber female Conservative MPs by about four to one. The misleading TV pictures are created by the Conservative Whips who arrange what is called 'a doughnut' of women MPs to sit behind the Prime Minister.

In other areas of public life individual women have been appointed to senior positions and the change has captured much media attention. Cressida Dick has become the first woman commissioner of the Metropolitan Police. This is good news but the press release recording a change at the very top should not be taken to suggest that the balance of power throughout the Met has been significantly changed. Men still hold almost all the other top jobs: nearly four in every five senior officers (Chief Inspector and above) is a man.

The Paradox

Looking at these facts of twenty-first-century life, most people might draw the reasonable conclusion that this is the way powerful men want Britain to be. After all, if they wanted things to change, these men could share power with the women in the organisations they lead and, working together, could transform the whole of British society. Instead, what we see is a sad paradox. The men at the top of organisations in Britain tell us that they are in favour of equality but in practice most of them have done little to correct the enormous difference in the power held by women and men.

A public commitment to equality is often expressed in a grand policy statement. We have read a number of such statements produced by government, private companies, public sector bodies and voluntary organisations. They tend to have a 'happy-clappy' quality, full of goodwill and rising optimism. When questioned about their policy, the top people in those organisations, mostly men, tell us how hard their organisation is working to give more opportunity to women and how conscientious they are in searching for women of the right calibre to promote into senior positions.

Unfortunately, in this respect as in many others, the public presentation rarely conveys the reality of what is happening in their organisations. In 2016, I (John) attended an event to celebrate an initiative to make women 'Board-ready', a rather patronising phrase that is widely used in the corporate world. The Head of Inclusion for a large bank explained to me that, although mistakes had been made in the past, he was proud of their new policies. A complete arsenal (his term) of measures were being adopted to increase the proportion of women in the bank's senior management team. He went through them[16] and they seemed very impressive. I asked about the outcome. 'Early days yet', he said.

After some gentle nagging, I got hold of a set of figures. They showed that that the proportion of women in the senior management team of the bank was increasing by about 1% a year. At that sluggish rate of progress, women would not make up even a quarter of the senior team until the 2020s.

Women on the Board

For many years before it became obligatory to claim a commitment to equality, the dearth of women at senior level in British business attracted little attention. However, a campaign was set up in the early 1990s, led by Elspeth Howe, to get more women into senior positions. It was originally called Opportunity 2000 because as, Elspeth Howe wryly remarked at the anniversary dinner,

> 'We set the year 2000 as the target date for achieving our ambition of 30% women in every Boardroom. It seemed a modest target at the time but we missed it by a mile.'

Elspeth Howe and her colleagues did not abandon their optimism. When the twentieth century turned into the twenty-first, the campaign – with a nice sense of irony – renamed itself Opportunity Now.

In due course, and after many unfulfilled promises, Opportunity Now joined up with the 30% Club of sympathetic Chairmen (sic) and managed to put greater pressure on government. Gordon Brown seemed inclined to take action but, after the Coalition Government took office in 2010, Vince Cable – the Business Secretary – gave Lord Davies, Labour peer and former Trade Minister, the task of leading an initiative to get more women into company boardrooms. No new laws were promised. Davies would have to persuade companies to make any changes that he thought necessary.

What followed gives another insight into the nature' of twenty-first century inequality. Male domination in British business has led to the adoption of methods of recruitment and promotion which make it much more difficult for women to reach the top than men. So the driving force for reform might be expected to have been the desire to make British business more equal in its treatment of men and women.

Lord Davies approached things differently. Both authors (Eva and John) went to a conference in Sheffield to hear Davies explain what he was trying to do. His core message was that it was good for business to have more women at the top of a company. An increased number of women in senior positions meant a better quality of decision-making, more resilience for the company and was likely to lead to greater profitability. All of this is no doubt true but surely, we thought, the initiative should be about much more than just gaining a commercial advantage. After nearly an hour of his session, we asked him why he had not mentioned equality. He gave what he later admitted was an incomplete answer.

At the end of the conference, Davies sought us out and explained in full. His task, as he saw it, was to persuade the men in the boardrooms of Britain to accept that promoting more women to the top was good for their business. He was presenting the argument in commercial terms because that was the best way to get a hearing from the decision-makers.

Over a cup of coffee in the station buffet, we pressed Davies further. Did he mean that, if he had based his case for more women on principles of fairness and equality, the businessmen would not have listened? They might have listened, he replied, but they would have been less likely to take the necessary action. That was why he was giving such prominence to the so-called 'Business Case' for change. Lord Davies has been Chairman of Standard Chartered Bank so he must know what British businessmen consider important.

Davies made a second significant decision about the direction of his initiative. Since almost all of the powerful jobs in British business are held by men, a successful reform programme should presumably aim to ensure that more women become chief executives and finance directors of our large companies. However, Davies decided to concentrate his attention elsewhere. Instead of trying to ensure the appointment of more female executive directors, he decided that priority should be given to increasing the number of *non*-executive directors who sit on company boards.

The distinction between executive and non-executive directors is important. Executive directors are full-timers who run the company on a month-to-month basis, have access to all company information and recommend strategy to the board. Non-executive directors are part-timers who consider those recommendations. One senior executive we know has described non-executive directors as, 'visiting dignitaries'. They are more than that but, because they have no continuous involvement in decision-making and no independent source of information, their influence is limited.

The first Davies Report set a target of increasing the proportion of women who sit on the hundred top company boards to 25% by 2015. There is no doubt that this change is worthwhile but the extent of the reform should not be exaggerated. To meet the target most companies had only to appoint one extra female non-executive to its board; a few companies had to appoint two. Even after the success of the Davies initiative, women on the board are still normally outnumbered 3:1 by the men. And, more important, very few changes were made in the gender balance of senior rexecutive directors who remained overwhelmingly male and continued to hold almost all of the power.

Once the 25% target was reached, there was a discussion about next steps. Although a number of radical ideas were put forward, it was eventually decided to stay with existing policy of trying to increase the proportion of female non-executive directors. A new target was announced calling for 33% (instead of 25%) women on boards by 2020.[17] That requires the number of women on boards of big companies to increase by not much more than 1% each year.

Judged on its own terms, the Davies initiative was a success. But men surrendered little power to women and the male domination of big business has scarcely been affected.

Having Children

Men are expected to be in continuous full-time work from the time they finish their education until they retire. Many working practices are built around the assumption that this is what constitutes a normal career. But a career pattern with no breaks does not fit the needs of most women. They require time off to have children and many also want to reduce their hours of work during years when their children are small and when they are needed to support dependent relatives. Over the decades since the Women's Liberation Movement, employers in both the public and private sectors have been under pressure to change their work practices to meet these requirements.

Unfortunately, the changes have tended to be grudging and have put women at a substantial disadvantage compared with most men. Some smaller companies have even declared that they cannot accommodate claims for maternity leave. When they were attacked for their unsympathetic attitude, Lord Alan Sugar rushed to their defence.

> 'I know of many outfits which won't recruit women who are likely to have children because they don't want the cost and staffing problems of maternity leave. Who can blame them?'

Sugar was criticised for his intervention. It was said that he should be helping companies to find solutions rather than acting as an apologist for discriminatory employers. Nevertheless Sugar is certainly right in his observation that a significant number of smaller companies are very reluctant to appoint women of child-bearing age.

Bigger organisations have made changes to meet new legal requirements but few organisations do enough to protect women from the problems that arise after a lengthy period of absence. It is good practice for organisations to keep in touch with women while they are taking maternity leave. In fact, few organisations do more than send out an occasional email. Women on long-term leave are not quite forgotten but their interests are rarely given much attention.

Even fewer organisations have a satisfactory procedure for handling the transition back to work. Spending all day looking after young children is fulfilling in some respects but after only a few months away from work many women have told us that they feel a loss of self-confidence and are worried that their social skills are withering away. As a minimum, women should be briefed thoroughly on their return to work and should be given continuing support during the early weeks. Instead, some companies can be very unsympathetic. One woman we interviewed had to attend a high-profile conference on the day after her return from maternity leave.

> 'My mind was somewhere else and I could not concentrate. I was just gibbering. It took me weeks to get back into the swing of things.'

When a woman has a child, she notices a change in the way she is regarded. People ask if she really wanted to return to work or whether she would rather be at home with her child. Assumptions are made. She suddenly finds that she is not considered for work that involves travel or an overnight stay. If that decision is questioned, she is told that, 'we know that you need to get home'. And, of course if a woman back from maternity leave asks to work flexibly or, even worse, requests a move to part-time hours, her fate is sealed. She is regarded as having admitted that work is no longer a priority in her life. She is not considered as a candidate for promotion and is typically expected to settle down into a job as someone's assistant or as part of the organisation's support staff.

The statistics show that women with children earn significantly less than men or women without children. The best estimate is that every child costs a woman about £4,000 a year.[18] Ambitious women try to minimise the disadvantage. A small minority decide against having children, but we found that was a small minority. More common was the decision to take very little maternity leave. Six months leave was typical but several women took only three months and the shortest period of maternity leave that we discovered was just over two weeks! One woman said,

> 'I rushed back to work because I did not want to be forgotten.'

Often this rapid return was coupled with a determination to avoid being categorised as a mother by not talking about the children. 'I made mine invisible', said one woman with a high-flying career. These stratagems expose one of the saddest features of twenty-first century inequality. Women are forced to pay a high price, emotionally and financially, for the natural and necessary act of having children.

Pay

The disturbing fact that women with children are paid less and promoted less partly explains why there is still a substantial gap between the pay of men and women. The office of National Statistics calculates the gender pay gap at just under 10% but this figure has been criticised for being based on unrealistic assumptions. If overtime payments and the lower hourly rate of part-time workers are taken into account and if the earnings of the highest paid men are included in the calculation, the size of the average gap is calculated at nearly 20%.

Employers are obliged by law to pay men and women the same for work of equal value. But this concept is difficult to apply unless there is a sophisticated job evaluation scheme in place and those are rare in British business. Bonuses and additional payments of all sorts make comparisons difficult and those extra payments are more often paid to men than to women. Many women have a vague but untested impression that their male colleagues get paid more. Often they are right. During our research one woman told us,

> "It was not until I got to see the Board papers that I realised that, for most of my career..., I was paid less than my male colleagues. I am not sure that it was discrimination but the difference was substantial."

Transparent salary systems and published earnings information would enable everyone to judge whether the Equal Pay Act is being observed or circumvented. Most employers prefer what they call 'confidentiality' on salary issues, claiming that this is what their staff prefer. In fact there is little evidence to support this assumption. Many public sector organisations have operated to published salary scales for years and in some countries even personal tax details are publicly available. The big problem that needs to be faced is that very many unfair and discriminatory practices can be concealed under the cloak of confidentiality. Secrecy is the enemy of equality.

Fragility

We recognise, of course, that in spite of all these difficulties there have been welcome improvements in recent years. The gender pay gap has shrunk a little. The number of women in parliament, at least in the Labour Party and the SNP, is now big enough to form a critical mass in support of reform. Many of the more public forms of discrimination have been outlawed by Act of Parliament. Almost all careers are open to both women and men. And there is no doubt that women are treated better than a generation ago. The trouble is that the pace of change is glacially slow and there is no guarantee that it will continue.

We are frequently reminded of the fragility of the gains made by women. The two most important politicians in Britain are the Prime Minister, Theresa May, and the First Minister of Scotland, Nicola Sturgeon. After a period of political turbulence, they met in Glasgow to discuss the terms of Britain's exit from the EU and whether Scotland should hold a second referendum on Scottish independence. Dominating the front page of the *Daily Mail*[19] the following day was a picture taken from an angle that focused on the legs of the two women leaders. Next to the picture was a caption which read:

'Never mind Brexit, who won Legs-it!'

The report of what May and Sturgeon said to each other at this important meeting was relegated to the inside pages, which also contained an article by journalist, Sarah Vine, commenting further on their legs, clothes and posture.

The front page was widely condemned but the *Daily Mail* responded in familiar fashion. The newspaper declared that the front page was intended as a joke, the critics obviously had no sense of humour and they 'should get a life'.

The hope is that, in time, even the *Daily Mail* will recognise that women should be taken seriously and that Britain should change its culture as well as its laws. Two decades ago there was a genuine feeling of optimism that Britain was moving, albeit slowly, in the right direction. Unfortunately there are now powerful forces pulling us back into a darker place. As we have shown earlier, social media has released a torrent of misogyny that previously had no ready form of expression. This is very serious but we are anxious that another feature of the internet might be more important in the longer term. The internet allows easy access to pornography for anyone with a smart phone, tablet or laptop. The result is that more males, including young boys, are watching more pornography than would have been conceivable even five years ago.

The women in pornographic films are not shown as worthy of respect; they are presented as sex-toys for the gratification of men. In the next chapter, we explore the effect of this insidious development on women, on men – particularly young men – and on the nature of relationships between the sexes. Our conclusions are very worrying.

The effect of pornography adds another layer of complexity to the gender politics of the twenty-first century. There is a feeling that we have reached a moment of great uncertainty. The optimism of the late 1990s has faded and unless new energy is injected into demands for greater equality, there are plenty of reasons to be pessimistic.

Resistance

In Chapter 6 we noted that since the Votes for Women campaigns there has been systematic resistance by men to policies to increase gender equality. The changes in board membership proposed by Lord Davies were modest and it was hoped that there would be no backlash from men. Unfortunately, in the last year or two we have seen a build-up of hostility to further changes. In spite of assurances from the Business Secretary, every ambitious man soon realised that appointing more women into senior positions would mean appointing fewer men.

Resistance was not immediately apparent. There was the familiar difference between public expressions of support for equality and private behaviour. In public, businessmen smiled benignly and complied; in private, the pressure to replace men with women was resented. But these private opinions got no public airing until John Allan, Chairman of Tesco, spilt the beans.[20] Allan said that the move to appoint more women (and people from what he called an 'ethnic background') has meant that,

> 'if you are a white male, ... you are an endangered species and you are going to have to work twice as hard'.

Figures subsequently published showed that, in Tesco at least, males are under less pressure than Allan suggested. The Tesco Board has 12 members. Only three of them are women and they are all non-executives. All the Executive Directors on the Tesco Board – the people with real power – are men.

When challenged, Allan said that his remarks 'were intended to be humorous'. Perhaps he really was just indulging in another piece of male banter. However his whole speech reads as if he had become very frustrated at the prospect of men losing their favoured place in the sun.

Other companies said little but resistance showed in their actions. Many big companies met the recommended proportion of women by keeping the same number of men on the board and simply adding an extra woman non-executive. Women replacing men was unusual. Companies also changed their governance arrangements by accelerating the transfer of effective power from the board, which now contained a higher proportion of women, to their executive (or management) committee, which is typically made up of executive directors, most of whom are men.

These events suggest that any new measure to transfer power from men to women, however limited, is likely to encounter further resistance. Powerful men are quite happy to sign high-flown policy statements in favour of equality or insert little homilies into their Annual Reports. However, just as happened in the Votes for Women campaign, when the debate stopped being about principles and began to be about implementation, the attitude of men hardened and the tactics of resistance which we described in Chapter 5, came into play. The commitment to equality is once more revealed as little more than skin deep.

In future the main battle is likely to be about enforcement. Will any future initiatives be voluntary or will they be backed by law. As we explained in Chapter 6, relying on voluntary action is an unfair and inadequate way of increasing equality of opportunity for women. Our suspicion, based on the experience of the past hundred years, is that many powerful men will not volunteer to share their power with women. There is a big risk that they will prevaricate in public and plan obstruction in private.

The Merit Principle

Whenever statements are made about the desirability of having more women in senior positions, powerful men often add a significant qualification. They talk about the importance of merit. The CEO of a large company explained his company's position like this:

> 'Of course we believe in giving women every opportunity to get to senior positions but we must be sure that we are getting the best person for the job, whether that is a man or a woman.'

Getting the best person for the job is a worthy objective and few people would disagree with the merit principle expressed in these terms. However the crucial question is about practice: do organisations take all reasonable steps to find the most able candidate for a senior position?

When we examined the recruitment practices of large organisations, we were surprised by what we found. There is no mystery about how to recruit successfully. The first task is to ensure that the details of any vacancy get to as many potentially suitable candidates as possible. Most public sector organisations and most charities meet this test by advertising in the publications that potential candidates are likely to read and on websites that potential candidates are likely to use. However we found that large private companies do things very differently.

The first surprise is the almost complete absence of open competition. Vacancies are rarely advertised. In 2003, the Review by Derek Higgs established that only a miniscule 1% of non-executive appointments in FTSE100 companies were filled by persons answering an advertisement. Davies looked at the figures again in 2011 and confirmed that little had changed. We could find no equivalent figures for the appointment of executive director but we know that the normal practice is for the company to place no advertisements but to ask a head-hunter to draw up a list for the chairman and the board to consider.

The second surprise is the informality of the selection process. Higgs found that only 4% of non-executive directors had attended a formal interview before appointment. Indeed, about half of the vacancies had been filled through personal friendships and contacts. The head-hunter, if one is used, operates in secret and the strong impression is of a very limited exercise where insiders have a considerable advantage. The weakness of this process is obvious and serious. Most potential candidates, including many well-qualified women, will not even know that a vacancy exists until after it has been filled.

No doubt many board members believe that an informal process with no advertising is a good way to find the best candidate. Impartial observers are likely to draw the opposite conclusion. Instead of focusing on merit, there seems to be a pervasive desire to preserve the exclusivity of board positions. This thought came strongly to mind when both authors attended a conference in the City of London to discuss the appointment of more women to the boards of large companies. At the end of the presentations, the chairman of the conference was asked why senior positions were not advertised. His answer was that many of these jobs have such high salaries and are so attractive that the company concerned would not be able to cope with the flood of applications. An HR specialist intervened to point out that assessing applications is exactly what a good HR department is equipped to do.

Private organisations must be allowed some independence of deci-sion-making but the public has rights as well. We are entitled to expect that private organisations apply the principles of fairness and equality that are meant to form the bedrock of our society. There is also the matter of integrity. Most private organisations continue to insist that fairness and equality are to the forefront of their value system; they have an obligation to demonstrate that those laudable principles are actually put into practice. Lastly, they should not try to escape their responsibilities by spurious argu-ments about merit when, in the appointment of senior people, what we see is not a commitment to rewarding merit but a system that gives a substantial advantage to insiders.

Public and Private

Twenty-first century sexism and inequality is less obvious than it was fifty or a hundred years ago. The orthodoxy of our times is that men and women should have equal rights and equal opportu-nities: that is the message that we hear from powerful people when they speak in public. But the more we look behind the public utter-ances, the more we find that this comforting unanimity conceals ambiguity, pretence and even hypocrisy.

In spite of the public commitment to equality, men still occupy a massive proportion of the most powerful positions in our soci-ety and they are resistant to the suggestion that they should share their power. In one disguise or another, misogyny still exists in the secret thoughts of many people. The desire of men to use their power over women did not evaporate as the princi-ple of equality gained more vocal support. Many men are still tempted to use sexist language and to abuse women. They feel a sense of entitlement and imagine that they are too powerful to be caught out.

Nearly a hundred years ago, Eleanor Rathbone observed that we not only need laws to guarantee equality but we also need a great cultural change to ensure that the rights of women are given as much attention as the entrenched rights of men. Nowadays we have better laws and, on the surface, a better recognition of the need to improve women's rights. But we still need that elusive cultural change which converts lip service into deep conviction. In the next chapter we discuss how women react to the sexism and inequality which are still such unpleasant features of our society.

8

Threats and Trepidation

Assaults

How are women reacting to the sexism, which is sadly still prevalent in twenty-first century Britain?

Here is the experience of one woman, a university lecturer, as told to the *Guardian* in March 2017:

> "The worst thing is that there are many people who are suffering under this professor. Simply putting in a formal complaint will not do anything but make life hell for me and other women. He will never be fired. Everyone I have spoken to confirms this."[1]

A junior university staff member told *The Guardian* that she had tried to raise concerns about sexual harassment in her department for five years, but no manager she contacted had taken action.

Having read this and further articles in *The Guardian* on sexual assaults in universities, we decided to investigate.

Caroline (not her real name), a former popular and well-respected lecturer at a London University College, bravely volunteered to tell us about her own experience of a sexual assault by a senior member of the teaching staff there.

She had had a good working relationship with this man for a few years: he had been her PhD supervisor and was now a colleague whom she considered to be a mentor.

In April 2011, she went to see him in his office to discuss some of her research. When the conversation came to an end he said, 'Turn around and look out of my window', which she did, thinking there was a view since the office was on the first floor.

That was when he attacked her.

> "He then launched himself on me from behind, put
> his hands under my arms and grabbed my breasts.
> I couldn't get him off me though I kept shouting
> 'Get off me. Get off me.' I stamped hard on his foot,
> used my elbows and tried to prise his hands off me
> but couldn't budge him. He eventually backed off.
> It was a frenzied attack."

She told no-one at first feeling 'utterly ashamed' and asking herself 'Have I been sending out the wrong signals?'

A colleague urged her to speak to Human Resources at the University, which she finally did after a further two months and then found herself having to tell her story to two *men* from HR, one whom she knew. The other man has subsequently been sacked by another university on the grounds of sexual abuse.

Her attacker was interviewed separately and denied the charge and the only sanction he received was that he should not enter the building where Caroline worked. She was offered therapy but when she felt unable to proceed with a tribunal, this was promptly withdrawn.

Caroline lost confidence, although she continued to work at the university for a further five years and then finally resigned in August 2016. 'I felt like a shadow', she told us. 'I became a shadow.'

Caroline was clearly still very upset when retelling her story even after 6 years. She feels that she was systematically undermined as a professional over several years.

Wendy (not her real name), a senior lecturer and union representative at the university who had helped to arrange this interview and was present throughout, told us,

> 'There are at least 6 more women who would be willing speak to you along similar lines.'

This is a shocking state of affairs and probably needs to be written about in a separate publication.

We are reading and hearing more and more stories of university students and junior staff members being sexually harassed or actually assaulted by senior colleagues.

Legal experts involved in the cases say that the numbers of allegations they are dealing with are the tip of the iceberg and that no universities,

> 'really tackle the issue squarely.... one Oxford college saying overtly that it wants to ensure that that there will be no adverse effect on the reputation of the college'.[2]

'Lad culture' and misogyny on student campuses are blamed for this predatory behaviour but many victims never report their harassment because they are, 'fearful of the impact on their education or careers'. If they do make an official complaint they are likely to find little support as the following *Guardian* report attests:

> "A graduate student who was sexually assaulted by a senior academic said she had been pressurised to drop her complaint. 'They offered me a settlement on the condition that I drop out of the programme and accept that no internal investigation on the member of staff would take place.' She refused but after an independent enquiry, despite all the evidence she gave, none of her complaints were upheld."[3]

In some cases, but not all, among the students themselves, the assaults happen after a great deal of alcohol has been consumed during rowdy sessions, particularly connected with sporting fixtures.

Sexual assault and violence are no more reprehensible in places of learning than anywhere else, but seem more shocking when discovered to be perpetrated in institutions normally regarded as safe areas of study and quiet contemplation.

What are the reasons for this apparent surge of unacceptable behaviour?

Was Germaine Greer right when she said so many years ago that 'women have very little idea how much men hate them...'[4]

Domestic violence has been reported for decades. Pressure has forced the police to respond with more speed nowadays, but too many disputes are settled out of court or dropped. But however violence is dealt with officially, the question remains: why are some men so angry? It has been suggested that the anger has been submerged in recent years because it has become politically incorrect to admit to it, but this explanation does not address the reason behind the rage itself. We gave what we feel to be part of the explanation in Chapter 7 but we feel sure that there must be more.

Social media may be partly to blame. It is so easy to generate and spread spite and hatred through the internet. But Joan Smith's *Misogynies* published in 1989, long before the advent of the internet, warned us of 'a simple, virulent loathing of the female' which seems to be accounted for through what she called 'anatomy-is-destiny' theories. She asks holders of this opinion,

> 'Can you shrug off the fact that women are routinely denigrated, despised, segregated, raped, mutilated and murdered? Are you saying, in fact, that it is natural for men to hate and fear women?'[5]

For women facing daily denigration and abuse, whether this is based on hatred or contempt or a fundamental disregard for their feelings, is understandably not uppermost in their minds.

Indeed at a conference at Birkbeck College, Hannana Siddiqui, who has worked with Southall Black Sisters for 30 years, did not attempt to address this issue, but talked with grave concern about the much more urgent problem caused by the cuts in services which has coincided with a rise in religious fundamentalism. Women who previously sought protection in refuges are now being returned to their homes where they can be abused and exploited by their whole family. Sometimes the excuse given for this dereliction of duty by authorities is a disinclination to 'interfere' in the culture of a community. They should be left to police themselves. The result is that vital intervention is not available to prevent abuse against vulnerable women. Hannana Siddiqui also made the point that not all Asians have a religious faith and that it is the secular feminist organisations which are facing closure as money is being diverted into the 'fight against terrorism'.[6]

In her much more recent book *Pimp State,* Kat Banyard takes the issue a stage further when she tackles prostitution: 'The money isn't a coincidence', she writes, 'it is a coercion'. And paid sex often leads to sexual violence. Her thesis is that commercial exploitation of women cannot be synonymous with a society in which men and women live as equals.[7] Banyard objects to the description of prostitutes as 'sex workers' arguing that it is not work, it is abuse. 'It's the ultimate invasion', says one prostitute whom she interviewed for her book, which is almost too unbearable to read at times in its honest descriptions of the lives of women living below the radar,

'They are in your head and they are in your body'.

Sarah Veale, former Head of Equality and Employment Rights at the TUC, is clear:

'In a civilised society sexual exploitation cannot be counted as a labour market activity: prostitution is sexual exploitation.'[8]

Pornography

Kat Banyard condemns the making and the use of pornography:

'There is a significant association between the using of porn and holding attitudes supporting violence against women.... There is a correlation between the behaviour of pimps and domestic violence perpetrators. It's about control, violence and isolation.'[9]

We are not suggesting that our society is full of brutal misogynistic men but the widespread use of pornography especially among younger boys must be helping to desensitise them to pain.

Twenty-nine year old Annabel Jones told us that,

> 'there is a veritable explosion in the use of internet porn
> among young men'.

One of the problems, she said, is that often young boys are watching
porn before their first sexual experiences, so that their expectations
are completely false. When they meet real women they often have
problems with erections because the women do not conform to,

> 'the ridiculous and idealised porn version of females: how
> they should look and behave particularly during sexual
> encounters'.

Women have to be totally hairless. As another young woman, Ashleigh James, told us,

> 'We're allowed to have hair on our heads and our eye-
> brows but nothing below the nose!'

There is something particularly worrying and unhealthy about this
apparent wish for pre-pubescent bodies, echoing John Ruskin's
apparent terror of pubic hair.

Young women are also undergoing cosmetic surgery to their labia.
What kind of perfection can they possibly be seeking when con-
senting to such drastic measures?

It does not take much imagination to see how this must have a
damaging effect on relationships between the sexes, both emotionally and physically.

Both Annabel and Ashleigh were adamant that every young man
they know watches pornography. It is very easy to access on their
phones and, whereas once looking at porn might have been a

secretive activity practised in private, Annabel told us that young men whom she knows openly share and discuss pornography.

Their views are shared by Jack Hodgkinson, a final-year student at a London university college. 'Watching porn is almost a rite of passage for boys.' At his college, with its heavy emphasis on sports, the men talk about the women they have had sex with 'in terms of numbers'. There is no affection or respect. The sex seems to be all about basic male gratification. Every year the 'sports lads' go on a week's tour which Jack describes as a 'booze/sex fest' and come back proudly announcing how drunk they got and how many women they had 'laid'.

Jack does not believe that these men are 'angry' but that they are brought up in a misogynistic world in which women's feelings are not properly valued and their attitude towards them is accordingly unthinking at best, more often brutally damaging.

In the face of such damaging male behaviour, the reluctance some young women may feel to challenge perceived inequalities is hardly surprising. Their feelings of low self-esteem and powerlessness are clearly not likely to motivate them to join movements demanding equality.

But the reaction of women is not just about sexual harassment, abuse and pornography.

The Need to be Liked

> 'One of the more crippling aspects of being a woman....
> is the continual and largely unconscious compulsion to be nice' complains Jill Tweedie.[10]

In *Teaching Men to be Feminist (2013)*. Anne Dickson warns that

'women are inclined towards conciliation rather than conflict' (and) 'An inordinate dependence on others' approval
becomes a major obstacle to emotional and physical
autonomy'.

'Teach her to reject likeability', advises Chimamanda Ngozi Adichie in answer to a friend who has asked her how to raise her
daughter to be a feminist.[11]

For most women, the need to be liked and the constant seeking of others' approval can act as a considerable brake on their
aspirations. Too often women swallow inconsiderate or even hurt-
ful comments rather than risk conflict because they are afraid of
losing a friend or an ally.

Likeability has obvious advantages in helping to make the world
go around more smoothly and sometimes avoiding confrontation
is the wiser option. But not always.

The need to be liked disempowers. It prevents honest responses. It
creates a vacuum that remains empty. It stunts the development of
lines of argument necessary to challenge inequality.

The American novelist Curtis Sittenfeld describes the problem thus:

> 'We could agree, or we could avoid discussion, and I was
> good at both; by generation, gender and geography, and
> above all by temperament, I was good at agreement and
> good at avoidance.'[12]

We are not advocating aggression but there is a place for asserting
one's rights. We can all point to women who have courageously
fought a lone battle against adversity and we are in their debt.
Much of their success, as demonstrated in previous chapters, is
won after years of dogged persistence. Most of us do not possess

their stamina or their courage, but if we are not brave enough to emulate their tactics, we can at least attempt to overcome our fear of disapproval by disputing minor infringements.

Every small favourable outcome adds to confidence in pursuing justice. It is often easier to engage in struggles on behalf of others because setbacks do not seem so personal, but eventually women have to fight unjust situations in which they themselves are involved and discover that being disliked may be significantly less painful when victory is the prize.

Femininity

Defining femininity remains a conundrum. But how serious is this in the grand scheme of things? Unfortunately the idea that being feminine somehow contradicts being a feminist has taken hold in many women's heads. We know that this came from the media's representation of all feminists being unfeminine in looks and behaviour. The fact that well-known feminists vary in their appearance: some glamorous and fulfilling the stereotypical expectation of what a feminine woman should look like and others simply uninterested in how they present themselves, is beside the point. What matters is what they have to say. So why has this become an issue at all?

More than two centuries ago, Mary Wollstonecraft wrote,

> "I once knew a weak woman of fashion who was more
> than uncommonly proud of her delicacy and sensibility
> who thought that a distinguishing taste and a puny appe-
> tite the height of human perfection...in short, those attrib-
> utes which men have deemed necessary as femininity..."[13]

Mary Wollstonecraft goes on to list these qualities of femininity as 'passivity, weakness, lassitude and dependency to frivolity, a fondness for dress and a dislike of serious purpose'.

A pretty damning indictment of femininity.

Indeed, trailing through numerous references to femininity from Aphra Benn and Mary Wollstonecraft onwards, it is virtually impossible to find a positive comment. As Marina Horner says,

'it is still a deeply entrenched conviction that intellectual competence cannot co-exist with femininity'.[14]

Angela McRobbie, who wrote extensively in the 1970s about the search for femininity and romance in magazines like *Jackie*, aimed at the teenage girls market, gives a wry answer in a more recent publication to the new longing for femininity:

'It is as though this is the vengeance of the younger generation who had to put up with being chided by feminist teachers and academics at university for wanting the wrong things.'[15]

Perhaps she has a point.

The irritation and impatience expressed by some feminist commentators is understandable if femininity is still to be described as disempowering but young women in the twenty-first century might quibble with such dogmatic assertions. Women are more visible in positions of power – not in great numbers, it has to be said – and although their dress is still commented on in ways that men's appearance is not, femininity may not be the barrier it once was. For Marie Bailey, a young university lecturer and feminist,

'Femininity need not signify powerlessness or dependence but can be celebrated in its own right as giving confidence in an alternative non-masculine way.'

Her views may be over optimistic but we need to take heed and encourage a less negative view of femininity if it also helps younger women to trust their feminist instincts.

Equality in the Home

How much real equality is there when it comes to domestic relationships?

In *The Second Shift* published in 1989, Airlie Hoschild boldly states:

> 'Women don't need wives – they need careers basically redesigned to suit workers who also care for families.'

Her book is based on years of painstaking research during which she interviewed 50 professional couples in Berkley, 12 of whom allowed her to observe them closely at home. The more successful women in the partnerships whom Airlie Hoschild observed,

> 'started to make up for their status at work by doing even more housework to salve their partner's ego!'

What she called 'the marital myth' of men taking greater responsibility in the home is borne out by current research. In November 2016, the Office of National Statistics published its findings on this subject and found that on average women are still spending 26 hours a week compared with men's 16 hours.

At a recent conference, when the feminist researcher Rosabeth Moss Kanter was asked what men could do to advance women's leadership, she answered tartly, 'The laundry'.

Anecdotally, men seem to be happiest when operating domestic machinery; the washing machine, the vacuum cleaner, the dishwasher. They will happily do the shopping if their wives prepare the lists. In fact many men are quite willing to undertake most tasks in the home as long as it is pointed out that they need to be done. The initiative they demonstrate at work seems to desert them when they reach their own front door.

What about the cult or mystique of motherhood? The sentimentality of the Victorian era and the dutiful housebound mother in a frilly apron of the 1950s are thankfully a thing of the past but an image of perfect motherhood still persists. It is very easy to fall below some ideal standard when a woman's reputation as a good mother can come under attack. Usually the criticism is self-inflicted and often unjustified. But women do feel under great pressure to conform to unachievable goals as mothers, particularly if they are employed.

For some, surviving on the bare minimum is hard enough without trying to provide nutritious meals, help with homework or just finding time to talk and play with their children. For those with demanding jobs and higher salaries, there is never enough time to give proper attention to the family. Beatriz Lees, a very experienced childminder, says:

> "I am told that the hours between six and nine in the evening are very fraught. The children don't go to bed meekly, leaving time to finish work and the mother is exhausted and unable to concentrate. She doesn't have time to talk to her husband."

To quote Gloria Steinem:

> 'You can't do it all. No one can have two full time jobs, have perfect children and cook three meals a day and be multi-orgasmic... the superwoman is the adversary of the women's movement.[16]

And then there is the problem with guilt. Guilt appears to be built in to a woman's DNA. It is corrosive and incapacitating. 'Women know all about guilt… it is our speciality', writes Ros Coward.[17] It seems to be ubiquitous. For Marxists like Juliet Mitchell domestic work is all part of the capitalist system, externally imposed, which helps to keep women subjugated, [18] but it is rare to find a woman who does not feel that her imperfections are her own fault.

A significant but usually unspoken factor causing guilt can be the relationship women have with men. Feminists want to live in equal partnership with men and this may be possible in the confines of the family, but in a society where men are still dominant there are bound to be unresolved tensions. Rudman and Glick's 2008 study *The Social Psychology of Gender* gives us some insights into the difficulties:

> "The stereotypes for male and female behaviour are very strong and persistent. Men's attitude towards women is guided by two desires: the desire for dominance and the desire for an intimate and interdependent heterosexual relationship. These desires are often in conflict."

Much has been written about the dominance of men in the working environment but the subtleties of private relationships are rarely exposed. To reveal tangled emotions would rightly be considered an infringement of trust but their existence is undeniable. When these problems are brought out into the open by women speaking together on their own there is often recognition but this is quickly followed by rueful resignation. And this reaction is surely understandable. In her writing over several decades, Sheila Rowbotham has always been clear: feminists are not man-hating harridans. They want to live in equal harmony with their male partners but women's relationships with men in an unequal society are bound to create strains which are difficult to overcome.

In *What Is a Feminist?* the influential feminist commentator, Dale Spender, writes:

> 'I do not believe for one moment that men are born with the value system that they generally manifest but, having acquired it, I have met very few men who are willing or able to discard it.'[19]

Sadly, over thirty years later, she would no doubt be reiterating the same sentiments.

Inequality in the Workplace

Advances have undoubtedly been made for women at work. The Equal Pay Act of 1970 made it illegal for women to be paid less than men for the same work and the guarantee was later extended to apply to jobs of equal value. The Sex Discrimination Act of 1975 was another landmark towards greater equality but, as we argue strongly in Chapter 6, neither of these essential laws has been adequately enforced.

The most robust calculation suggests that the gender pay is still close to 20%. And some of the discrimination against women is very severe. The Fawcett Society has found that,

> 'unfair treatment of women especially around maternity has resulted in 54,000 women currently leaving their jobs after having children'.[20]

A large part of the problem for women seeking justice in cases of discrimination is that unless they have support, financial and moral (most often through membership of a trade union), they have to take their grievance to Tribunal and fight it alone. A daunting prospect, made worse by recent legislation demanding considerable payment for the necessary tribunal hearings. Inevitably under these circumstances, only a small proportion of such challenges are embarked upon. Indeed, as we revealed in Chapter 5, the Employment Tribunal system, has lost almost all credibility with women as a way of settling inequality claims. Lawyers are cautioning women against taking cases to Tribunals, even if their cases are strong.

However, it is not just the nature of the inequality problem that we need to address. The question has to be asked: how are women feeling and reacting to inequality? The honest answer is complicated. In our research, we found that women usually regard work very differently from men. For most men, particularly those with significant ambition, pay and status are the main objectives. Most women care much less about status and, particularly at senior levels, rather less about pay. Their priorities are much more social that economic. They want their work to be satisfying and they want to share a workplace with colleagues whose company they enjoy. If those conditions are met, we found that most women are unlikely to challenge their employer over unequal pay; win or lose the effect would destroy the prospect of a contented workplace that most women value highly.

On the other hand, we found that many women feel strongly about unfairness, particularly when it seems to give men a much greater opportunity for promotion. Some women become very cynical about claims that gender is of no account in the modern workplace. While at Cranfield University, Ruth Sealy interviewed women in the banking sector.[21] Those in the early part of their career were happy to accept that their large investment bank operated as a meritocracy, rewarding skill and achievement regardless of gender. On the other hand, those women who were further on in their career were much more sceptical. The stories they told were of women being bypassed when the best assignments were allocated and of women being overlooked for executive positions.

Most of these women felt that they were being undervalued by the bank.

In many workplaces the view of the women is that the culture of the company will not change and that the only sensible option is to move on. Of the senior women interviewed by Ruth Sealy, half were considering leaving. We found the same attitude in many of the women from the corporate sector whom we interviewed. If the company has a style that does not suit women, best to resign, give an anodyne reason and look for a workplace that is more congenial.

In Chapter 9, we return to the issues of job satisfaction and to how work can be transformed to meet the social needs of women.

Challenging the Status Quo

Few people, women or men, would disagree with the proposition that equality is needed and long overdue. That in itself is an achievement. When Harriet Harman successfully introduced the Equality Act in 2010, 'to ensure that everyone has a fair chance in life', it was generally supported as a just and sensible measure. Reading through the Act, the requirements, though unequivocal, are straightforward: banning age discrimination, transparency in the workplace, consideration of the diverse needs of the workforce, extending positive action, to mention just a few.

Years of research and consultation had gone into framing the Equality Act before it was presented and eventually passed, despite repeated attempts by Theresa May, then Shadow Home Secretary, to frustrate its progress, objecting to it as 'unnecessarily onerous on business'.[22] However, although legislation is necessary to begin the process of tangible change, applying it is a different story. As the eminent human rights lawyer and campaigner Helena Kennedy told us,

'A lot has happened, but not enough has changed.'

Why should this be?

Having made substantial gains, unthinkable before both the major campaigns we describe in Chapters 3 and 4, what is preventing further progress?

Power

When we interviewed women for our earlier book,[23] we noticed how often they were wary of the word 'power'. Some said they preferred to use the word 'influence'. But these two words are not synonymous. It is possible to have 'influence' in persuading others to take on new ideas or in pursuing a course of action but power is an altogether stronger concept. Power gives us the authority to make a real difference. Winning the vote gave women the power to take part in democratic processes; campaigning collectively in the Women's Liberation Movement gave women the power to demand rights. Now we must use power to continue the work of previous generations of feminists.

To quote Helena Kennedy again,

'We should stop pussyfooting and seize power. Stop being afraid of that word.'

Roseanne Barr says,

'...the thing women have yet to learn is that nobody gives us power. You just have to take it'.[24]

The advantages of using power will be considered in Chapter 9, when we look to the future, but it might help to consider why some women find the word 'power' so unpalatable. It may simply be the image of strength used in ways that are undemocratic or with little consultation. It might be the fear of wielding unquestioned authority which can be used abusively. It might simply be fear of the unaccustomed ability to authorise measures that affect people's lives. We owe a great deal to women who have wielded power and have not been afraid to use it judiciously, usually with beneficial effects.

In Chapter 5 we recognised the work of powerful women parliamentarians like Margaret Bondfield, Ellen Wilkinson, Barbara Castle, Jenny Lee, Shirley Williams and Margaret Thatcher and Theresa May. Harriet Harman and others carry the torch forward today.

During the last twenty years a new generation of women has broken through into positions of power in many other sectors of society: academics like Mary Beard and Susan Greenfield, prominent women in the arts like Jude Kelly, Vanessa Redgrave and Deborah Bull, Dr Wendy Savage, a pioneer in gynaecology, Kate Allen, Director of Amnesty International and Frances Crook, CEO of the Howard League of Penal Reform. Some others have been the first woman to reach a particular position of power, like Brenda Hale, the first female judge in the Supreme Court, Cressida Dick, the first woman Metropolitan Police Commissioner and Frances O'Grady, the first woman General Secretary of the TUC. We recognise their names because they make sure we hear their voices. They understand the necessity of gaining power and of using it to support their causes and ours.

External Pressures

When faced with a choice of emotional upheaval in our lives or putting up with some injustice, most of us feel tempted to settle for what we are used to. Centuries of being reared to be compliant, not to confront and, more seriously debilitating, not to show anger, are bound to undermine women's urge to act. Louise O'Neill rails against,

> 'The manacles of a lifetime of cultural conditioning...
> (that) are more difficult to shake off than I would like'.[25]

Continuing to live with a familiar identity that feels comfortable as a woman is easier than making a stand against inequality. Added to which is the risk of making oneself unpopular. Challenging conventional attitudes causes discomfort, especially if one lacks support. Adopting new and unaccustomed beliefs is risky. It can be liberating but usually requires a shift in self-concept, which feels like acquiring a new identity with which we are unfamiliar. Having taken the plunge however, initial wariness soon wears off and one of the important legacies of the Women's Liberation Movement is the sisterhood between women which can be called upon to sustain us in moments of self-doubt.

As Miriam David writes in *Reclaiming Feminism* (2016),

> 'Becoming a feminist was not an easy ride: it was a challenging struggle, personally, politically and also professionally.'

Miriam David is a feminist academic with a long history of standing up for women's rights, particularly in the field of higher education. Her own introduction to feminist beliefs came as a result of being part of a wave of women studying sociology when the Robbins Committee was tasked with expanding the number of universities in Britain. The original intention behind the expansion of universities was to create more economists but this was a period of new intellectual initiatives and one unexpected consequence was, as we mentioned in Chapter 6, the number of women studying sociology far outweighed the men.

Miriam David tells us that

> 'In our class of 1966, the year we graduated, there were
> over 50 sociologists of whom about a tenth were men.'[26]

Obviously, studying a subject like sociology which questions institutions and their functions, will involve the need to throw light on attitudes to equality. It requires students to unpick taken-for-granted assumptions about society. The appeal of sociology for many of us lies in the fact that 'sociologists have a hunger for addressing moral issues'[27] and the position of women in society would surely count as exactly that kind of moral issue.

'It was the Zeitgeist', Miriam David told us when describing why women in the late 1960s and 1970s became feminists.

What did the zeitgeist consist of? And how has it changed?

The influence of the liberal arts curriculum in the 1970s was a factor in encouraging people to extend their vision. A new world of exciting ideas was opening up. Academic research was becoming less competitive and was being shared. There was an explosion of feminist theatre companies such as The Raving Beauties, Cunning Stunts, Beryl and the Perils, Monstrous Regiment and Spare Tyre mounting provocative productions. Feminist novelists of a slightly earlier period like Doris Lessing and Margaret Drabble were joined by Margaret Atwood, Marilyn French and many more. They were all asking us to see the world through different lenses. It is clear that in a society where such changes in perspective were welcomed, feminism could flourish.

Nowadays, with less funding for the arts generally, a narrower school curriculum and without the loud approving background noises of the 1970s to inspire confidence, it may feel easier to slump into inertia. Whatever the temptation to do nothing, it has to be resisted. We owe future generations of women a more equal chance in all aspects of their lives. In Chapters 9 and 10 we will endeavour to show how this might be achieved.

Revolution not Reform

In conversation with younger women it is not uncommon to hear them say that the main struggle for women's equality is over, that there is little left to do and that the rest will come about through voluntary action. In Chapter 7, we show how unlikely this is. Many men still actively resist genuine progress; others think that by stating their support for women's equality they are not obliged to make sure it happens. Those men who campaign alongside women deserve encouragement. Their numbers are growing and that is to be welcomed, but ultimately women themselves have to decide how to move forward effectively.

In 1972 Ann Oakley wrote:

> 'There is still a disparity between belief and practice. Professed egalitarian beliefs are belied in practice even in women.'[28]

It would surely be an indictment if nearly half a century later that same criticism could still be levelled. Even though, as we have demonstrated, we can understand hesitation when it comes to campaigning, we have to convince ourselves and others that there is still work to do.

> "Equal pay, more nurseries... in its contemporary form reform is wholly divorced from any fundamental critique of women's condition... it represents a tepid embellishment of the status quo."

Juliet Mitchell's dismissive reaction to the efforts of early feminists of the Women's Liberation Movement[29] may be unduly harsh, but in order to rebut her accusation we need to prove that we are ready to face the insecurities as well as the benefits that fundamental change will bring.

Most women involved in the Women's Liberation Movement did not adopt a strong political stance, like the Marxist or Anarchist feminists, and neither did they have much in common with the self-styled radical feminists who blamed gender inequality on patriarchy alone. It is true that many of the prominent figures of the women's movement in the 1970s were on the left: some, like Sheila Rowbotham openly espousing and advocating socialism as the inspiration and driving force behind their feminism. As we illustrated in Chapter 4, other women had no particular political allegiance but simply wanted to create a fairer society. This spread of opinions very probably reflects today's attitudes.

Any new movement will always attract a variety of enthusiasts. Most use their energy to further agreed causes but some threaten to derail the central purpose of its members. So it was with the Women's Liberation Movement, which in the end was not able to withstand the conflict of opposing factions in its ranks.

But whatever the individual motivations, one of the lessons of that time was participatory politics. Women came together in committees and in more informal groups determined to make a difference.

Working together was effective and helped allay the fear that some women have about taking what is seen as political activity and therefore being labelled in a way that makes them feel uncomfortable. Collective action was and remains a start. In our next chapter we discuss the motivations and methods for building on this impetus with optimism.

9

New Writing on the Banner

"All is for the best in the best of all possible worlds."[1]

This advice to Candide from his tutor Pangloss (*Candide* by Voltaire 1759) may seem deluded in twenty-first century Britain but his optimism is enviable. To make progress we all have to believe that our thoughts and actions count and the only way we can prove that is by taking risks and making ourselves heard.

Utopia

Lynne Segal in *Radical Happiness: Collective Joy* (2017) quotes a defiant slogan from the French demonstrations of 1968:

'Be realistic – demand the impossible.'

While we understand the irony behind these words they should make us stop and think. Of course we all realise the tenacity and sheer hard work needed to achieve even what is possible. We have illustrated this with numerous examples in the preceding chapters but let us indulge briefly in imagining utopia. We might find that at least some of what we want is within our grasp.

What does utopia look like?

When parents are asked what they most want for their children they often reply that they want them to be happy. Superficially this may sound like a glib response, because of course we all want much more than that, but it is worth trying to unravel what happiness might consist of.

In his book, *Happiness*,[2] Richard Layard lays out the seven factors affecting happiness: family relationships, financial situations, work, community and friends, health, personal freedom and personal values.

We may disagree with Layard's list or wish to add to it, but it would be difficult to argue against the fact that it contains the most important ingredients vital to feelings of wellbeing. None of his suggestions is particularly revolutionary and yet if proper attention is paid to them all our lives would undoubtedly be happier. So, how does our current society encourage us to develop them? We would contend that in a harshly competitive world it is easy to ignore this list and that is to our detriment.

This book is about women and how they can attain their aspirations, gain more control over their working lives and live with greater fulfilment and less unnecessary stress. For them utopia would involve the ability to make decisions without constantly defending their rights. In 'the best of all possible worlds', there would be greater honesty and transparency in personal and public relationships. Genuine choices would be made unhampered by obstruction or disapproval.

One of the banners on the 1971 demonstration, described in Chapter 2, proclaimed,

'Equal pay is not enough – we want the Moon.'

What do we hope to find there?

We would hope to break the repressive chains of stereotyping, leaving us all free to plan our lives to give maximum satisfaction. We need to re-order and reconstruct society from birth, through education, jobs and leisure into a more contented retirement. The linear path we now follow allows few of us the opportunity to spread our wings and develop all our talents. We need time to reflect upon our trajectory through life so that we have a greater choice over our destinations instead of accepting current impositions.

A good start would be for women and men to share power and work in equal partnership at home and in the workplace. This does not imply constant harmony – dissension is often desirable and healthy – but it does mean genuinely listening and hearing arguments and not simply waiting to put one's own point of view.

In Britain, we are fortunate to live under a hard-won democratic system. Political engagement is the best way to instigate and maintain desirable alternatives to what seems like immutable systems. In previous chapters, we have stressed on the necessity of political involvement to achieve sustainable progress. For various reasons, politics in this country has become tainted and people are wary of expressing their opinions through visible political activity. This has not always been the case and is not inevitable.

We should be brave enough to reclaim our democratic right to protest publicly. Apart from other considerations, collective action can be invigorating and fun. Laughter is a great unifier. To quote Lynne Segal again, we find joy,

> 'when we are most fully absorbed or lost in something clearly bigger than ourselves'.

Later on she describes the power of joy as,

> 'the force of collective energies, drawing people together as communities'.[3]

Joy should never be underestimated. We need time to savour to the full whatever makes us happy or contented.

Changing the Culture

Even this tiny glimpse of utopia indicates just how much of our present-day culture needs to change. However, if we do it well, we can win a glittering prize. We will not only enrich the lives of women but we can also liberate men from some of the emotional and material burdens that they heaped on themselves during the many years when they were expected to take sole responsibility for everything outside the kitchen and the cot.

Sharing power with women has often been seen by men in terms of what they lose. However it would be better viewed as a way of sharing the onerous responsibility of running the country, of managing companies and many other organisations, of leading the intellectual and cultural life of the nation and, of course, of providing for community and family. There would be immense relief as well as great comfort if we could redefine the relationship between men and women not as a competition for power but as a collaborative effort in which problems are solved together, with both sharing the joy of success and, if things go badly, both accepting a share of the blame.

Changing the culture of any society is difficult even if the outcome is highly desirable. As we showed in earlier chapters, our existing cultural norms are sustained by a host of customs, conventions and stereotypes. A belief that reform is inevitable, and will eventually come without any great effort on the part of women, is comforting but fallacious.

Deborah Mattinson, who is Chair of the Young Women's Trust, believes that we might even be slipping backwards. She is particularly concerned that

> "Nowadays, young working class women are the most reviled group in Britain. They are routinely portrayed as feckless, drunken and promiscuous single mothers. They make up the largest proportion of young people who do not have a job and are not in education or training. They get very little support. If they manage to get an apprenticeship it will most likely be in the beauty sector, where job prospects are poor and pay is low."[4]

When we met Carole Easton, the chief executive of the Trust, she drew our attention to a statistic which we found shocking:

> 'More than a quarter of young Mums have used a food bank due to financial struggles.'[5]

Based on the history of the past century, and on several hundred years before that, it is clear that there is no strong dynamic in our society that will take us to a better place. The lesson of our history is that women must intervene to secure their own liberation.

It is also tempting to believe that all the necessary reforms can be achieved by politicians passing Acts of Parliament. Sadly, that is another comforting illusion. Laws that are well designed and properly enforced can achieve a great deal but, unless they are supported by a substantial body of public opinion, they risk being as ineffectual as that long-forgotten Act of Parliament with the grandiose title that was passed in 1919: the Sex Discrimination (Removal) Act. In any event, the government of the day and the

House of Commons will need to be convinced that changes in the law are warranted. The history of the last hundred and fifty years demonstrates how difficult that can be.

This analysis points to the overwhelming need for a new liberation campaign, which will build support for the necessary changes in our society and will win political backing for new legal rights to buttress a more just system. This conclusion may seem uncongenial to the many women who do not see themselves as campaigners and are fearful of reaching for the moon, but it is unavoidable. If current trends continue, women will still be waiting for equality at the end of this century and into the next. The desirable reforms will not happen by accident. They will have to be fought for.

Protection

We will also have to fight against wickedness. Any worthwhile campaign must be utopian in its aims, but before we raise our eyes to the sky we have to remember, with great anger and perhaps with more than a little shame, that there are some women in Britain whose lives are blighted by violence and misery. They might dream of equality but their urgent need is for help and protection.

In Chapter 8, we described some dreadful incidents of sexual assault. They are not rarities. To repeat the figures quoted earlier:[6]

> "In the year 2015/2016 the Police in England and Wales recorded 23,851 cases of adults being raped, almost all of them women. In the same year 11,947 cases of rape against children were recorded, mostly against girls. Latest figures show that the Crime Prosecution Service has also prosecuted nearly 12,000 individuals for sexual assaults

other than rape and has taken nearly 13,000 cases of harassment and stalking to court. Recorded rapes, against both adults and children, have doubled in the last four years. Rape Crisis (England and Wales) estimates that only 15% of incidents of sexual violence are reported to the police. If that estimate is correct, nearly 200,000 women suffer sexual violence each year in England and Wales."

These figures are horrific but the figures for domestic abuse of women might be five or even ten times higher. On the basis of its surveys the Office for National Statistics (ONS) estimates that 1.8 million people had suffered abuse[7] by a partner, ex-partner or family member. Abuse of women accounted for two-thirds of this total. However, once again the figures understate the extent of the problem. Estimates based on the Crime Survey for England and Wales show that four out of five victims of partner abuse did not report it to the police.

A civilised country cannot just wring its hands and express regret at the violence that is all around us. Many women suffer pain, guilt and despair. Even worse, unless we take action, more women will be murdered.

Melinda Korosi was an English Language teacher living in Carlisle with her two children. Early in 2016, Miklos Verebes, her erstwhile partner, was sent to prison for assaulting her. A week before he was released, Melinda Korosi told the police of her fear at what might happen. On 13 September, Verebes was released on licence. Two days later he broke into Melinda Korosi's house and killed her with a sharpened rock. After the murder trial Melinda Korosi was described by the police as,

> 'a quiet and unassuming member of the local community... (with) a kind nature'.[8]

Every week two women in the UK die like Melinda Korosi at the hands of their partner or ex-partner.

Domestic Violence

When a woman is repeatedly assaulted by her partner the first question that occurs to people is rarely why her partner is violent. Instead they wonder why she stays with him. This reaction reveals a great deal about our culture. When the victim is a woman, society seems to assume that she must be at least partly to blame. And women in this desperate plight are ready to accept the judgement of others. The usually feel guilty and ashamed.

The truth is that many women living with a violent man have few options. If they leave their home, they lose any remaining financial security and, if they have children, they may put them at extra risk. Flight might not end the violence. She might be found, dragged back and assaulted more severely. In any event, for many women the possibility of leaving is entirely theoretical: they have nowhere safe to go.

Senior officers tell us that the police are now better trained and better equipped to deal with domestic violence; reports are taken more seriously and followed up more assiduously. This policy of less tolerance and more prosecutions is to be commended. As well as going some way towards protecting the abused woman, it is an important declaration about the standards of behaviour that society requires of men. But it is not a sufficient response. A woman suffering abuse often recoils from the dreadful ordeal of giving evidence in court, facing her one-time lover, experiencing the familiar fear and advertising her misery to the world. Over half of unsuccessful prosecutions fail because the woman decides not to give evidence.

What a woman in this situation requires is a secure place to stay and extensive support, both financial and emotional. Sometimes this can be provided in the family home but in many cases a better solution is for the woman to move into a women's refuge to recover from her ordeal and plan the beginnings of a new life. Unfortunately there are too few refuges, those that exist are under-funded and two-thirds of those that remain face closure unless the government protects them from the repercussions of a continuing series of welfare cuts.

Julie Walters, actor and patron of Women's Aid England, expresses the anger and distress of the refuge movement.

> 'Refuges save lives: it is as simple as that. The government must exempt them from these welfare reforms – or live with the consequences of more women being killed and more families traumatised by domestic abuse.'[9]

The provision of an adequate network of women's refuges, nation-wide and properly funded, should be one of the first objectives of a new liberation campaign.

Sexual Assault

The reality of sexual violence is very different from the way it is often portrayed in the media. According to Rape Crisis (England and Wales) about 90% of those who are raped knew the perpetrator. Assaults by strangers occur too often to be ignored but rape is a crime typically committed by acquaintances, colleagues, friends, partners and relatives.

If intercourse is proved, the defence normally offered by the accused is that sex was consensual. Often the defendant really seems to believe that the women had consented: perhaps he had known her for some time, he thought that she fancied him and, in any event she did not resist, well not very much. Most male defendants seem to make no distinction between consent and acquiescence. The possibility that a woman might not put up a fight because she is very frightened rarely seems to occur to men charged with rape.

Disagreements about consent reveal much about the relationships between men and women in our society and the extent to which these relationships are governed by power. What many men find difficult to accept is that men have no rights when they are seeking to have sex with a woman. The power of decision rests entirely with her. This is a very unusual situation for men who have been taught from infancy that they should be in control. So it is not surprising that men invent their own miserable rules about what constitutes rape. It is not rape, they say, unless the woman is badly hurt; it is not rape if she seems to enjoy it; it is not rape if the act has been committed by a husband or a partner or a boyfriend.

The issue of consent is of enormous importance. Woman will not achieve a secure place in our society until it is universally accepted that every woman has the unconditional right to decide with whom she has sex and when it will take place. If there is any doubt about the woman's consent – if she is asleep or drunk or stoned – the man has no right to proceed and, if he does, he is guilty of rape. The principle of equality allows no concession to male notions of power or entitlement. It is her body and her decision.

The key question is how to embed this principle in our culture. In Chapter 8 we revealed the appalling behaviour of some men in universities and colleges. The incidence of abuse and assaults is rising and many institutions seem more concerned to avoid damaging publicity than to protect students and staff. Universities and colleges are not the only places where women are at risk but, if we intend to roll back this tide of male sexual exploitation, it is a good place to start.

Many female students seem to have lost faith in the possibility of a fair hearing. One woman explains:

> 'When I filed, "a formal complaint... I was told by members of staff that sexual harassment is something that happens to women in academia and that I simply needed to learn to put up with it."'[10]

This negligent and damaging attitude must be changed. We propose that every university and college appoint a nominated member of staff charged with receiving and investigating complaints of sexual abuse or assault, whether from students or staff. She should be outside the normal management structure and should report directly to the chancellor or principal. If she finds that a complaint is justified, she will refer the matter to the appropriate disciplinary body for further action. The outcome will be reported to her and she will compile regular reports for the Department for Education which, in turn must be required to publish an annual report covering the whole of further and higher education.

The nominated member of staff must be fully trained to support and advise complainants. She should maintain close contact with the relevant voluntary organisations, including Rape Crisis. The decision as to whether an incident is reported to the police will rest, of course, with the complainant but, if she decides to do so, the nominated member of staff must ensure that she is given all necessary assistance.

Parallel with these structural changes should be a determined campaign to change the culture inside universities and colleges. Every student should be required to attend a detailed briefing explaining the new structures and the standards of behaviour that are expected. This would also be an opportunity to explain the institution's objections to sexist initiation rites and other objectionable practices. It is very important that women and men attend the briefings together so that members of both sexes receive the same messages and hear the same explanations. Similar arrangements should be made for staff.

These provisions may not work perfectly and should be regularly reviewed. Nevertheless, they should ensure that some cool clean air blows through the university and college sector.

Once a satisfactory model has been developed, similar arrangements might be developed for other organisations which have a bad reputation, particularly those that are more or less closed to outside scrutiny. A new liberation campaign will want to identify places where there is the greatest need.

A government initiative is urgently needed. If Britain's decision-makers cannot see the need for comprehensive and vigorous reform to protect the women of Britain, we must replace them with people who have more determination and more humanity.

Equality

For more than a century most female activists have focused on the need to achieve equality with men. The women's suffrage societies famously demanded the same voting rights as men and two of the demands framed by the Women's Liberation Movement at the Ruskin Conference were for equal pay and for equal educational opportunities.[11] Although circumstances have demonstrated the limitations of this objective – an issue we return to later – the claim for equality with men is important and compelling.

Every time a government insists that it has done enough to settle the issue of gender equality, the legislation fails to deliver what has been promised. We argued earlier that the two great Acts of the 1970s – the Equal Pay Act and the Sex Discrimination Act – have failed because they rely on individual women taking cases to employment tribunals where lawyers representing their employers usually give them such a miserable time that, win or lose, they feel humiliated and demoralised. The enforcement of important social legislation should not depend on the willingness of individual women to accept public martyrdom.

The solution is straightforward. Most of the responsibility for enforcement should pass to a specialist public agency, which would identify apparent breaches of the legislation and threaten action at Tribunal against the organisation concerned. We suspect that, faced with this challenge, most organisations would take corrective action without going to Tribunal. The public agency would be able to take class actions on behalf of groups of women. The right of an individual to take her case would remain and the public agency should have the authority to represent her if it judged that her case stood a reasonable chance of success.

The next requirement is a high level of transparency. Ideally all organisations should be required to publish the numbers of men and women at different levels in their structure and the numbers of men and women on each salary grade. An experienced eye will quickly unravel the story behind the figures. Is there a gender pay gap and, if so, how is it explained? Does the organisation provide equal opportunities or are most of the women parked in the more junior jobs with the lowest pay? Heavyweight intervention might be reserved for the worst offenders but the public agency will want to remind a number of chief executives about the requirements of the law.

Unfortunately, instead of applying the law with rigour, the government is introducing a rather feeble compromise. Organisations with over 250 employees will have to publish an annual report on the salary levels of male and female staff. This requirement is less detailed than we would like but the crucial weakness is that there will be no specialist public agency to follow up the figures with pressure on organisations to comply with the law. Sam Smethers, chief executive of the Fawcett Society, is not optimistic that this limited approach will change the culture of pay setting in Britain, and neither are we. Much more likely is that each organisation will publish its information with a little homily telling us how hard they are working to eliminate inequality. And they will repeat those warm words next year and every year into the future.

More resolute action is needed. A public agency is essential to ensure that all those warm words about future intentions are implemented. It should be able to require further information and if there is serious doubt about an organisation's intentions, the public agency should have the power to insist on the production of a detailed improvement plan. Beyond that, the public agency should have the authority to take legal action against the worst miscreants.

If companies complain about this level of intrusion into their affairs, the response from campaigners should be robust. The Equal Pay Act and the Sex Discrimination Act have been on the statute book for over forty years and the requirements of the law should surprise no one. Transparency is very important because secrecy can conceal so many unacceptable practices. When the BBC published the salaries of its stars and presenters, a disgraceful level of gender pay discrimination was revealed. There is good reason to think that a similar pattern of discrimination exists in most other organisations. As we concluded in Chapter 7, secrecy is the enemy of equality.

And so is complacency. To believe that employers, after years of inaction, will now eradicate discrimination, simply because they have to publish a report on pay in their organisation, stretches credibility beyond breaking point. A dedicated public agency is needed to test their figures, identify failures, require improvement and, in the worst cases, to take the issue to Tribunal or to the courts.

After forty years of inadequate enforcement, it is now time for parliament to deliver the rights which they enacted in the 1970s. Having willed the ends, parliament should, at long last, will the means.

New Opportunities

The case for reform would be strengthened if the public knew more about the casual and discriminatory manner in which senior appointments are made in the private sector. A vacancy at board level in a big company is almost never advertised and candidates are very rarely assessed in any formal manner.[12] In this closed and exclusive little world, the men on the board tend to appoint men whom they know and feel comfortable with. In twenty-first century Britain, such casual disregard for equality of opportunity is outrageous. Most well-qualified candidates never hear about a vacancy until after it has been filled.

Reform is long over-due. We believe that the advertising of all board-level positions and all senior posts in the largest 350 companies in Britain carrying a salary of over £100,000 a year should be made mandatory and that appointments should only be made after a formal procedure of assessment and interview. These rules should also apply throughout the public sector and, as soon as possible, to the charity sector. This modest change will open up new opportunities to thousands of ambitious women, and also – it should be noted – to large numbers of ambitious men.

This new requirement might also be resisted by some in the business community. If so, it would provide a good opportunity to reduce the influence that big companies have traditionally exercised on gender-equality issues. There have been too many occasions in our history when a lack of enthusiasm from powerful men has delayed women's progress. Everyone wants Britain to be 'business friendly' but deference to the business community is entirely misplaced if it allows inequality to continue.

Something Better

So far so good, but feminists who think deeply realise that achieving equality with men can only be the beginning of a much bigger revolution. As Joan Bakewell explains:

> 'Feminism isn't a single issue. It is nothing less than a change to history.'[13]

For Kat Banyard, what is needed is,

> 'a total transformation of society at every level...'[14]

Equality with men will end the most obvious signs of unfairness but it will certainly not bring us very close to utopia. Equality with men sometimes means little more than joining men in their own distress.

Equal pay is a worthwhile objective if the men are well paid but it brings little joy if the men earn no more than the legal minimum wage or, even worse, if they have a zero hours contract in the gig economy. Equality in education is much needed but many working class men still have little opportunity to go to university. Unless that unfairness is corrected, equality in education means that young women from the poorest families are likely to suffer the same class-based disadvantage as many young men.

Female activists of the 1930s saw the desperate way in which women and men were treated during the Depression. When so many men were unemployed and downtrodden, feminist campaigners knew that their objective had to be more ambitious than merely demanding equality. There was less misery in the 1970s but the Women's Liberation Movement drew a similar conclusion. Equality was a strong initial demand but they could not accept that the aspirations of women should be limited to what men had, especially when some men had very little. What was needed then, and is needed now, is a more radical change in the system so that all discrimination is eliminated, and that means not just the disadvantage suffered by women but also the disadvantage suffered by those men whose life chances are shrunken by poverty and class prejudice.

This realisation takes a liberation campaign deep into political controversy. Equality between men and women is something that people across the political spectrum have eventually come to accept, but a programme to make the whole of society more equal, not just in terms of opportunity but also in terms of wealth and status, may only appeal to people on the left of politics. Yet the conclusion is inevitable. If arrangements in our society allow men to be left behind, women will be left behind too. If we desire utopia for women, our utopian vision must include men.

In 1927, the National Union of Societies for Equal Citizenship, the main organisation representing women in Britain, split apart.[15] Those who thought equality with men should be the sole aim, and that women should not campaign for any special treatment, left to join the Open Door Council. Most of those who stayed called themselves New Feminists and advocated a different approach that has great resonance today. Women should not focus on men; they should focus on themselves. Women, they said, should not be content with what men have. Instead, as Sheila Rowbotham, told us very firmly when we interviewed her last year:

'In future we should campaign to secure what women need.'

This is a crucial change of approach. The claim for equality with men should not be jettisoned but should be regarded as no more than a step on the way to a happier destination. From the outset, a new liberation campaign should set itself the objective of meeting the needs of women. If that involves revolutionary change in the society that men have created, then so be it. A better life for women will also mean, if they have the eyes to see it, a better life for most men.

Childcare

The need to focus on the needs of women is demonstrated in many aspects of public policy. Some feminists argue that women will not achieve equality until the rearing of children becomes the equal responsibility of both parents, with men having as much involvement as women. This notion makes us nervous.

Most of the women we have interviewed certainly want male partners to offer greater help on household matters like cleaning and laundry. But as we pointed out in Chapter 6, women also want to retain the right to be the default decision-maker on matters that affect their children. Sharing the work is one thing but ceding control would not be welcome. In time, a redistribution of power in respect of child rearing might be accepted but for the time being it is quite evident that this is not what mothers want or need.

Once women are accepted to be the primary carer, public policy must be planned accordingly. A failure to provide adequate childcare means that a woman's employment choices are seriously compromised. Choosing to work part-time to spend more time with your children is a reasonable decision but to be forced to work part-time because no-one else is available to look after the children is an assault on the right of women to lead a fulfilling life.

Unfortunately childcare provision in Britain has become a political game. Every unhelpful option has been considered from vouchers to tax relief. The current political trick is to offer a measure of free childcare and then fail to fund the system so that the childcare either never materialises or it has to be part-funded by paying poverty pay to the workers who look after the children. Britain's childcare policy is heavily criticised by the feminist writer Bea Campbell:

> "Britain is almost unique in Europe: it abolished universal child care after World War 2 and has never recovered from that. It has the lowest level of public child care among its European equivalents. That makes unequal distributions of paid and unpaid work inevitable, and it renders economic equality impossible. No Parliamentary party has made this a priority – and that's a disgrace."[16]

We agree. Adequate, well-funded and flexible childcare arrangements, free at the point of use, are essential if women are to have reasonable opportunities in life and at work.

But of course a society that puts the needs of men above the needs of women is unlikely to deliver the public policies that women require. Women cannot rely on favours of indulgences from powerful men. They must become decision-makers in their own cause. And they must have the necessary power to influence events, both economic and social.

Sharing Power

The word 'power' is a problem for most women. In our research we have found that securing more influence holds no fears but the prospect of having greater power evokes apprehension and some distaste. When we probe these feelings it becomes clear that what is so off-putting is not power itself but the way in which power has traditionally been exercised by men in this country and throughout most of the world. Male power is too often used to assert dominance. Men want to be in control of the people around them and that dominance tempts men to exercise power with arrogance and with a lack of respect for the rights and feelings of others. Women understand very well where the assertion of dominance can lead, because it is women who usually suffer its worst consequences.

However, when women actually achieve power in our society it is notable that they tend to consult more than men, strive harder to reach a consensus and show greater concern for people who are the potential losers in any decision they take. One experienced HR specialist told us that

> 'Women are more prepared to give more time to think through the consequences while men come to a conclusion quickly and cannot see the point of long discussion.'[17]

Not all women operate in this way; some apparently believe that there is no alternative to the male way and act accordingly. But female leadership at its best, while sometimes scorned by gung-ho men, brings a level of humanity to the exercise of power that some of our most celebrated 'captains of industry' very obviously lack. If, as we argue, increasing happiness takes us a step closer to utopia, then the female manner of exercising power must be the better model for the future.

Language is important and women rarely speak of 'taking power' from men. Women have little interest in replacing men as the dominant sex in our society but they want to escape from the historical cul-de-sac where women are considered to be less important than men and where women's interests and concerns are routinely neglected or ignored. The concept that is in harmony with the aspirations of most women is that our society should be redesigned so that the needs of women and men should have equal importance. Dominance by one sex should be replaced by a fairer and more beneficial model based on the sharing of power.

In the rather macho world of British business this might seem like a soft option. Some powerful men might hear the phrase 'power-sharing', raise their eyebrows slightly and imagine that, as long as they promote a few more women, they can carry on as before. That is a delusion which should be quickly dispelled. Throughout these pages, we have described the many disadvantages suffered by women. It is not just that most of the power is held by men: women have to fit into structures and institutions that have been designed by men for the convenience of men; women are judged more by their looks than by their abilities; women are expected to accept that men should be the leaders and that their role is to assist and support; at work, women are paid less and promoted less; at home, women are expected to do most of the cooking, cleaning and laundry as well as being the default carer; when women have children their difficulties intensify. Power sharing means that all this and much else has to change.

Seeing is Believing

An Institute of Management Survey[18] has found that women are much more optimistic about the prospects of promotion if they could see women at the top of their company. Seeing is believing, and few women will believe that power is being shared if the top jobs continue to be held overwhelmingly by men. If we are to change our culture, we need to put more and more women into senior positions and to do it quickly.

In Chapter 7, we told the story of Lord Davies' valiant attempt to increase the number of women in the boardrooms of Britain's biggest companies. It was a voluntary programme and we noted that some companies were reluctant to volunteer.

The Norwegian Government also tried a voluntary approach but got tired of waiting for progress. Its solution was to impose a quota system by law. Women were guaranteed a certain number of seats around the boardroom tables of companies quoted on the Oslo Stock Exchange.

All sorts of predictions were made about the awful consequences of such a move. There would be too few suitably qualified women; shareholders would no longer invest in Norway's industry; quotas would reduce economic growth and ruin the Norwegian economy.

Rather than accept the truth of these rumours we decided to ask the Norwegians themselves. At the beginning of 2013, we arranged for five Norwegian experts to speak to a conference of MPs and others at the House of Commons.[19] The speakers told us that the rumours were completely untrue. The introduction of quotas enforced by law had proved such a success that even previously sceptical Norwegian businessmen are now supporters.

Apparently Une Amundsen had originally poked fun at the proposal. He even said that he might have to go to an escort agency to get enough women to serve on the board of his company! But nowadays he describes the quota law as 'a very positive move'. Board meetings are now more business-like and, in a surprise revelation, Amundsen told a leading Norwegian newspaper that the increase in the number of women board members means that,

> 'Men spend less time fooling about and there is much less
> dirty talk!'[20]

Norway's quota law is a model of power sharing. Identical guarantees are given to women and to men. Both sexes must have a minimum of 40% of the places in the boardroom of the biggest companies.

The comparison with Britain is stark. Norway achieved more in two years than Britain is likely to achieve in fifteen. The evidence strongly suggests that we should follow Norway's example. A new liberation campaign should support the introduction of a quota law in Britain based on the Norwegian model.

The Public Sector

It would be easy to extend the principle of power sharing to the public sector. Government at national and local level has the authority to make the appointments to the governing bodies of hundreds of public-owned and publicly funded organisations. There is no need to adopt a formal quota system. Control of the appointment process should be used to achieve gender parity as soon as possible and to maintain parity thereafter.

The same procedure should be used to ensure that the chairs of public bodies should be gender-balanced over time. However, progress will need to be carefully monitored. During the period of the coalition government, the cabinet office launched an initiative to improve the gender balance of public sector appointments. The advice was almost completely ignored by government departments.

The aim of these moves is to create a fresh culture in Britain in which gender power sharing becomes the norm and organisations which persist in retaining a preponderance of men on their governing bodies will, as a matter of course, be called out to explain and justify their apparently discriminatory practices. In time, and with the right level of public pressure, such organisations will come to be regarded in the same way as sports clubs which only accept male members: unfriendly, ridiculous and out of touch with the modern world.

Flexibility

Clearing the way for more ambitious women to reach the top has many advantages and those who are successful might begin to build a better future. But transforming society to the advantage of women is more than a numbers game. As Miriam David explains with characteristic sharpness:

> 'More women does not mean more equality. This is misogyny masquerading as metrics.'[21]

We believe that allowing more women to reach senior position is valuable but we accept that the reform cannot be said to bring early benefit to the millions of women who have little aspiration to reach the top but who suffer significant disadvantage and discouragement throughout their working lives.

Most employers have never really come to terms with the needs of women workers. Men are expected to work continuously on a full-time basis from the end of their education until retirement. This is regarded as the norm and working practices are based on that expectation. But most women have a very different career pattern. Women need time off to give birth and, when they are the primary carer, to rear children. As their caring commitments change over time, many women also want flexible working arrangements which allow them to change their hours from full-time to part-time and back again.

Maternity leave is a legal right but many employers still regard such breaks as a great nuisance and a few are downright unhappy with the need to keep a job open until the mother returns to work.

A long-serving councillor in the home counties complained bitterly to me (John) about the behaviour of one of the women who provided support to the elected members of his Council. She had just returned from a year of maternity leave.

> "We used temps to cover her job for all that time. But now she is coming back to work and wants to switch to part-time hours. That just causes us even more problems. We were loyal to her but she has shown no loyalty at all to us."

I asked him, rather provocatively, which was more important, giving birth or looking after his Council's elected members. He gave no answer but looked at me as if I had gone mad.

In practice the responsibility to look after elderly relatives and other family dependants also falls on women. There is no right to take leave from work to attend to these duties. The best that is being suggested is that the employer might allow the carer to take up to a year of unpaid leave but, once again, that would be at the employer's discretion.

A more routine problem is securing time off at short notice to deal with the illness of children, the collapse of childcare arrangements and other emergencies. Once again the discretion of the employer is involved and most women do not have the time or the inclination to argue the point, particularly when it might involve discussing matters that most people would want to keep private. As a result many women pretend that they are sick – a harmless subterfuge until they are caught and the white lie suddenly becomes the cause of disciplinary action.

Given goodwill, these issues could be easily settled. A period of emergency leave could be a matter of right rather than discretion. The availability of a range of more flexible hours would enable women to plan their lives so that domestic commitments could be better accommodated. Job-shares could be offered more often. In some places, a more relaxed attitude to working at home could be adopted, switching the commitment away from attendance to a requirement to complete an agreed schedule of work.

Across the business community there are dozens of bright ideas that would reduce stress and raise productivity but most are rarely used unless shortages of staff become so acute that employers have to improve their offer to potential recruits. Without that pressure, the world of work clings to hidebound practices which cause no great difficulty to men but which impede women like an assault course designed by a male with limited imagination.

Predictability

Flexibility is generally helpful to women but it can be a slippery concept and needs to be handled with care.

Denise (not her real name) works as a care assistant in a residential home in West Sussex. She is paid the minimum rate allowed by law and is contracted to work 5 shifts of 8 hours, some of which are at weekends. Her shifts are often changed at short notice to cover busy periods and she is sometimes expected to work well beyond her normal finishing time. She has three children and often cannot tell her aunt, who mostly looks after the children, when she will be able to pick them up.

Denise and her colleagues wanted to be given early warning about changes in their hours so they could sort out their childcare cover. They were told that 'working flexibly' is for the benefit of the residents and is part of the job.

Very many women work for low pay in demanding jobs. Denise is lucky because at least she has a fixed-hours contract. Cathy works for an agency on a zero-hours contract and does not know from one week to the next whether she will have any work or pay. In 2017, she told a conference in London[22] that she has no paid holiday and no company sick scheme. Work is often offered at the last minute and Cathy is worried that if she says no, she will be marked down as unreliable and will be offered fewer shifts in the future. If there is any hint of complaint, her boss tells Cathy and her colleagues that she must 'work flexibly'.

Sally Brett, Head of Equality, Inclusion and Culture at the British Medical Association, warns employees to be wary of flexibility that is under the control of management.

> "Of course women welcome flexibility if it means they are allowed to make changes that allow them to balance work with family life, but it is often managers who switch things around at short notice and that means that women cannot plan their daily lives. When I worked at the TUC, one trade union representative from the retail sector, told me that what many women need most is not flexibility but predictability. At the BMA now, I see huge challenges for women junior doctors who are sometimes given very little notice of their placements and rotas, and are often expected to work extra hours at the end of shifts to meet service demands."[23]

Many of our current working practices should not exist in a civilised country. As trade union membership has declined, the notion that pay, hours and conditions of work should be a matter of agreement between employer and employees has faded. In many places, pay is too low, working hours are too long and the right to challenge unfair decisions by management has all but disappeared.

Men suffer too but by and large women bear the bigger burden because they do the worst paid jobs in the least regulated parts of the economy.

In Chapter 3 we criticised Winston Churchill for his unsympathetic attitude to women's suffrage but at least he had enough humanity to set up Wages Councils to protect workers from exploitation in industries where they were most vulnerable. Women need a new system of protection very badly – and so do an increasing number of men.

Disrupt the System

Incremental reform can be very helpful but if we really want men and women to have the same level of opportunity, much more radical change is needed. Merely adapting a system which is firmly based on male patterns of life will not be enough to meet the needs of women.

The main problem is that our current employment practices penalise women who take breaks from work to have children. Many employers regard the taking of breaks as an indication of unreliability – 'she will be off again next year to have another baby' – and, of course, while she is on leave, the men gain experience and apply for better jobs. When a woman returns to work, she generally finds that she has been left behind by her peers and has to play catch-up.

The best way to remove what amounts to indirect discrimination is to disrupt the current system by ensuring that all employees, male and female, take breaks from work as a matter of course during their working lives. Instead of being a female phenomenon, work breaks should become a normal feature of employment.

Like all the best reforms, work breaks would bring a multiplicity of benefits. Babies born this month are likely to live to a hundred and this implies that the average working life will increase to about sixty years. With rapid changes in technology, breaks from work to train and retrain will be essential to ensure that the workforce is adequately equipped. People will also want to change the direction of their career, try something new or deepen their knowledge by taking a degree course. They might just want a period of reflection after decades of work, or they might wish to indulge a new interest or spend some time working as a volunteer. The possibilities are legion.

These opportunities should be open to both men and women. They can accommodate childbirth and if breaks become routine and carry no penalties, men will be much more willing to share the obligation to look after their young children or to support older dependants.

The significant additional benefit is that career breaks will be enormously popular with men. Over the years I (John) have lost track of the number of men who have told me that they feel trapped in their present job. Maybe the work turned out to be different from what they expected, maybe the management has changed and the workplace has become less congenial, maybe they are bored and want more stimulating work, or maybe they want to escape from what they regard as unacceptable pressure. The reasons are many but the symptom is the same. Going to work becomes a bigger and bigger burden.

For many men it is a problem that has no ready solution.

'I don't want to look as if I am giving up.'

'I cannot afford to be out of work.'

'How will I pay the mortgage?'

'Where can I find a better job?'

'I don't have the skills to move to the job I would really like.'

So they soldier on, unfulfilled, miserable and sometimes sliding into depression. Offering these men career breaks of one, two or three years during which they could plan a better future would be like handing them the key to their cage.

Of course the breaks will have to be properly paid and, to avoid unreasonable pressure on individual employers, the state will have to bear the cost. This seems revolutionary until people realise that all that is proposed is the creation of something like a new pension entitlement, to be taken during each person's working life instead of at the end of it.

Some misanthropes will ask where the money will come from. We should remind them that the people taking the paid breaks will have the burden of working for an increased number of years, and will be paying taxes for a much longer period. In any case we need to disrupt a tired old system of work which penalises women and often traps men in jobs they no longer want to do. We should design something better.

We believe that this policy is not only necessary but will also bring the much-needed humanity to the world of work. A person will be able to find a new direction in life, follow a private passion, take a second or third chance at higher education or just spend some time thinking about life and smelling the flowers.

This policy would make women and men happier; it might even be called utopian.

10

Living the Impossible Dream

Our programme to secure a better life for women is extensive and might, in the fashion of our times, be dismissed as little more than a wish list.

Women are accustomed to this brand of cynicism. In the years before the First World War women were repeatedly told that they did not need the vote. Fifty years later they were ridiculed for suggesting that discrimination against women should be against the law. Yet they won the vote and sexual discrimination is now illegal.

The victories took time and, as Joan Bakewell has shrewdly observed,

> '(it is) a long slow process... Like the tectonic plates it will buck and shudder. But it cannot come to an end. It cannot be written off. We are, after all, half the human race.'[1]

Creating a society that gives as much importance to the needs of women as to the needs of men and where power is more equally shared between the sexes is not easy. It will entail overturning the cultural norms that sustain male supremacy and changing the way women and men see themselves. It must be understood for what it is. We are not proposing some modest process of reform. This is a revolution.

Political Power

A new liberation campaign with great and utopian ambitions will need strong political support. The women's campaigns stalled in the 1920s and again in the 1980s because there were too few women in parliament to sustain progress. As late as 1996, there were only 60 women in the House of Commons, sitting among 590 men. An important objective of a new liberation campaign must be to achieve a much better gender balance in parliament.

The number of women MPs has increased significantly in the last twenty years and this has created the impression that the problem of under-representation has been solved. This is an illusion. As a result of the 2017 General Election, women MPs make up less than a third of the House of Commons. What this means in practice is that there are over 200 more men in the Commons than women. As a result, there are more men than women on all the important committees, more male speakers in all the important debates, more male MPs commenting to the media and of course, many more men than women in the Cabinet. And when political priorities are discussed, the male view is almost certain to get the greater support.

The main political parties are in very different positions. Women Labour MPs make up 45% of the Parliamentary Labour Party. On the other hand, women MPs in the Conservative Party comprise a small minority: only 21%. The reason why the Labour position is very much better is because the Labour Party decided over twenty years ago to use all-women shortlists in the selection of many parliamentary candidates.[2]

In 2005, the Conservative Party reviewed its position and decided that it was not in favour of all-women shortlists or other 'equality guarantees'. The Conservative Party prefer,

> 'to use equality rhetoric and promotion measures to increase the number of its women candidates'.[3]

The result of this policy has not been encouraging. There was no increase in the proportion of Conservative women MPs elected in 2017 and Conservative women are still outnumbered 4 to 1 by male Conservative MPs.

The effectiveness of the various methods of increasing the number of women MPs has been assessed by researchers such as Rosie Campbell and Sarah Childs. They concluded that rhetoric and promotion are much less effective in increasing the number of women MPs than 'equality guarantees' like all-women shortlists.[4]

When he was Prime Minister and Leader of the Labour Party, Gordon Brown reinforced this conclusion. He told the Speaker's Conference that,

> 'under representation of women historically, we have found, can only be addressed by all-women shortlists'.

Other solutions have been proposed. The Women and Equalities Committee of the House of Commons recommended that 45% of each Party's candidates should be women. This recommendation is supported by the Fawcett Society. Sam Smethers, the Society's Chief Executive, believes that the disappointingly small increase in women MPs resulting from the 2017 General Election shows that

> 'The time has come for a legally enforceable target to achieve the radical and sustainable change we need.'[5]

We do not believe that a new liberation campaign needs to spend much time prescribing the precise method of selecting candidates. Much more important is the outcome. If the Conservatives can discover some other system that delivers the same improvement as all-women shortlists, they should be free to use it. However, a new liberation campaign should insist that, within a reasonable period, all parties should achieve gender parity in the House of Commons. Since election results are not altogether predictable, a small amount of leeway might be allowed.

Of course an added complication is that not all of the new women MPs will be feminists or even believe that parity of representation in parliament is desirable. Candidates with the biggest doubts tend to say the least; they should be prompted to say more. A new liberation campaign should ask every female candidate whether she supports the aims of the campaign. If the answer is no or, more likely, if the question is ignored, campaigners should ensure that every elector in the constituency knows that the candidate does not take gender issues seriously. This was an approach that worked well in the Votes for Women campaign and it should be used again.

Campaigners are more likely to gain strong support in parliament if the politicians feel that the public are ready for substantial change. Encouraging that change will require great energy from the campaigners and the enthusiastic encouragement of the more progressive forces in our society.

Virginia Woolf describes the first time she set eyes on Ethel Smyth, the composer of the suffragette anthem 'March of the Women':

'bustling down the gangway of the Wigmore Hall, in tweeds and spats, a little cock's feather in your felt hat and a general air of angry energy'.[6]

Ethel Smyth takes us back to Voltaire:

"Success and happiness are by no means synonymous but I am certain that 'cultivating your garden' is the sole way to be happy. Only you must dig and plant with all your heart, for doing things by halves is the most boring thing to the mind."[7]

The Role of the Arts

Elsewhere in this chapter we have said that in order to facilitate sustainable change there will need to be a significant cultural shift. Evidence seems to suggest that in order to challenge and excite people's imagination we need to turn to the arts.

The movement of the arts has to run in concert with the movement of politics.

Inspiration for an improved society is often initiated by what we see and hear in films, theatres, galleries and concert halls. These experiences release our imagination, dusting away familiar, stultifying cobwebs.

'Without leaps of the imagination we lose the excitement of possibilities. Dreaming is after all a form of planning.' says Gloria Steinem.[8]

During the two women's campaigns theatre, dance, music, painting and sculpture flourished. This was not a coincidence. During periods of intellectual revolution and political upheaval we tend to find what energises us.

Members of The Actresses Franchise League, founded in 1908, coached women unused to public speaking to project themselves

and they helped to choreograph and stage some of the political spec-
tacles of the campaign. Plays by former actresses turned playwrights,
like Cicely Hamilton and Elizabeth Robinson, were commissioned
by women who briefly took over the running of theatres in the early
1900s. Women supporting the campaign for women's suffrage toured
with agit-prop comic realist monologues and duologues which were,

'accessible, politically structured and entertaining'.[9]

The artistic experiences that endure in our minds tend to be based
on an underlying optimism about the human spirit. We are invited
to see ourselves through the lives of characters on the screen or the
stage or in the pages of a novel.

Life Interpreted Through the Arts

The First World War has been portrayed extensively in plays,
music, literature and film. The poems of Wilfred Owen published
in 1918 are lasceratingly beautiful. They were later set to music by
Benjamin Britten in his War Requiem as an eloquent pacifist plea,
and first performed in 1962 in the newly restored Coventry Cathe-
dral, bombed almost to destruction during the Second World War.
The poignant final image of the young German soldier in the 1930
film All Quiet on the Western Front (1930) killed while reaching
up to a butterfly flying above his trench symbolises the pitiless
brutality of that war in a way that no amount of scenes of battle
ever could.

Joan Littlewood's production of Oh What a Lovely War caused a
theatrical sensation in 1969. Her method is to lull us into a false
sense of security through laughter at the ritualistic antics of the
army top brass before jerking us back to reality by projecting on a
screen behind the actors the numbers of men who died fighting over
the few hundred yards lost or gained in the carnage of the Somme
and Ypres. As actor David Whitworth told us,

'There is an emotional connection in the theatre between performers and the audience.'

The context of these artistic expressions is grim but, in asking us to read, watch, hear and absorb their message, they are presented in the hope that we will not repeat the same mistakes.

Predating the Women's Liberation Movement, *A Taste of Honey* by the nineteen-year-old Shelagh Delaney was staged by Joan Littlewood in 1958. It told the story of Jo, a young working class girl, effectively abandoned by her feckless mother, pregnant after a one-night stand with Jimmie a black sailor. She is looked after and cared for by her gay friend Geof 'this pansified little freak' as her mother calls him, which probably exemplifies the majority opinion at the time. The play forces us to confront prejudices about lifestyle, class, race and homophobia. Art presaging changes in attitude.

Joan Littlewood described Shelagh Delaney as the antithesis of London's 'Angry Young Men':

'She knows what she is angry about.'

Delaney was followed among others by the socialist feminist Caryl Churchill whose plays were put on through the 1960s and 1970s and who is still writing today.

Nell Dunn's novels, *Up the Junction,* in 1963[10] and *Poor Cow*[11] in 1967 were turned into successful films under the direction of Ken Loach.

'Live performances capturing a communal vividness'[12] continued to be staged by feminist theatre groups and companies like Spare Tyre, Monstrous Regiment, Cunning Stunts and Red Ladder who took to the stage to poke fun at men and masculinity.

Companies like these prospered throughout the 1970s after which, under the unsympathetic Thatcher government, funding was withdrawn and many companies and theatre groups folded.

These examples illustrate the influence of the arts during the two central women's campaigns of the twentieth century, but we all have individual ways of cultivating our personal gardens and most of us would agree that making or listening to music, watching or acting in a play or successfully finishing a painting alone or with others enables us, temporarily at least, to shake off external worries or burdens.

Conversely they might in fact serve the useful purpose of helping us to face the problems that are troubling us, but at a distance. They give us precious time and space to be absorbed in a parallel world. They may also help us to focus on new ideas. They give us the opportunity to contemplate alternatives to the way we conduct our lives.

Theatre Points the Way

The plays of contemporary women playwrights like Timberlake Wurtenbaker, Lucy Prebble and Laura Wade have received critical acclaim.

David Whitworth again:

> 'Women's role in the theatre has changed. When I started in the 1960s the assistant stage managers were always women. There are now far more women stage managers and also directors.'

When we interviewed Paul Miller, Artistic Director of the Orange Tree Theatre in Richmond he said,

'Plays by men about women are not enough. Theatre directors are very conscious of diversity and gender and are staging plays with gender blind casting – women cast in male roles.'

He also told us that theatre is where change begins and is then taken up by television which is more conservative, but will eventually follow theatre's lead. Writers for the hugely popular Sunday night slot like Sally Wainwright (*Happy Valley*) and Heidi Thomas (*Call the Midwife*) started in the theatre and are now telling stories which,

'have helped to alter people's consciousness. They have enabled discussion and debate'.

Theatre and Opera Director, Sophie Gilpin, said of Phyllida Lloyd's all-female productions at the Donmar Theatre of Shakespeare's *Julius Caesar, Henry 1 V and the Tempest*,

'It was probably the most wonderful theatrical experience of my life.'

The reviews for this brave enterprise were universally ecstatic as were those for the more recent National Theatre production of *Twelfth Night* with Tamsin Greig playing Malvolia.

Exciting and original casting teach us to think about gender in new ways.

The most striking example of the arts influencing and merging with politics is that of the dissident playwright Vaclav Havel who, having spent several years in prison because of his political opinions, was elected President of Czechoslovakia in 1989 and then of the Czech Republic in 1993.

The Effect of Films

The films and television shows which are the most effective in making us think about the way we choose to live are fundamentally affectionate and slightly anarchic.

In his 1950s films, *Monsieur Hulot's Holiday* and *Mon Oncle*, Jacques Tati asks us to consider a more congenial life style. Through his gauche innocence, Monsieur Hulot creates unwitting havoc in a sedate French seaside resort. His unworldly enjoyment of simple pleasures is juxtaposed to the American businessman who is constantly and manically answering long-distance phone calls.

In *Mon Oncle*, Monsieur Hulot is bemused by his sister and brother-in-law's modern but sterile lifestyle, largely controlled by gadgets. By contrast, Monsieur Hulot resides at the top of a somewhat ramshackle house. As he climbs the stairs he passes a silent canary in a cage. In a symbolic gesture, he carefully turns his window pane round so that the bird can bask in the reflection of the sun and the bird, though still incarcerated, instantly starts to sing loudly and joyfully. Its spirit is liberated.

This example (and there are countless others) invites us to consider the possibilities, albeit constrained, of a different way of seeing the world.

Freedom from convention may be fleeting but it is alluring.

Our participation in these moments of illicit rebellion are admittedly transient but our memory of them is surely lodged somewhere in our emotions.

The Power of Television

Lighter and easier to digest, but no less forthright and compelling is the work of female comedians.

Victoria Wood and Jo Brand stand out as women performers challenging convention. They have made provocative television series, forcefully reminding us about the role women are expected to play in our society.

The late Victoria Wood was self-deprecatingly and unsparingly funny about the accumulated personal indignities and frustrations faced by women. Her audiences wince but laugh with her.

Jo Brand is more openly antagonistic in confronting the way women are treated by many men. Like Victoria Wood, her humour is self-deprecating, but she is not afraid to express herself in language and mannerisms that mirror the vulgarity she is criticising.

Dave Jones was used to producing successful television documentaries about a variety of serious issues. However, as he said,

> 'I think a better way to get people to think and do something is through drama.'

He felt that the viewer could more readily identify with the characters on the screen. The result was his 1991 series, *GBH*, through which, as a Liverpudlian himself, he attacked the corruption on Liverpool Council at that time. He was correct in his view that this was a more direct way of reaching his audience. The series had a big impact. It made people think and talk and perhaps it even changed the nature of local politics in Liverpool.

Olivia Colman playing DS Ellie Miller in the television drama series *Broadchurch,* watched by millions, reacts with undisguised fury when she finds pornographic images on her son's mobile phone. No amount of homilies by parents and teachers could have the same impact.

From his television film *Cathy Come Home* in 1966 right through to *I, Daniel Blake* released in cinemas in 2016, Ken Loach has been a consistent critic of successive governmental measures blighting the lives of vulnerable people.

The domestic abuse of Helen in *The Archers*, though fictional, made headline news for several days. The desperation of this one woman in a popular radio series, mirroring that of the many referred to earlier in this chapter, caught the public's imagination in a way that the statistics rarely can.

Classical Music Lags Behind

The world of classical music still has some way to go in terms of gender equality. In our discussion with professional singers Elizabeth Roberts and Christopher Foster, it was clear that they felt optimistic about future possibilities. In Chapter 1 we quoted Elizabeth saying,

'The arts reflect back to us what is and also what could be.'

But both have reservations about the current situation. Christopher told us that it was a teacher at his comprehensive school who recognised his musical ability and sent him home with an Eb Horn. 'But those opportunities for children in state schools are diminishing now', he said.

Both reminded us of disturbing tales of abuse by people in positions of authority – conductors and directors – which go unchallenged because musicians are understandably concerned about the effect of 'whistle-blowing' on their own careers.

More positively, Elizabeth told us that when she was teaching in a girls' school she encouraged girls 'to find their own voice and carry that through to other area of their lives'.

We hope that her pupils found the confidence to heed this valuable advice.

We need to look further afield to find an effective fusion of politics and classical music. The East-Western Divan Orchestra was founded by Jewish conductor Daniel Barenboim and Palestinian philosopher, Edward Said. The orchestra is made up of young musicians from Israel and surrounding Arab countries determined to work for peace by learning to play together in an atmosphere of trust and respect. After a concert in Ramallah in 2004, with tensions running high, Daniel Barenboim declared,

> 'Either we kill each other or we share what there is to share. This is the message we come here to bring.'

Artists and Art

If asked to name artists, most of us can reel off the names of many male painters. Female painters do not come to mind so easily.

Until this century, women in the art world were models, mistresses or muses, some eventually becoming painters in their own right, like Berthe Morisot and Suzanne Valadon. This situation has improved and we can point to Freda Kahlo and Georgia O'Keeffe through to contemporary female artists like Marlene Dumas and Tracey Emin. Between 2010 and 2016 four winners of the prestigious Turner Prize were women and Maria Balshaw, the newly appointed director of Tate Modern has a history of championing women artists.

The impact of the visual arts is immediate and our emotions are instantly engaged.

When better to begin to introduce the enjoyment of art in all its forms than with young children?

> 'The art experience should be irresistible ... it should stimulate children's curiosity, creativity and excitement',

says Suzy Tutchell leader of Primary Art Education at Reading University. While they are at university, her (mainly female) students see themselves as artists and she hopes that this message can be conveyed to their pupils when they start on their careers in schools. 'However', she told us, on her visits to school she finds 'classrooms where art is disappearing'.

The art of Ricky Romain and Heather Fallows[13] is intentionally and overtly political. They create work about the displaced and the dispossessed, in particular telling the stories of refugees.

> 'My figures carry nothing with them other than their memories', says Ricky. 'The artist's palate is empathy. It is our responsibility to use our platform through our paintings.'

Heather agrees and adds,

> 'artists create and hook into the zeitgeist'.

Their exhibitions are enhanced by events such as talks and workshops so that their message can be discussed and then more widely disseminated through social media.

Literature

Affection and anarchy are the staples of Babette Cole's gently teasing books questioning gender stereotypes. Children fall on *Princess Smartypants*[14] and *Prince Cinders*[15] with joy – and so do adults. The prolific children's writer Michael Rosen is a tireless campaigner for children's rights and he attacks injustice through his writing in a way that appeals but is not didactic.

There are so many novelists to choose from who have strong women as their main characters. Mary Anne Evans had to write under the pseudonym George Eliot in order to find a publisher in the nineteenth century and her novel *Middlemarch* published in 1871, exposes the status of women and their aspirations.[16] She is unlikely to have called herself a feminist but the message of her novels undoubtedly still rings true to feminists today. Similarly, Winifred Holtby is hailed by many as a feminist for her 1936 novel *South Riding*[17] but she herself only reluctantly submits to that description. Writing in the *Yorkshire Post* in 1926 she says firmly,

> 'While inequality exists, while injustice is done and opportunity denied to the great majority of women, I shall have to be a feminist.'[18]

Our current poet laureate has no such qualms. Carol Ann Duffy is unequivocally an unrepentant feminist. The concept of a gay woman poet laureate would have been totally unthinkable even 50 years ago. Without the predecessors above, to whom she is the heir, she would not hold this post now. And good use she makes of it.

The more recent extraordinary statements and tweets issued by President Trump caused a huge rise in the sales of George Orwell's *1984*.[19] Incredulous about the crass utterances of the most powerful man in the world, people turned to dystopian literature in order to believe that such apparent disregard for the sensitivities of women in particular was possible.

The arts have the potential to change our view of the world.

We believe that the cuts in the funding of the arts in schools is nothing less than a betrayal of the next generation.

Philip Hedley was the Artistic Director of Theatre Royal, Stratford East for twenty-five years, having originally worked there with

Joan Littlewood. He always actively encouraged and was engaged with local schools in London's East End. He told us,

> 'Drama is being dropped in many schools. Drama was the only subject that young people in Newham excelled in above the national average.'

A future liberation movement needs to develop a mutually supportive campaign to preserve the arts in education. We would all benefit from such action.

As the playwright Alan Plater used to say,

> 'The most precious asset a nation has is the imagination of its children.'[20]

Organising the Campaign

We have advocated a far-sighted and perhaps utopian agenda of policies, an expectation of social progress stimulated by the arts and a strong cohort of women MPs. If the new liberation campaign is to succeed, these conditions must be used to best advantage. The campaign itself has to be designed and organised with great care.

In Chapter 6, we set out the lessons from the suffrage struggle and from the Women's Liberation Movement. We concluded that the new liberation campaign should be democratic to the core, run by women for women, encouraging local initiatives rather than enforcing central control. Its appeal must cross the boundaries of class and ethnicity so that it is seen to represent the interests of women from all backgrounds. It will need the resilience of Millicent Fawcett's suffrage societies, the imaginative presentation that kept Emmelene Pankhurst's WSPU constantly in the news and the compelling vision of revolutionary change that energised the Women's Liberation Movement.

The task is momentous and the temptation is to ignore what already exists and start afresh. That was the aim of a group of feminists who formed the Women' Equality Party (WEP). In spite of considerable advice about the weaknesses of their initiative, the founders decided to go ahead. Their first problem was that the large number of women activists in other political Parties, were effectively excluded from the WEP. Political parties do not allow their members to support the candidates of other parties, so before female activists in the Labour Party or the Lib Dems or the SNP could do anything to help the WEP, they would have had to resign from their own party. Understandably most declined to do so.

When WEP candidates contested the 2017 General Election they confronted the second problem. Voters are reluctant to 'waste' their vote on a party that has little chance of winning. In the event WEP fielded seven candidates and they all lost their deposits. None achieved even 2% of the vote and the average was under 1%. Sophie Walker, the WEP Leader, said she did not expect to win when she stood in Shipley but she wanted to attract publicity for WEP policies. When asked if these policies might not be better pursued through the bigger parties, she said that she,

'would be delighted if other Parties stole (WEP) policies'.

Perhaps the most constructive way forward is for WEP to seek a commitment from the other parties that they support the WEP's seven core propositions.[21] It is likely that, with the exception of the Conservatives, every major party would be sympathetic.

Rather than disregard the work that is already being done, the best approach is surely to build on it. We have identified over a hundred organisations which represent women. Some are small and local, some see their purpose as information exchange, a good number represent women in particular occupations and a few support particular magazines. However, about thirty are national organisations engaged in campaigning, principally for better reproductive rights, against rape and sexual assault, against domestic violence, against pornography, for more effective control of the internet, for improved rights for women from particular ethnic and religious communities, for specific changes in the law and for greater representation of women in parliament. Women's groups in trade unions and women's sections in some political parties are also engaged in extensive campaigning.

Much good work is being done and there is strength in this diversity. But the weakness is obvious. There is little coordination of aims and activities. If the campaigns worked together and applied collective pressure, the influence of female activists would be greatly increased. What is missing is a truly national campaign bringing together women from all backgrounds and demanding change not just in respect of particular detriments but focusing on the massive transformation which is necessary to improve the role and status of women. When we interviewed Sarah Veale, Equality and Human Rights Commissioner and for many years a leading strategist for the TUC, she spoke of the need to,

'draw the threads together'.

This is exactly the approach that the new liberation campaign should take. Individual campaigning organisations should not lose their purpose and their autonomy: what is needed is not a reduction in the number of campaigning groups but a much greater acceptance among female activists that they must work together to maximise their strength. As Natasha Walter has argued,

'if we want to see changes, we ... need solidarity and action'.[22]

The key to solidarity is mutual trust and that has to be built with diligence. A few feminists have suggested that a big conference of all campaigning organisations should be convened and all the participants should be urged to commit themselves to work in unity. Conferences can be triumphant but they can also be fraught. At the right moment a well-run conference can increase morale and inspire the participants, but perhaps it is better planned for the second stage, after a period of cooperative endeavour and when the case for working together in solidarity has already won strong-hearted support.

Rather than a blanket approach, we prefer the metaphor of the snowball, rolling forward and growing incrementally in size. The most representative women's campaigning organisation is the Fawcett Society. It has an enthusiastic membership, a strong record of campaigning on a range of issues important to women and, of course, its name is a constant reminder of past success.

We suggest that the Fawcett Society approaches the principal campaigning organisations, proposing that they begin to form a new confederation. The discussions should be sisterly and it should be stressed that the idea is not to create some tightly unified structure but to form a cooperative venture of mutual support. The leadership might rotate between the membership organisations but, applying the lessons from the Women's Liberation Movement, the new Liberation Campaign should always have representative spokeswomen. We suggest three specialist officers: a spokeswoman to communicate with the media, a political officer to liaise with women MPs and trade unions and an officer to connect with people in the Arts.

In full knowledge of the criticism which was directed at earlier campaigns, the confederation should establish and maintain a diversity of membership. It must not be seen to be captured by one

class, by one ethnic community or by one energetic group. Close
contact with the trade unions should help to ensure a deep knowledge of working practices and how they affect women.

The new liberation campaign will need to decide early priorities
and some of these might produce limited reforms. They should
be celebrated but no one should pretend that a cluster of specific
reforms will deliver utopia or anything like it. Mary Stott has
asked the key question,

> 'If women's liberation concentrates on "reformist"
> demands, can it really achieve its aims of changing funda-
> mental attitudes?'[23]

As we have insisted, the aim of the new liberation campaign has
to be revolutionary. It should be guided by the mantra of the new
feminists. The demand is not just for equality with men but for
everything that women need to live a fulfilling life. And if they
need the Moon, that should be the truth that the new liberation
campaign must speak in the citadels of power.

Cultivating Our Gardens

If we agree with the feminist composer Ethel Smyth, that we
need to cultivate our gardens and that these need to be plenti-
fully stocked with flourishing arts, what other seeds do we need to
plant? And if we are also to act upon her advice that we need to
'dig and plant with all our hearts' what will motivate us to strive
energetically to create the kind of society we want to live in?

As Susie Orbach warns,

> 'Knowing what you don't want is one thing. Discovering
> what you do want is an entirely different adventure.'[24]

How do we prepare ourselves to embark on this adventure with the 'enthusiasm and creative power', 'unbridled optimism' and 'evangelical power' that Lois Graessler, Catherine Hall and Micheline Wandor[25] found during the Women's Liberation Movement? Is it possible or desirable to go beyond what Mary Stott called 'reformist demands' to 'changing fundamental attitudes'? In our view, unless we are brave enough to take that step, unnerving and unpredictable though the results might be, we are short-changing future aspirations of girls and women.

Sheila Rowbotham and Lynne Segal, respected pioneers of the Women's Liberation Movement, direct us to 'visions of a better life, of what might be'. If we share John Stuart Mill's belief in human progress, it is up to us to pave the way. Michelene Wandor urges us to,

> 'keep believing change is possible. We're not dead. We're just waiting'.

We cannot afford to wait any longer.

If we are serious about creating a new and more equal society it seems sensible to begin with education.

Nicholas Hytner, former director of the National Theatre, makes a strenuous appeal to politicians not to ignore the creative arts.

> 'Politicians talk up our world-beating arts scene, then cut the classes teaching creativity.'[26]

As we have seen, in state schools drama, art, dance and music are suffering from cutbacks in teachers with the enthusiasm, qualifications and skills to teach these subjects. The emphasis is on test results and targets in maths, science, English and technology which are felt to be of more practical use in a world where success is measured by the values of a competitive, unforgiving enterprise culture. Even in academia, Jessica Ringrose is concerned about the

> 'relentless focus on performance, competition and achievement'.[27]

There is no doubt that girls have overtaken boys in school in terms of examination results and they are gradually becoming more visible in top jobs but, asks Angela McRobbie, at what cost? Are young women satisfied with what they have achieved? If she is correct, they are beset by anxieties about their performance in the workplace and a prey to a rampant consumer culture preaching perfection. As Marie Bailey, a young and successful academic, told us:

> "As women we are educated to sacrifice in order to get on, but the sacrifice isn't worth it. The need to be perfect in every way has made things worse. There is a constant fear of failure: physically, emotionally, socially and financially."

This is not what previous generations of feminists have fought for.

Perhaps part of the problem may be the way we are forced to behave in schools now. For many years teachers have been encouraged to teach and show respect. This is not something they should just preach in school assemblies or personal and social education lessons, but should be a necessary aspect of their whole bearing and approach. Most teachers will attempt to fulfil that obligation (after all, getting the best out of children is why they entered the profession) but they feel harassed by the pressure of unreasonable amounts of paperwork and pushing pupils in directions they have little sympathy with. Listening takes time and time is a casualty of a new, increasingly sterile regime. If we really believe in the importance of educating future generations, then the resources and support have to be made available.

Cuts continue to bite, leaving schools desperate for cash at the most basic level. Alarming numbers of teachers and support staff are being made redundant. We read stories of head teachers leaving the profession exhausted and disheartened by the levels of commitment required of them to sustain a system in which they have lost faith.

In Chapter 8, we touched upon the damaging use of pornography by children as young as eleven years. This is a difficult and sensitive issue for teachers to raise with their pupils but, without the time, resources and skills to do so, the potential influence of some wise adults is lost and more abuse goes unchallenged.

In 1938, Virginia Woolf asked:

> 'What is the aim of education, what kind of society, what kind of human beings should it seek to produce?'[28]

Her question is still relevant today.

The feminist literary critic Elaine Showalter quotes Susan Sontag declaring:

> 'The first responsibility of a liberated woman is to live the fullest, freest and most imaginative life she can. The second responsibility is her solidarity with other women.'[29]

In order to live up to the first of Sontag's responsibilities, women need to attend to their own aspirations, desires and comforts. They need to try to overcome their fear of disapproval, of conflict, of personal criticism. They need to have the courage to stop being,

> 'adept at keeping the show on the road, coping, functioning and presenting an outside image of confidence'.[30]

They need to believe that the world will continue to exist if they cease seeing themselves in the role of supporting a system which usually works against their interests. They need to take a hefty spade to their own gardens instead of tending to the gardens of others.

Solidarity

Susan Sontag's second requirement is more thorny, but we should not shy away from it. Pauline Barrie, a university union representative, spoke to us about the disheartening effect of women colluding against other women. And she was not alone in making this accusation. Mary Daly is convinced that,

> 'members of an oppressed or minority group do in fact become inferior – just the way society desires, the prejudice reinforced'.[31]

Her argument certainly seems logical and carries weight. There is much evidence that women feel betrayed when they lose the support of members of their own sex. Such betrayal is more likely to happen in a harshly competitive atmosphere.

So we need to challenge the ambience to make it gentler and more receptive to the sisterhood that existed in the Women's Liberation Movement.

Sam Smethers, the CEO of The Fawcett Society said to us, 'Working lives have got to change' and we have suggested disrupting current employment practices that discourage anything other than an unbroken linear progression in our working lives.

By reclaiming and reinventing feminism we can reproduce the cooperation and sisterhood of the Women's s Liberation Movement. We need to remind ourselves that,

> 'in the early days of the women's movement we felt ourselves to be part of a supportive feminist community'.[32]

That is the spirit we have to recapture. Seasoned feminists working together with younger ones.

Libby Brooks notes that,

> 'when older women remind younger ones about the his-
> tory of the movement, it's because many of the answers to
> our present day questions can be found there'.[33]

Deborah Mattinson suggested to us that one way forward would
be to set up a group of older experienced feminists with younger
interested and committed women. They could work together to
produce a manifesto for women's equality.

Ivana Bartoletti and Christine Megson of the Fabian Women's Network have developed a successful mentoring scheme for women
from all walks of life who are keen to become councillors and MPs.

Katie Learmonth, a young feminist told us that she seems to exist in
'a perpetual state of outrage'. Her friends (both men and women)
are feminists and she is an active member of a women's group
at her work in the Environment Agency but equality still seems
elusive outside her immediate circle. Ashleigh, the 23-year-old
working in the publishing industry, whom we quoted in previous
chapters, agrees:

> "Feminism is essential for equality. My friends and I spend
> a lot of time talking about women's equality. We were
> walking up Helvellyn recently and as we puffed out way
> to the top it was the main topic of conversation!"

Like Katie, she is becoming impatient with the hesitation among
women of her age to describe themselves as feminists.

How much of this reluctance can be laid at the door of social
media? Communication by text and email rather than face-to-face
conversation must take its toll. Messages posted on Facebook,
usually promoting positive lives full of fun, described to us by

undergraduate Jack Hodgkinson as 'an alternative fantasy world which must be stressful', ultimately has the effect of advocating conformism. A recent report concluded that internet access is considered more vital than a swimming pool by young people on holiday.

It would be ridiculously narrow-minded to pretend that we have not benefited from technological advances but pressing buttons instead of speaking in person is affecting the ability of some young people to form close personal bonds. However, we should remember to take heart from activity we have witnessed instigated by the internet during recent periods of intense political pressure.

Some activism is only known to a few local residents. Sarah Veale gave us an example of young women cooperating successfully in a just cause. In Lewisham they are fighting to retain their play centre. This activity has made them quite militant and if they succeed they will have formed a group with the confidence to demand other facilities in the borough.

In her book, *A Passion for Friends* (1986), Janice Raymond claims that

> 'social and political life stem from values, choices and activities that are defined with clarity and exercised with commitment'.

Her words encapsulate what we have been advocating in this chapter. This is how we can set about cultivating our precious gardens but Janice Raymond does add an important rider which we should acknowledge and try to rectify:

> 'There has not been much talk or writing about happiness in the women's movement.'[34]

So let us take a final leaf out of Lynne Segal's optimistic book,[35]

'Simply being together is empowering. Bringing a certain audacity and energy to life.'

She goes on,

'Happy endings can be joyfully pursued when we feel empowered together with others, although ... they can never be said to have finally arrived'.

Women's struggle for a better life has not yet reached its happy ending but we should honour the struggles of feminist campaigners in earlier years, celebrating their great victories and uniting in sisterhood to complete their work. And as we labour to reach our utopia, we should remember the closing words of Sylvia Pankhurst's autobiography:[36]

'Great is the work that remains to be accomplished.'

NOTES

Chapter 1: The Two Great Anniversaries

1. Metro on 3 April 2017.

2. A statue of Emmeline Pankhurst was erected in 1930 in Victoria Tower Gardens, near to the parliament. It was unveiled by Stanley Baldwin, the Prime Minister. The cost was paid by private subscription.

3. Denby, D., *Great books*. Touchstone, 1996.

4. Campbell, B., *The end of equality*. Seagull, 2013.

5. David, M., *Reclaiming feminism: Challenging everyday misogyny*. Policy Press, 2016.

6. Obituary in National Union of Societies for Equal Citizenship Annual Report.

7. Obituary assessment.

8. Interview with Ethel Smyth, BBC, 1937.

9. Sealy, R., *Meritocracy*.

10. Tichenor, V. J., *Earning more and getting less: Why successful wives can't buy equality*. Rutgers University Press, 2005.

11. Kelly, J., in *Fifty Shades of Feminism*, Appignanesi, Lisa et al. (Eds.).

12. Hale, B., in *Man-Made, why so few women are in positions of power*. Tutchell, Eva & Edmonds John. Gower, 2015.

13. Mosse, M. in Pepe, Victoria et al., *I call myself a Feminist*, Virago, 2015.

14. Nash, K. in Pepe, Victoria et al., *I call myself a Feminist*, Virago, 2015

15. Segal, L., *Radical happiness: Moments of collective joy*. Verso, 2017.

16. Anderson, G. D., in *Fifty Shades of Feminism*, Appignanesi, Lisa et al. (Eds.).

Chapter 2: Days of Hope

1. Pankhurst, E. S., *The suffragette movement*. Book VI Chap 2. (reprinted Virago, 1931).

2. Pankhurst, E., *My own story*. Book 2 Chap 2. Eveleigh Nash, 1914.

3. *Ibid*. Book 2 Chap 2.

4. *Ibid*.

5. Pankhurst, E. S., *The suffragette movement*. Book VI Chap 2.

6. 27 February 1908.

7. Times, 22 June 1908.

8. *Daily Express*, 22 June 1908.

9. Pankhurst, E., *My own story*. Book 2 Chap 2. Eveleigh Nash, 1914.

10. Rowbotham, S., *Once a feminist*. Wandor, Micheline. Virago, 1990.

11. Tweedie, J., Women march for liberation, *Guardian,* March 1971.

12. Stott, M., *Guardian*, January 1971.

Chapter 3: Winning Votes for Women

1. Blackburn, Helen: *Women's Suffrage: A record of the Women's suffrage Movement in the British Isles with Biographical Sketches of Miss Becker*, 1902. See also the report by Parliament's Vote 100 Project team.

2. The first petition to parliament calling for votes for women was presented by Henry Hunt, MP, for Preston in 1835, but did not spawn a campaign. Hunt, or Orator Hunt, as he was known – usually sarcastically – was famous for organising what came to be called the Peterloo Massacre and Hunt spent two years in prison. Hunt called himself, 'the only radical' in the House of Commons yet even Hunt went no further than supporting votes for unmarried women, with married women having to rely on their husbands for representation.

3. The young Millicent Fawcett had helped to collect signatures for the petition and was in the House of Commons when Mill spoke.

4. Fawcett, M., *The women's victory – and after*. Chap 10. (reprinted, Cambridge University Press, 2011).

5. Pankhurst, E., *My own story*. Book 1 Chap 2. Eveleigh Nash, 1914.

6. Fawcett, M., *Women's suffrage*. Chap 2. (reprinted, Amazon, 1912).

7. Pankhurst, E., *My own story*, 1914.

8. Pankhurst, E., *My own story*. Book 1 Chap1.

9. Pankhurst, E., *My own story*. Book 2 Chap 8.

10. Mitchell, H., *The hard way up*. Faber and Faber, 1968.

11. Letter from Disraeli to William Gore Langton MP, 1873. Quoted in M. Fawcett, *Women's suffrage*. Chap 2.

12. Henry Labouchère is mostly known for the amendment that bears his name and was used to prosecute Oscar Wilde. In 1877, he set up a journal titled *Truth,* which he used to campaign against feminists and Jews. After failing to secure the political or diplomatic posts that he thought his due, he retired to Italy in 1906.

13. Fawcett, M., *Women's suffrage*. Chap 3.

14. *Ibid.,* Chap 5.

15. Pankhurst, E., *My own story*. Book 1 Chap 1.

16. *The Nineteenth Century Magazine* in June 1889, quoted in J. Marlow (Ed.), *Suffragettes*.

17. Remark by Janet Courtney. Quoted in J. Marlow (Ed.), *Suffragettes*.

18. Fawcett, M., *Women's suffrage*. Chap 5.

19. *Ibid.*.

20. Penguin Classics, *The Suffragettes*.

21. Fawcett, M., *Women's suffrage*. Chap 3.

22. Several scholars have suggested that the tract may have been written jointly with his wife, Harriet Taylor Mill.

23. Fawcett, M., *Women's suffrage*. Chap 3.

24. Statement by Lord Cromer in 1909, quoted in J. Marlow (Ed.), *Suffragettes*.

25. Punch ran a long series of cartoons. Some ridiculed the suffrage campaigners but most were sympathetic.

26. Pankhurst, E., *My own story*. Book 1 Chap 4.

27. Pankhurst, E. S., *The suffragette movement*. Book lll Chap 2. 1931 (reprinted Virago, 1977).

28. *Ibid*. Book VI Chap 8.

29. Labour leader, December 1912. Quoted in J. Marlow (Ed.), *Suffragettes*. See also Bondfield, Margaret, *A life's work*.

30. Pankhurst, E., *My own story*. Book 1 Chap 4.

31. *Ibid*. Book 1 Chap 4.

32. Fawcett, M., *Women's suffrage*. Chap 6.

33. See Chapter 6.

34. The term suffragette seems to have been coined by the *Daily Mail*.

35. Pankhurst, E. S., *The suffragette movement*. Book V Chap 1.

36. Pankhurst, C., *Unshackled. The story of how we won the vote*. Hutchinson, 1959. Quoted in J. Marlow (Ed.): *Suffragettes*.

37. Manchester Guardian report, October 1905. Quoted in J. Marlow (Ed.): *Suffragettes*.

38. Pankhurst, E., *My own story*. Book 2 Chap 6.

39. Billington-Greig, *Fragment of autobiography*. Quoted in J. Marlow (Ed.), *Suffragettes*.

40. Pankhurst, E. S., *The suffragette movement*. Book V Chap 4.

41. Speech by Israel Zangwill, February 1907. Quoted in J. Marlow (Ed.), *Suffragettes*.

42. Letter by George Bernard Shaw to *Times*, June 1913. Quoted in J. Marlow (Ed.), *Suffragettes*.

43. 27 February 1908.

44. Pankhurst, E., *My own story*. Book 2 Chap 3.

45. Pankhurst, E. S., *The suffragette movement*. Book VIII Chap 3.

46. *Ibid*. Book VIII Chap 3.

47. Fawcett, M., *Women's suffrage*. Chap 6.

48. Memorial sent by 116 Birmingham doctors. Quoted in J. Marlow (Ed.): *Suffragettes*.

49. Pankhurst, E., *My own story*. Book 2 Chap 7.

50. *Ibid*.

51. Statements collected by Henry Brailsford and sent to the Home Office. Quoted in J. Marlow (ed): *Suffragettes*.

52. Marlow, J. (Ed.), *Suffragettes.*

53. Lansbury had called on Labour to oppose every government measure until women secured the vote. He got little support from other Labour members who described the policy as impractical. So he resigned his seat and, with the active encouragement of the WSPU, fought a bye-election on the issue of women's suffrage. Unfortunately he had not consulted members of his local party who saw no need for a bye-election and the WSPU gave him less effective organisational support than he expected. He lost. See also Chapter 6.

54. Pankhurst, E. S., *The suffragette movement.* Book VII Chap 3.

55. Report by the *Daily Express*, February 1909. Quoted in J. Marlow (Ed.), *Suffragettes.*

56. Kenney, A., *Memories of a militant.* Edward Arnold, 1924.

57. Statement by Franklin. Quoted in J. Marlow (Ed.), *Suffragettes.*

58. Letter from Millicent Fawcett to David Lloyd George, quoted in Grant, Jane W., *In the steps of exceptional women. Fawcett Society,* 2016.

59. Kenney, A., *Memories of a militant.*

60. Pankhurst, E. S., *The suffragette movement.* Book VII Chap 3.

61. *Ibid.* Book lX Chap 4.

62. Pankhurst, E. S., *The suffragette movement.* Book VIII Chap 3.

63. *Ibid.*

64. *Ibid.* Book IX Chap 8.

65. *Ibid.*

66. *Ibid.*

67. *Ibid.*

68. Adele Pankhurst, sister to Christabel and Sylvia, was working for pacifist causes in Australia and she was also repudiated by Emmeline.

69. Pankhurst, E. S., *The suffragette movement.* Book IX Chap 11.

70. Emmeline Pethick Lawrence denounced the discrimination in the *Daily News.* Quoted in E. S. Pankhurst, *The suffragette movement.* Book IX Chap 11.

Chapter 4: The Women's Liberation Movement

1. Wandor, M., *Once a feminist*. Virago, 1990.

2. *Ibid.*

3. *Ibid.*

4. *Ibid.*

5. *Ibid.*

6. *Ibid.*

7. *Ibid.*

8. *Ibid.*

9. Cochrane, Kira. (2010). 40 Years of women's liberation. *The Guardian.*

10. Wandor, *Once a feminist.*

11. Interview.

12. Spender, D., *For the record: The making and meaning of feminist knowledge*. The Women's Press, 1985.

13. David, M., *Reclaiming feminism: Challenging everyday misogyny*. Policy Press, 2016.

14. BBC interview in 2016.

15. Rowbotham, S., et al. (Eds.), *Beyond the fragments*. Merlin Press (Third edition, 2013).

16. *Ibid.*

17. Wandor, M., *Once a feminist.*

18. *Working class wives*. (Introduction to the 2nd ed.)

19. Gavron, H., *The captive wife: Conflicts of housebound mothers*. Routledge and Kegan Paul, 1966.

20. Oakley, A., *The sociology of housework*. Pantheon Books, 1975.

21. Interview in, *The Guardian*, 1976.

22. *Ibid.*

23. Guardian interview, 8 June 2012.

24. Mitchell, J. & Oakley, A., *What is a feminist*. Blackwell, 1986.

25. Cochrane, K. (Ed.). (2010)., *Women of the revolution: Forty years of Feminism*. Guardian Books,.

26. Firestone, S., (1970). *The dialectics of sex*. William Morrow.

27. M. Wollstonecraft. (1792), *A vindication of the rights of women*. J. Johnson.

28. Quoted by D. Spender (1982), *Women of ideas and what men have done to them*. Routledge and Kegan Paul.

29. Brownmiller, S., (1986). *Femininity*. Paladin, Grafton Books,.

30. Morgan, R. (Ed.), (1970). *Sisterhood is powerful: An anthology of writings from the Women's Liberation Movement*. Random House.

31. Cochrane, K., *Women of the revolution*.

32. Pepe, V., et al. (2015). *I call myself a feminist*. Virago

33. Wandor, M., *Once a feminist*.

34. Raymond, J. (1986). *A passion for friends*. The Women's Press.

35. Morgan, R., *Sisterhood is powerful*.

36. Greer, G. (1970). *The female eunuch*. Harper Collins.

37. Oakley. A. (1972)., *Sex, gender and society*. Temple Smith.

38. Rowbotham, S., *Beyond the fragments*.

39. *Ibid*.

40. David, M., *Reclaiming feminism*.

41. Rowbotham, S., *Beyond the fragments*.

42. Raymond, J., *A passion for friends*.

43. Cochrane, K., *Women of the revolution*.

44. Rowbotham, S., *Beyond the fragments*.

45. Private letter.

46. Raymond, J., *A passion for friends*.

47. Pepe, V., *I call myself a feminist*.

48. Wandor, *The way we were and will be*.

49. See also Chapter 7.

50. Rowbotham, S., *Beyond the fragments*.

51. Interview.

52. Bates, L., *Everyday sexism*. Simon and Schuster, 2014.

53. Banyard, K., *Pimp state: Sex, money and the future of equality*. Faber and Faber, 2016.

54. Hobbs, M. (1976). *Born to struggle*. Quartet.

55. *Ibid*.

56. Kennedy, M. (2001) One woman's reflections on the Ruskin Conference. Celebrating the Women's Liberation Movement 30 years on. *Women's History Review*, 10(2).

57. Wrench, J. & Solomos, J. (Eds.), *Black feminism in the United Kingdom*, 1995.

58. *Ibid*.

59. *Ibid*.

60. Truth, S. (1981). *And ain't I a woman?* from *Black women and feminism*. Bell Hooks, South End Books.

61. Carby, H. (1982) *White women listen! Black feminism and the boundaries of sisterhood: The empire strikes back: Race and racism in 1970s Britain*. University of Birmingham.

62. Southall Black Sisters website.

63. Wrench, J., and Solomos, *Black feminism*.

64. Carby, H., *White women listen!*

65. Wrench, J., and Solomos, J., *Black feminism*.

66. *An Open Cupboard Policy* in Issues in Race and Education Spring, 1984.

67. Mitchell J., & Oakley, A., *What is a feminist*.

68. Schneir, M. (Ed.),. (1995). *The vintage book of feminism*. Vintage

69. Pepe, V., *I call myself a feminist*.

70. *Ibid*.

71. Desert Island Discs, 20 March 2016.

72. *What is feminism?* Op. cit.

73. Stuart, J. M. (1869)., *The subjection of women.*

74. *Ibid.*

75. Oakley, A. (1972). *Sex, gender and society.* Temple Smith.

Chapter 5: How the Revolutions Stalled

1. Fawcett, M., *Women's suffrage.* Chap V. (reprinted, Amazon, 1912).

2. Constance Markievicz is sometimes assumed to be remote from the suffrage cause. In fact, she was the sister of Eva Gore Booth who was active with the Radical Feminists in the North West of England.

3. 24 February 1920.

4. Selvik, A., in Tutchell, Eva and Edmonds, John (Eds.). (2013). *Made in Norway.*

5. NUSEC Annual Report, 1919.

6. Fawcett, M., *The women's victory and after.* Chap VIII. (reprinted, Cambridge University Press, 1920).

7. Phillips, M. (Ed.) (1918). *Women and the Labour Party.* Headley.

8. There was also the mostly unspoken concern that every time a woman was recruited, the man she replaced would be called up to join the carnage in Belgium and France.

9. Thom, D. (1998). *Nice girls and rude girls.* Chap 2. Tauris.

10. *Ibid.* Chap 8.

11. Thom, D., *Nice girls and rude girls.*

12. *Ibid.* Chap 6.

13. *Ibid.* Chap 9. Deborah Thom points out that personal grief might have contributed to Mary Macarthur's pessimism. 'She had been very ill, her husband had died and she had failed to win a seat in Parliament.'

14. Fabian Women's Group Survey had shown just before the war that many women were breadwinners.

15. Emmeline Pankhurst was accused of becoming rich from the suffragette campaign. In fact, when she died her estate amounted to only
£86.5.6d.

16. Stott, M., *My commonplace book*.

17. Obituary, National Union of Societies for Equal Citizenship Annual
Report.

18. *Time and Tide*, November 1929.

19. Rowbotham, S. (1997) *A century of women – A history of women
in Britain and the United States*. Chap 4. Viking.

20. Blog by Catherine Brown.

21. Eleanor Rathbone's insistence on marriage as a requirement for
family rights alienated some on the Left.

22. Rowbotham, S., *A century of women*, Chap 4.

23. Wilkinson, E., *The town that was murdered*. Gollancz, 1939.

24. *The ladies bridge*, documentary directed by Karen Livesey, 2013.

25. Rowbotham, S., *A century of women*. Chap 5.

26. Carruthers, S. L. (2000). *The media at war: Communication and
conflict in the twentieth century*. St. Martin's Press.

27. Rowbotham, S., *A century of women*. Chap 5.

28. Braybon, G., & Summerfield, P. (1987). *Out of the cage. Women's
experiences in two world wars*. Routledge.

29. Rowbotham, S., *A century of women*. Chap 5.

30. Tutchell, E. & Edmonds, J. (2015). *Man-made, why so few women
are in positions of power*, Chap 2. Gower.

31. Judith Hart MP was the Secretary of State for Overseas
Development.

Chapter 6: Lessons From Our History

1. Penny, L. (2014), *Unspeakable things: Sex, lies and revolution*.
Bloomsbury.

2. Bates, L. (2014). *Everyday Sexism*. Simon and Schuster.

3. Liddington, J. & Norris, J. (1984). *One hand tied behind us*. Virago.

4. *Ibid*.

5. Pankhurst, C. (1959). *Unshackled: The story of how we won the vote*, Hutchinson.

6. Liddington, J., & Norris, J., *One hand tied behind us*.

7. Billington-Greig, T. (1978). *The non-violent militant*. Routledge and Kegan Paul.

8. See Chapter 3.

9. Brownmiller, S. (1986). *Femininity*. Paladin, Grafton Books.

10. Wandor, M. (1990). *Once a feminist*. Virago.

11. Mitchell, H. (1968). *The hard way up*. Faber and Faber.

12. *Ibid*.

13. Harman, H. (2017), *A woman's work*. Allen Lane.

14. *Ibid*.

15. Pankhurst, E. S. (1931). *The suffragette movement*. Book VIII Chap 2.

16. WSPU was disbanded in 1917.

17. Harman, H., *A woman's work*.

18. David, M. (2016). *Reclaiming feminism: Challenging everyday misogyny*. Policy Press, 2016.

19. British Library Archive: Women's Liberation Movement.

20. *Votes for Women* magazine, 1908. The colours were worn for the first time in that year.

21. Harman, H., *A woman's work*.

22. Obituary of Jo Richardson, Independent newspaper, 1994.

Chapter 7: Twenty-First Century Sexism and Inequality

1. Most newspapers and particularly *BBC online*, 3 April 2017.

2. *Guardian online*, 7 December 2015.

3. *Telegraph online*, 20 May 2014.

4. According to the Daily Mirror, others also sent emails to Scudamore containing sexist material, including David Dein, the former vice-chairman of Arsenal and former vice-chairman of the football association.

5. *Independent*, 14 June 2017.

6. Shane Sutton left before Jess Varnish's allegations were investigated.

7. This division apparently happens in the household of the Prime Minister. On the TV programme, the One Show in May 2017, Phillip May said that he does the 'manly' jobs.

8. Rowbotham, S. (1973). *Woman's consciousness, Man's World*, Pelican.

9. Bates, L. (2014)., *Everyday sexism*. Simon and Schuster.

10. In total, Demos found over 9,000 aggressively misogynistic tweets sent per day worldwide, with 80,000 Twitter users targeted by this trolling. This study reflects the findings of the Demos 2014 report, in which women were described as being as comfortable using misogynistic language as men.

11. *Sounds Familiar*. Results of survey reported on Fawcett Society Website.

12. Mill, J.S, (1869). *The subjection of women.*

13. *Washington Post*, 7 October 2016.

14. Previously Deputy President, Lady Hale became President in 2017.

15. Research by the authors.

16. They included new recruitment arrangements, targeted training, extensive mentoring, improved succession planning and tighter control of promotional procedures.

17. Hampton-Alexander Review, November 2016.

18. Gangl, M. & Ziefle, A., Motherhood, labour force behaviour and women's careers. *Demography*, 2009.

19. On 28 March 2017.

20. *Guardian online*, 11 March 2017.

Chapter 8: Threats and Trepidation

1. Sexual assaults at universities reach epidemic proportions. *The Guardian*, March 2017.

2. *Ibid.*

3. *Ibid.*

4. Greer, G. (1970). *The female eunuch*. Harper Collins, 1970.

5. Smith, J. (1989). *Misogynies*. Faber and Faber.

6. Feminist Emergency, Birkbeck College, 23 July 2017.

7. Banyard, K. (2016). *Pimp state: Sex, money and the future of equality*. Faber and Faber, 2016.

8. Interview.

9. Banyard, *Pimp state*.

10. Cochrane, K. (Ed.) (2010). *Women of the Revolution: Forty Years of Feminism*. Guardian Books.

11. Adichie, C. N. (2017). *Dear Ijeawele – or a feminist manifesto in fifteen suggestions*.

12. Sittenfeld, C. (2008). *American wife*. Random House.

13. Wollstonecraft, M. (1792). *A vindication of the rights of women*. J. Johnson.

14. Spender, D. (1982). *Women of ideas and what men have done to them*. Routledge and Kegan Paul.

15. McRobbie, A. (2009). *The aftermath of feminism: Gender, culture and social change*. Sage.

16. Sandberg, S. (2013). *Lean in – women, work and the will to lead*. WH Allen.

17. Coward, R. (1984).*Female desire: Women's sexuality today*. Paladin.

18. *Women: the longest revolution*, New Left Review, 1966.

19. Mitchell, J. & Oakley, A. (Eds.) (1986). *What is a feminist?* Blackwell.

20. *The gender pay gap*. Fawcett Society, 2015.

21. Sealy, R. (2010), Changing perceptions of meritocracy in senior women's careers. *Gender Management*.

22. *This woman can*, Fabian Society, 2017.

23. Tutchell, E. & Edmonds, J. (2015)., *Man-Made, why so few women are in positions of power*. Gower.

24. Pepe, V. et al. (2015). *I call myself a feminist*. Virago.

25. *Ibid*.

26. David, M. (2016). *Reclaiming feminism: challenging everyday misogyny*. Policy Press.

27. England, P. (1999). The importance of feminist thought on sociology. *Contemporary Sociology*.

28. Oakley, A. (1972).*Sex, gender and society*. Temple Smith.

29. Mitchell, J. (1966). *Women: the longest revolution*, New Left Reviews.

Chapter 9: New Writing on the Banner

1. Voltaire, *Candide*. Sirfene, 1759 (reprinted as Penguin Classic in 1950).

2. Layard, R. (2005). *Happiness*. Penguin.

3. Segal, L. (2017). *Radical happiness: Collective Joy*. Verso.

4. Interview.

5. Interview.

6. In Chapter 7.

7. The abuse that is recorded ranges from threats to sexual assaults and beatings.

8. *Guardian*, 2 June 2017.

9. Women's Aid Website.

10. Bates, L. (2014). *Everyday sexism*. Simon and Schuster.

11. See Chapter 3.

12. The figures are given in Chapter 7.

13. Appignanesi, H. R. & Orbach, S. (Eds.) (2013). *Fifty shades of feminism*.

14. Banyard, K. (2016). *Pimp state: Sex, Money and the future of Equality*. Faber and Faber.

15. See Chapter 5.

16. Interview.

17. Interview for *Man-Made*.

18. Vinnicombe, S. & Bank, J. (2003). *Women with attitude*. Routledge.

19. *Made in Norway*, report of conference held in House of Commons, January 2013.

20. *Ibid*.

21. David, M. (2016). *Reclaiming feminism: challenging everyday misogyny*. Policy Press.

22. Insecurity at work conference, TUC, June 2017.

23. History & Policy Forum Seminar, King's College, April 2017.

Chapter 10: Living the Impossible Dream

1. Appignanesi, H. R. & Orbach, S. (Eds.) (2013). *Fifty shades of feminism*. Virago.

2. Decision of 1993 Labour Party Conference.

3. *Women at the top*, Conservative Party, 2005.

4. Sarah, C. (2008). *Women and British party politics*. Routledge.

5. Fawcett Society website.

6. Letter from Virginia Woolf to Ethel Smyth, 1940.

7. *A final burning of the boats etc.* 1928.

8. Used by Gloria Steinem many times and repeated after the Women's March in January 2017.

9. Aston, E. & Reinelt, J. (Eds.) (2000). *A Cambridge companion to modern British women playwright*. CU Press.

10. Dunn, N. (1963). *Up the junction*. Hart, Davis McGibbon.

11. Dunn, N. (1967). *Poor cow*. McGibbon Kee.

12. Wandor, M., in *A Companion etc.* op. cit

13. Interview.

14. Cole, B. (1996). *Princess smartypants*. Puffin.

15. Cole, B. (1997). *Prince cinders*. Puffin.

16. Eliot, G. (1871). *Middlemarch*. Blackwood.

17. Holtby, W. Riding, South, Gollancz, Victor, 1936 (posthumously).

18. Holtby, W. (1926). *Yorkshire Post*.

19. Orwell, G. (1949). *1984*. Secker and Warburg.

20. As quoted to us by Philip Hedley.

21. They are: Equal representation in parliament, equal pay and opportunity, equal parenting and care-giving, equal education, equal media treatment, an end to violence against women and equality in healthcare and medical research.

22. Appignanesi, H. R. & Orbach, S. (Eds.) (2013). *Fifty shades of feminism*.

23. Stott, M., Guardian, 1971.

24. Appignanesi, H. R. & Orbach, S. (Eds.). *Fifty shades of feminism*.

25. Cochrane, K. (Ed.) (2010). *Women of the revolution: Forty years of feminism*. Guardian Books.

26. *Guardian*, June 2017.

27. David, M. (2016). *Reclaiming feminism: challenging everyday misogyny.* Policy Press.

28. Woolf, V. (1938). *3 Guineas*.

29. Appignanesi, H. R. & Orbach, S. (Eds.), *Fifty shades of feminism*.

30. Dickson, A. (2013). *Teaching men to be feminists*. Quartet Books Ltd.

31. Morgan, R. (Ed.) (1970). *Sisterhood is powerful: An anthology of writings from the Women's Liberation Movement*. Random House.

32. Rosenfeldt, D. & Stacey, J. (1987). Second thoughts on the second wave. *Feminist Studies*, Summer, 1987.

33. Cochrane, k., *Women of the revolution*.

34. Raymond, J. (1986). *A passion for Friends*. The Women's Press.

35. Segal, L. (2017). *Radical happiness: Collective joy*. Verso.

36. Pankhurst, E. S. (1931). *The suffragette movement* (reprinted Virago, 1977).

SELECT BIBLIOGRAPHY

Adichie, Chimamanda Ngozi. (2017). *Dear Ijeawele – Or a feminist manifesto in fifteen suggestions.* Fourth Estate.

Appignanesi, Holmes Rachel & Orbach, Susie (Eds.) (2013). *Fifty Shades of Feminism*, Virago.

Aston, Elaine & Reinelt, Junelle. (Eds.) (2000). *A Cambridge companion to modern British women playwrights.* CU Press.

Banyard, Kat. (2010). *The equality illusion: The truth about women and men today.* Faber.

Banyard, Kat. (2016). *Pimp state: Sex, money and the future of equality.* Faber and Faber.

Bates, Laura. (2014). *Everyday sexism.* Simon and Schuster.

de Beauvoir, Simone. (1949). *The second sex, first published in 1949 as Le Deuxième Sexe.* Paris: Editions Gallimard.

Berger, John. (1972). *Ways of seeing.* BBC and Penguin Books.

Billington-Greig, Teresa. (1978). *The non-violent militant.* Routledge and Kegan Paul.

Blackburn, Helen. *Women's Suffrage: A record of the Women's suffrage Movement in the British Isles with Biographical Sketches of Miss Becker*, Williams & Norgate, 1902.

Bondfield, Margaret. (1948). *A life's work*, Hutchinson.

Brah, Avtar. (1995). *Black feminism in the United Kingdom – Racism and migration in western Europe.* In J. Wrench & J. Solomos (Eds.), Berg Publishers.

Braybon, Gail & Summerfield, Penny. (1987). *Out of the cage: Women's experiences in two world wars.* Routledge.

Brownmiller, Susan. (1986). *Femininity.* Paladin, Grafton Books.

Campbell, Beatrix. (2013). *End of equality.* Seagull.

Carby, Hazel. (2014). *Black British feminism then and now.* Media Diversified.

Carby, Hazel. (1982). *White women listen! Black feminism and the boundaries of sisterhood – the empire strikes back: Race and racism in 1970s Britain.* University of Birmingham.

Carruthers, Susan L. (2000). *The media at war: Communication and conflict in the twentieth century.* St. Martin's Press.

Castle, Barbara. (1987). *Sylvia and Christabel Pankhurst.* Penguin.

Childs, Sarah. (2008). *Women and British party politics.* Routledge.

Cochrane, Kira. (2010). *40 Years of women's liberation.* The Guardian 26th February 2010.

Cochrane, Kira. (Ed.). (2010). *Women of the revolution: Forty years of feminism.* Guardian Books.

Cole, Babette. (1996). *Princess smartypants.* Puffin.

Cole, Babette. (1997). *Prince cinders.* Puffin.

Coward, Ros. (1984). *Female desire: Women's sexuality today.* Paladin.

Dangerfield, George. (2012). *The strange death of liberal England.* Smith and Haas, 1935 (reprinted Serif).

David, Miriam. (2016). *Reclaiming feminism: Challenging everyday misogyny.* Policy Press.

Denby, David. (1996). *Great books.* Touchstone.

Dickson, Ann. (2013). *Teaching men to be feminists.* Quartet Books Ltd.

Dunn, Nell. (1963). *Up the junction*. Hart, Davis McGibbon.

Dunn, Nell. (1967). *Poor cow*. McGibbon Kee.

Dyhouse, Carol. (2014). *Girl trouble: Panic and progress in the history of young women*. Zed Books.

Eliot, George. (1871). *Middlemarch*. Blackwood.

England, Paula. (1999). *The importance of feminist thought on sociology. Contemporary Sociology*, 28(3), May.

Fawcett, Millicent. (2011). *The Women's victory – and after*, 1920 (reprinted),. Cambridge: Cambridge University Press.

Fawcett, Millicent. (1912). *Women's suffrage* (reprinted). Amazon.

Figes, Eva. (1970). *Patriarchal attitudes – Women in society*. Faber.

Fine, Cordelia. (2010). *Delusions of gender*. ICON.

Firestone, Shulamith. (1970). *The dialectic of sex*. William Morrow.

Freeman, Hadley. (2014). *Be awesome – modern life for modern ladies*. Fourth Estate.

Friedan, Betty. (1963). *The feminine mystique*. Harper Collins.

Gangl, Markus & Ziefle, Andrea. (2009). *Motherhood, labour force behaviour and women's careers: An empirical assessment of the wage penalty for motherhood in Britain, Germany and the USA. Demography*, 46(2).

Gavron, Hannah. (1966). *The captive wife: Conflicts of housebound mothers*. Routledge and Kegan Paul.

Graessler, Lois, Hall, Catherine, Wandor, Micheline. In K. Cochrane *Women of the revolution: Forty years of feminism*. Guardian Books 26th February 2010.

Grant, Jane W. (2016). *In the steps of exceptional women,*. Fawcett Society.

Greer, Germaine. (1970). *The female eunuch*. Harper Collins.

Harman, Harriet. (2017). *A woman's work*. Allen Lane.

Heilman, Madeline. (2001). *Description and prescription: How gender stereotypes prevent women's ascent up the organisational ladder. Journal of Social Issues, 57*.

Hobbs, May. (1976). *Born to struggle*. Quartet.

Holtby, Winifred. (1936). *South Riding* Victor Gollancz (posthumously).

Honeyball, Mary. (2015). *Parliamentary pioneers: Labour women MPs 1918–1945*. Urbane Publications.

Hoschild, Dr Airlie. (1989). *The second shift*. Piatkus.

Kanter, Rosabeth Moss. (1977). *Men and women of the corporation*. Basic Books.

Kennedy, Mary. (2001). *One woman's reflections on the Ruskin Conference: Celebrating the Women's Liberation Movement 30 years on. Women's History Review*, 10(2).

Kenney, Annie. (1924). *Memories of a militant*. Edward Arnold.

Kynaston, David. (2010). *Family Britain 1951–75*. Bloomsbury.

Layard, Richard. (2005). *Happiness*. Penguin.

Liddington, Jill & Norris, Jill. (1984). *One hand tied behind us*. Virago.

Marlow, Joyce. (Ed.) (2000). *Suffragettes*. Virago.

McRobbie, Angela. (2009). *The aftermath of feminism: Gender, culture and social change*. Sage.

Meulenbelt, Anja. (1980). *A creative tension, explorations in socialist feminism*. South End Press.

Mill, John Stuart. (1869). *The subjection of women*.

Millett, Kate. (1969). *Sexual politics*. Doubleday.

Mitchell, Juliet & Oakley, Ann. (Eds.) (1986).*What is Feminism?* Blackwell.

Mitchell, Hannah. (1968). *The hard way up.* Faber and Faber.

Mitchell, Juliet. (1966). *Women: The longest revolution.* New Left Review.

Morgan, Robin. (Ed.). (1970). *Sisterhood is powerful: An anthology of writings from the Women's Liberation Movement.* Random House.

Oakley, Ann. (1972). *Sex, gender and society.* Temple Smith.

Oakley, Ann. (1975). *The sociology of housework.* Pantheon Books.

Opportunity Now: *Breaking the barriers – women in senior management.* 2000.

Orwell, George. (1949). *1984.* Secker and Warburg.

Pankhurst, Christabel. (1959). *Unshackled: The story of how we won the vote.* Hutchinson.

Pankhurst, Emmeline. (1914). *My own story.* Eveleigh Nash.

Pankhurst, Estelle Sylvia. (1977). *The suffragette movement,* 1931 (reprinted). Virago.

Penny, Laurie. (2014). *Unspeakable things: Sex, lies and revolution.* Bloomsbury.

Pepe, Victoria, et al. (Eds.) (2015). *I call myself a feminist.* Virago.

Phillips, Marion. (Ed.) (1918). *Women and the labour party.* Headley.

Raymond, Janice. (1986). *A passion for friends.* The Women's Press.

Rice, Margery Spring. (1981). *Working class wives.* Penguin, 1939 (republished by Virago).

Rossi, Alice C. (Ed.) (1970). *Essays on Sex Equality, John Stuart Mill and Harriet Taylor Mill.* University of Chicago Press.

Rosenfeldt, Deborah & Stacey, Judith. (1987). *Second thoughts on the second wave. Feminist Studies.*

Rowbotham, Sheila. et al. (Eds.) (2013). *Beyond the fragments* (3rd ed.). Merlin Press.

Rowbotham, Sheila. (1973). *Woman's consciousness, man's world.* Pelican.

Rowbotham, Sheila. (1979). *The trouble with patriarchy.* New Statesman.

Rowbotham, Sheila. (1997). *A century of women – A history of women in Britain and the United States.* Viking.

Rowbotham, Sheila. (1999). *Threads through time.* Penguin.

Rudman, Laurie & Fairchild, Kimberley. (2007). *The F word: Is Feminism compatible with beauty and romance? Psychology of Women Quarterly, 31.*

Rudman, Laurie & Glick, Peter. (2008). *The social psychology of gender.* Guilford.

Russell, Dora. (1975). *The tamarisk tree: My quest for liberty and love.* Putnam.

Sandberg, Sheryl. (2013). *Lean in – Women, work and the will to lead.* WH Allen.

Schneir, Miriam. (Ed.). (1995). *The vintage book of feminism.* Vintage.

Sealy, Ruth. (2010). *Changing perceptions of meritocracy in senior women's careers. Gender Management, 25(3).*

Segal, Lynne. (1999). *Why feminism?* Polity.

Segal, Lynne. (2017). *Radical Happiness: Moments of Collective Joy.* Verso.

Sittenfeld, Curtis. (2008). *American wife*. Random House.

Smith, Joan. (1989). *Misogynies*. Faber and Faber.

Smyth, Ethel. (1928). *A final burning of the boats etc.* Longmans Green.

Spender, Dale. (1982). *Invisible women – The schooling scandal*. Writers and Readers Cooperative.

Spender, Dale. (1982). *Women of ideas and what men have done to them*. Routledge and Kegan Paul.

Spender, Dale. (1985). *For the record: The making and meaning of feminist knowledge*. The Women's Press.

Steinem, Gloria. (1983). *Outrageous acts and everyday rebellions*. Henry Holt.

Stott, Mary. (1971). *The Guardian,* 15th January 1971.

Suffragettes, (The) (2016). Penguin Little Black Classics No 94.

Tannen, Deborah. (1994). *Gender and discourse*. Oxford: Oxford University Press.

Taylor, Hazel. (1984). *An open cupboard policy – issues in race and education*.

Thom, Deborah. (1998). *Nice girls and rude girls*. Tauris.

Thomson, Peninah & Lloyd, Tom. (2011). *Women and the new business leadership*. Palgrave Macmillan.

Tichenor, Veronica Jarvis. (2005). *Earning more and getting less: Why successful wives can't buy equality*. Rutgers University Press.

Truth, Sojourner. (1981). *And ain't I a woman?* From *black women and feminism*. Bell Hooks, South End Books.

Tutchell, Eva & Edmonds, John. (2015). *Man-made, why so few women are in positions of power*. Gower.

Tutchell, Eva & Edmonds, John. (Eds.) (2013). *Made in Norway*, the report of the Conference held in the House of Commons in January 2013. Website of Fabian Society (Fabian Women's Network).

Tweedie, Jill. (1971). Women march for liberation. *The Guardian,* 8th March 1971.

Vinnicombe, Susan & Bank, John. (2003). *Women with attitude.* Routledge.

Voltaire (1950). *Candide.* Sirfene, 1759 (reprinted as Penguin Classic in 1950).

Wandor, Michelene. (1990). *Once a feminist.* Virago.

Wilkinson, Ellen. (1939). *The town that was murdered.* Gollancz.

Wollstonecraft, Mary. (1792). *A vindication of the rights of women.* J. Johnson.

Woolf, Virginia. (1928). *A room of one's own.* Hogarth Press.

Woolf, Virginia. (1938). *3 Guineas.* Blackwell.

NOTES ON AUTHORS

Eva Tutchell is an expert on gender issues, advising public authorities on challenges and solutions. Starting out as a secondary school teacher, Eva's work has covered all age groups. Her book, *Dolls and Dungarees* is recommended reading for primary school teachers, she has researched the attitudes of teenagers and particularly of teenage boys, has published guidance for schools and colleges on disordered eating and has developed and taught a module on gender for use in universities.

John Edmonds is a trade unionist and specialist in work organization. Until 2003, John was general secretary of the 700,000 member GMB trade union where he increased the representation of women throughout the union. He also served as TUC President. More recently, John has focussed on environmental issues and on a more inclusive system of education and training. He is a Visiting Fellow at King's College, London, studying labour markets and gender equality.

This is the second book that Eva and John have written together.

Their earlier book, *Man-Made: Why So Few Women Are in Positions of Power,* was published in 2015.

INDEX

Downing Street, 21, 24, 50, 51, 56, 61
Drabble, Margaret, 233
Drake, Francis, 109
Drummond, Flora (the WSPU "General"), 18
Duffy, Carol Ann, 281
Dumas, Marlene, 279
Dunbar, Roxanne, 92
Dunkirk, 126
Dunn, Nell, 273
Dyhouse, Carol, 72

Eagle, Angela, 195
Earl, Mary, 55
East London Federation of Suffragettes
foundation, 39–42
expulsion from WSPU, 41–42
deputation to Asquith, 49–51, 67
campaigning for Universal suffrage, 34–37, 39–42
Easter Rising 1916, 108
East-Western Divan Orchestra, The, 278–279
Easton, Carole, 241
Education, 24, 29, 37, 76, 93, 101, 122, 132, 133, 134, 149, 164, 201, 216, 232, 239, 241, 247, 248, 252, 260, 266, 280, 282, 287, 288, 289
Education Act (1870), 37
Edward Said, 279
Election, 'Flapper', 120
Eliot, George, 280
Emancipation Bill, 118
Emin, Tracey, 279
Employment Protection Act, The, 165
Employment Tribunals
career damaging, 265, 266
Humiliation of applicants, 249
inadequate enforcement process, 173
reluctance to take cases, 136, 227–228
Enforcement of legal rights
inadequate enforcement of 1970s Acts, 251
no enforcement of 1919 Act, 135
no enforcement of 1919 Commons Resolution, 173, 118
Equal Educational opportunities, 24, 76, 248
Equal Franchise Act, 1918, 118
Equal Pay
Commons Resolution, 1919, 118, 173
Equal Pay Act, 2, 92, 134, 135, 163, 165, 173, 204, 227, 249, 250
Royal Commission on Equal Pay 1944, 128
Ruskin Conference demand, 76
secrecy of salaries, 204–205
undertakings in First World War, 126
War Cabinet in Second World War, 127, 173
Equality and inequality
at work, 141, 143, 227–229
e. does not happen by accident, 176–178
e. is'good for business', 199
e. with men, 4, 7, 70, 121, 123, 124, 248, 252, 253, 254, 286
in the home, 224–227
policy Statements, 208
something better than equality, 252–254
Equality Act, The (2010), 229
Equality and Human Rights Commission, 195, 284
Exeter Hall meeting, 47–49
Fabian Women's Group Survey, 303n14
Fabian Women's Network, 291
Falklands War, The, 132
Fallows, Heather, 280
Family Allowances, 89, 123, 130
Fascism, 123
Fawcett Society, The, 192, 227, 250, 269, 285, 290, 299n58, 307n20
Fawcett, Henry, husband of Millicent Fawcett, 42
Fawcett, Millicent
admires courage of hunger strikers, 53

and equality, 28
believes War work will change
    status of women
    permanently, 114
compared to Emmeline
    Pankhurst, 2, 42–43
early life, 43
exposes contradictions in
    position of Antis, 35
funeral, 118–119
generosity to suffragettes, 43–44
holds high moral ground, 62
inspired by J S Mill, 306n12
leader of National Union of
    Women's Suffrage Societies,
    42, 48, 61, 65, 157, 162, 174
lives to see all women having
    vote, 1, 28, 41, 42, 167
makes alliance with Labour
    Party, 65
marriage, 42
part of Establishment, 42
personality, 2, 43
presses case for suffrage during
    war, 68
respected and loved by
    colleagues, 40–41, 43
shields cause from consequences
    of campaign of arson and
    bombs, 61
statue, 1
Tributes, 43
wide range of interests, 44
women "thrown overboard"
    by Gladstone, 32–34
Female leadership, 256
Femininity, 222–224
Feminism
    and suffrage campaign, 5–8, 28,
        152, 153, 172, 174
    f. and Women's Liberation
        Movement, 78–79
    slurs, 40
    and young women, 3, 6, 9,
        141, 154
    New Feminists, 121, 123,
        253, 286
    radical feminists, 95, 147, 235
Fifties, the (1950s), 73
Figes, Eva, 87

Films
    *All Quiet on the Western
        Front*, 272
    Brief Encounter, 73
    I, Daniel Blake, 277
    Poor Cow, 273
    Mon Oncle, 276
    Monsieur Hulot's Holiday, 276
    *Seven Brides for Seven
        Brothers*, 73
    Suffragette, 2
Finance Directors, 200
Firestone, Shulamith, 85
First World War
    changes only temporary, 114
    expectations of change, 112
    Government Agents, 113
    home Front, 129
    legacy, 115–117
    motherhood first, 225
    return to domesticity, 116
    women's work, 116
Flexible working (see also Zero
        hours contracts)
    control by managers, 263
    job sharing, 262
    potential advantages, 260
    rethinking work patterns, 260
    unpredictable hours, 261–262
Football Association (FA), the, 180
Ford strike at Dagenham,
        1968, 74, 163
Foster, Chris, 278
Fragility of gains by women,
        205–207
France, demonstrations in 1968,
        237
Franklin, Hugh, 61
Franz Ferdinand, Archduke, 68
Free Trade Hall, 45
French Open Tennis, 182
French, Marilyn, 233
Friedan, Betty, 74, 143
FTSE Cross Company Mentoring
        Programme, 186
FTSE100, 210
FTSE350, 196
Fugard, Athol, 12, 177
Further and Higher Education, 247
Fury, Tyson, 180

Garrett Anderson, Elizabeth, 47, 81
Gavron, Hannah, 82, 83, 300n19
Gay's the Word bookshop, 78
Gender Pay Gap (see also
        Equal Pay)
    penalty of being a mother, 264
    secrecy of salaries, 204–205
    size of gap, 134, 204–205
Gender roles (see stereotypes)
General Election 1918, 69
General Election 1929, 109
General Strike, 122
General Synod 1975, 165
Gilpin, Sophie, 275
'Girls' and 'boys', 154
Girton College, Cambridge, 102
Gladstone, Herbert, 19, 50
Gladstone, William
    agricultural labourers, 32–33
    anxiety about women's
        delicacy, 38
    helpful speeches, 32
    refusal to include women in
        1884 Reform Bill, 28
    splits Liberal Party, 34
Gladstone, Catherine: wife of
        William Gladstone, 36
Goldsmith's University, 80
Gore Booth, Eva, 146, 147
Graessle, Lois, 77, 287
Greenfield, Susan, 231
Greenham Common Cruise missile
        site, 133
Greer, Germaine, 75, 87, 143, 159,
        216, 301, 307
Greig, Tamsin, 275
Grunwick strike, 98
Guardian newspaper, The, 25, 213,
        216, 296n11, 296n12, 300n9,
        300n21, 300n23, 307n1,
Guilt felt by women, 36, 51, 226

Hain, Peter, 177
Hale, Brenda, 10, 195, 231, 295n12
Hall, Catherine, 71, 92, 153, 287
Hamilton, Cicely, 272
Hardie, Keir, 18, 39–40, 46, 47, 59
Hardy, Mrs Emma: wife of Thomas
        Hardy, 18

Harman, Harriet, 11, 14, 105, 110,
        156, 157, 163, 176, 229, 231
Hart, Judith, 304n31
Havel, Vaclav, 275
Haverfield, Evelina, 56
Hedley, Philip, 281, 310n20
Higgs Review (2003), The, 209
Hills Committee (1919), The, 114
History Workshop, 76, 90
Hobbs, May, 97
Hobsbawm, Marlene, 71
Holloway Prison, 51
Holtby, Winifred, 281
Home Rule for Ireland, 34, 52
Honeyball, Mary, 102
Hope, Bob, 79, 172
Horner, Marina, 223
Hoschild, Airlie, 153, 224
House of Commons, lay out of, 174
House of Lords, 33, 34, 52, 118,
        123, 135, 176
Housewives and housework, 81–85
Howe, Elspeth, 198
Hunger strikes, 5, 52, 53, 58, 62,
        63, 64, 67, 161
Hyde Park Demonstration of 1908
        Chapter 2: passim, 50
Hytner, Nicholas, 287

Identity, 8, 9, 92, 132, 140, 152, 232
Inclusion (see Diversity)
Independent Labour Party (ILP), 39
Infant Custody Act, The, 30
Infant Welfare centres, 81
Institute of Management Survey, 257
International Marxist Group, 76, 94
International Socialists, 76
Internet, 134, 191, 193, 206, 217,
        219, 284, 292
Inverdale, John, 180
Isle of Man, 34

Jackie magazine, 223
James, Ashleigh, 104, 219
James, Selma, 84, 85
Jarrow Crusade, The, 125
Jewson, Dorothy, 120
Jockey Club, The, 135
Jones, Annabel, 219